Before

Jay Sarno was very clever. When I was younger, I had a hard time seeing through his bombastic and carefree personality–he didn't look like an artist. He wasn't quiet and sensitive. He was a party guy. You don't associate that with Renzo Piano and Santiago Calatrava and Frank Lloyd Wright and Walt Disney. You wouldn't think that Jay could dream up what he did until you started talking to him. If anybody changed Las Vegas, it was Jay Sarno.

Steve Wynn, Chairman and CEO of Wynn Resorts

He was basically the founder of what Las Vegas is today. I don't care what anybody says. He was a man before his time who, of course, designed Caesars Palace and Circus Circus. The Grandissimo was even further before its time. And he was bigger than life.

Oscar Goodman, former mayor of Las Vegas

His themed hotels took us into the modern era and the creation of a massive amount of investment that gave Las Vegas the infrastructure to surpass places like Orlando or anywhere else as a destination resort.

Elaine Wynn, Director, Wynn Resorts

Jay always had an imagination. But that Grandissimo, how he described it to me was just—it was like he saw into the future.

Allen "Ace" Greenberg, Wall Street legend and lifelong Sarno friend

I think Las Vegas owes Jay Sarno a lot. The themed resorts. A very colorful character, lived life, as many people will tell you, to the absolute fullest, didn't miss many things.

Larry Ruvo, Senior Managing Director, Southern Wine and Spirits of Nevada

He was so far ahead of his time in Las Vegas. I mean he just knew everything, everything about gamblers and what made people work. And every day was a learning day for Jay Sarno, every day.

Evel Knievel, legendary daredevil and lifelong Sarno friend

How Jay Sarno Won a Casino Empire, Lost It,
and Inspired Modern Las Vegas

THE FIRST EMPEROR OF LAS VEGAS

DAVID G. SCHWARTZ

WINCHESTER

WINCHESTER BOOKS
Las Vegas, Nevada
www.winchesterbooks.net

Grandissimo
The First Emperor of Las Vegas

Library of Congress Call Number HV6710.3.S27 S38 2013
Paperback edition ISBN 978-0-9900016-0-7

Cover design and interior art by Charles S. Monster, 15-North

Interior layout by David G. Schwartz
Set in Adobe Caslon Pro

Designed and printed in the United States of America

For

Jeff Simpson (1960-2011)
Like Jay, he loved to shoot craps

Hal Rothman (1958-2007)
Like Jay, he changed the way we see Las Vegas

Stuart Mason (1935-2012)
With Jay, he moved a mountain

Contents

ℋ
Acknowledgements

In the six years or so it's taken to bring *Grandissimo* from idea to paper (or screen, if you've got the ebook), I have had plenty of help. Michele Jaffe lent a sympathetic ear and helped provide clarity in the book's earliest stages. My agent, Susan Ginsburg of Writer's House, offered sage advice along the way, and I am grateful to her for introducing me to Jane Cavolina, who helped me tremendously in editing the manuscript into its current form.

My day job at the University of Nevada, Las Vegas affords me a great launching pad for all kinds of projects, and for that I'd like to thank UNLV Libraries Dean Patricia Iannuzzi, Special Collections director Michelle Light, and the entire Special Collections faculty and staff: Delores Brownlee, Su Kim Chung, Michael Frazier, Peter Michel, Joyce Moore, Tom Sommer, Claytee White, and Barbara Tabach. Some other UNLV folks who deserve thanks are Cory Lampert, who gave me invaluable photo assistance, and Alec Madriaga, who put together a great video trailer for the book. Kathy Rankin was enormously helpful in giving the book its Library of Congress Classification Number, the call number that you'll find this book listed under in many academic libraries. Ginny Poehling and Kelli Luchs at the Las Vegas Convention and Visitors Authority were extremely helpful and accommodating in my quest for pictures, and Debbie Munch at Caesars Entertainment helped me by arranging a few interviews and expediting a photo request.

And at my evening job, my friends and colleagues at *Vegas Seven* helped me quite a bit too—particularly publisher Phil Hagen, and editor Greg Blake Miller, who has been a literary influence for the better in so many ways.

Several of my colleagues at UNLV Libraries helped tremendously by proof-reading the manuscript. They are: Aaron Abbey, Angela Ayers, Kristen Costello, Carrie Gaxiola, Amy Hunsaker, Ericka Jeschke, Annie Sattler, Susie Skarl, and Fran Smith. As on several other projects, Meg Daniel has proven to be a tremendous indexer (and great backstop proofreader as well).

Through the life of this book, I've gotten to know and interview many fascinating, quite different people with one thing in common; they'd all known Jay Sarno. They include several relatives: Phyllis Dunetz, Jonathan Sarno, Ellen Jean Rosenbloom, Larry Corash, Paul Sarno, Jan Corash, and Marian Portman. Then there are the friends and business associates: Steve Wynn, Elaine Wynn, Larry Ruvo, Allen "Ace" Greenberg, Al Einbender, Mel Larson, Stanley Mallin, Murray King, Arlene Bates, Evelyn Spinks Cappadonna, Joey Trujillo, Oscar Goodman, Carolyn Goodman, Flora Mason, Burton Cohen, and Kirk Kerkorian.

I would also like to give a heartfelt acknowledgement to a few people who aren't with us to see the book's publication, but who were generous with their time and recollections of Jay: Stuart Mason, Robert "Evel" Knievel, Lillian Sarno, and Bob Stupak. Those four very different people, for me, tell the story of how many worlds Jay Sarno spanned.

When I started this project, I was convinced that his two casinos were Jay Sarno's greatest accomplishment. Having gotten to know each of his four children in the last six years, I can say I was wrong—the four very different, very wonderful children he helped raise are his finest accomplishment. Jay, September, Freddie, and Heidi were incredibly generous with their time and recollections, and held up admirably under the sometimes-uncomfortable scrutiny I devoted to their father's life and their family's history.

I brought this book to the public in an untraditional way. Being unable to find a home for it with a publisher (at least on the terms that I wanted for it), I decided to publish it myself. Like many other creative artists, I decided to turn to Kickstarter to get the money I would need to put the book out. The campaign went better than I could have imagined—I reached my initial goal in less than four hours—and put some wind in the sails as I steered *Grandissimo* home.

I'd like to thank the following people for their generosity in helping fund this book: Aaron J. Byram, Peter Erickson, Christine & Sheldon Smith, Marc Knowlton, Chris Lynn, Gordon Clark, Pete & Heather Kennedy, John & Ute Lowery, João Ramos Graça, EConnect of Las Vegas, Don Kelley, Mike Winkler, 360 Vegas Podcast, William F. Pittock, Brian "BC" Chevrier, Jim Muszynski, Mark Lister, Craig A. Kellogg, TalkVegas.com, Doug Montgomery, Erik Hummel, Vice Lounge Online, Skip Bronson, Justin Evans, Reed Nolen, Oliver Lovat, Jim Goodman, Mark Bollman, Connor Knight, Jay Laine, Travis Forbes, Justin Kettel, Giulio DiCicco, Barton Kellogg, Richard Greenberg, Robert Kline, Paul Shanahan, Michael Storino, Janss Laurence Adams, Peter A. Machon, Steve Grantz, John Gruber, Daniel A. Greenspun, Jeff Leatherock, Matthew Farley, Brendon Wagner, Don McDonald Esq, Aaron Holland, Mark & Diane Moormann, Admiral Hunter Hillegas, Brandon Griffiths, the Blue Tide Whales, John A. Hall, Ricardo Rodriguez, Mark Ickert, Phillip Samano Jr, Chris Hall, Eric C. Whitaker, Ryan Hess, Doug Montgomery, Nicole Parthum, Roy Parpart, Steven R. Brown, Rob Taylor, and Tim & Michele Dressen.

One of the big reasons that the Kickstarter campaign was a success was the unstinting, unapologetic support of a group of Las Vegas fans and enthusiasts known as the Vegas Internet Mafia. My cohorts on the Vegas Gang podcast, Hunter Hillegas and Charles S. Monster, have been unbelievably supportive friends—Mr. Monster also produced the incredible book cover. Tim and Michele Dressen, co-hosts of Five Hundy by Midnight, gave me a great forum to spread the word about the book. Scott Roeben artfully snapped the author photo that graces this book. It's great fun interacting with so many people who are so passionate about this city that I study and call home.

And of course, my deepest gratitude goes to my wife Suni and our two children (who weren't born yet when I started writing this book but are here to see me finish it) each of whom helped keep me grounded, focused, and mercifully distracted just when I had to be. I love you all.

Who Is Jay Jackson Sarno?

Jay Sarno should be the patron saint of Las Vegas. More than twenty-five years after his death, it's still a city built in his image.

Before anyone else, he knew that Las Vegas should be about one thing: *action.* That word, to Jay and others like him, meant a combination of excitement, risk, and pleasure that no one had quite bottled up in one place before.

Do you sometimes like things that are bad for you? So did Jay. Do you still want them? So did Jay. And millions of others, of course, but Jay did something about it: he built a casino, Caesars Palace, around the idea that not only was it okay to indulge yourself, but that you should celebrate doing it. Gambling, eating, enjoying pleasure more than you should, this was action as delivered by Jay Sarno.

Whether it was the way the craps tables were laid out in the oval casino or the thrill of being served by wine goddesses who peeled grapes for and massaged the temples of male guests, visitors realized that Caesars Palace gave them something they wanted that they'd never known they were missing. The casino was a success, but Sarno's management of it wasn't, thanks to some of the promises he'd had to make to get it built. His solution? Build another casino, one that turned the circus into a gambler's paradise.

That casino, Circus Circus, struggled. Yet Sarno stuck with it and bucked the conventional wisdom that no one could make it work. By the time he was forced to step away from running the casino (for a small legal complication stemming from his admittedly paying the largest bribe in IRS history to an undercover agent), the framework for its future success was set.

And when Sarno needed a reason to go on living, after his legal problems were behind him and he had enough to remain materially comfortable for the rest of his life, he tried to build another casino. Called the Grandissimo, it would have started the mega-resort era in Las Vegas a decade before the 1989 opening of The Mirage. Its design would anticipate the generation of resorts that transformed Las Vegas in the 1990s. The Grandissimo would have updated the fantasy elements that Sarno had pioneered with Caesars for the mass-market era. As it stands, others, like his protégé Steve Wynn, took that step, carrying Sarno's influence on Las Vegas into the 21st century. In fact, as the city re-invented itself in the new century to better appeal to adult tastes, it returned to the ambience first supplied by Caesars Palace in the 1960s.

"What happens here," the official watchword for Las Vegas freedom for the past decade, began with Jay Sarno.

But where did Jay Sarno start? The man he became in Las Vegas was the culmination of a lifetime of reinvention. A business student at the University of Missouri when the United States joined World War II, Sarno joined the army—not out of any great patriotism, but because his awful grades left him few other options. He had been too busy selling ice cream at games, running a laundry service, and gambling with the proceeds to go to most of his classes, though he had paid some attention in art history.

But he didn't have his own name yet.

Sarno was calm as he was fingerprinted, examined, and admitted into the Army Air Force. It was September 1942: Men were dying overseas, but he wasn't worried. Standing in line, he mused that the army couldn't be tougher than his childhood in the slaughterhouse district of St. Joseph, Missouri—if he could find the right angle. Still, everything was so serious, so regimented.

The inductee ahead of him finished, and Sarno stepped in front of the overworked sergeant who was processing the recruits.

"Give me your last name, first name, middle name," he said, pen at the ready. Sarno's first problem. Middle names were a luxury that his *shtetl*-born parents had not lavished on their children. The immigration inspectors had only demanded two names: why would you need more? When Sarno stammered that he didn't have a middle name, the sergeant grew livid.

"You've got thirty seconds to come up with one, or you're not joining the army," he shouted.

"Jackson," Sarno said after only a moment's pause. "My name is Jay Jackson Sarno." The name had a certain Southern grace. It fit. Whether Sarno knew it or not, his new namesake, Andrew Jackson, had once pawned his clothes to settle a gambling debt. Sarno would do the same in a few years.

Growing up, Sarno had been alternately known as Jake, Jay, and Jack. Now he told the world what he wanted—what he demanded—to be called. In one stroke, Sarno erased his uninspiring father and became "Jack's son," his own man.

Choosing his name set the tone for a life that Sarno organized around living for the moment and chasing, like all gamblers, action. It wasn't about winning or losing, necessarily: it was about the *chance* to win or lose. Sarno would have gladly bet $100 to win $1 on 100 to 1 odds, if it was the only game in town.

Does this sound unhealthy? It was, and Jay knew it. But it was *action*.

By his own definition, Sarno was a "gambling degenerate." Today, doctors would call him a compulsive gambler. He was compulsive about everything: eating (only the best food, and lots of it), playing golf (just about every day, naturally betting big), and chasing women (to his wife's chagrin, until the divorce). Even his friends considered him crass, arrogant, and supremely difficult to get along with. He didn't need to be a nice guy. He knew that money could buy him anything he wanted and he was convinced that he could get that money by building better hotels than anyone else. The key was knowing what people wanted: to be told that it was okay to eat too much, gamble too much, look for happiness outside of your marriage.

And, though it galled his enemies, who included some of the city's most powerful men, to admit it, Sarno was right. His places worked. Caesars Palace ruled Las Vegas high roller scene until Steve

Wynn opened the The Mirage, and his second casino, Circus Circus, opened the Strip to the mass market.

So why isn't Jay Sarno better known today? Why isn't he part of the pop culture mythology that surrounds the city?

Las Vegas, after all, has no problem honoring flawed men. Marginal mobster Bugsy Siegel has been wrongly canonized as the city's founding father, and flipped-out billionaire Howard Hughes as its corporate savior. Building casinos with money borrowed from the Teamsters, facing down the federal government, refusing to accept the status quo—these are things that Las Vegas celebrates, not scorns.

But today's Las Vegas is uncomfortable with Sarno, despite the drama of his story and his enduring legacy. Why? He committed the only unpardonable sin in that corner of America: he was honest about his weaknesses. Jay Sarno pushed everything Las Vegas stands for to its farthest extremes; he shows what happens when too much of a good thing turns bad. For this, he has been cast out from the pantheon.

But Sarno's life tells us everything we need to know about how the Las Vegas we all know today came into existence: it's the story of how a determined man looking for action can change the world, and even make himself an emperor—for a while, anyway.

"Courage is moving from failure to failure without losing enthusiasm."

Winston Churchill, at the height of the Battle of Britain

"Don't worry, I'll get them tomorrow."

Jay Sarno, after losing $50,000 shooting craps
for the fourth consecutive night

ONE

Much Ado about Miami Beach

In shorts and sandals, shirtsleeves and sunburns, the crowd held its collective breath.

The two gin rummy players had started for a dime a point earlier in the afternoon; they were now up to five dollars a point. In a few minutes, one of them would be several hundred dollars richer, and the other would be cursing his bad luck.

Jay Sarno looked at his cards. He didn't like what he saw—what might be the start of a run of hearts, but not much else. But the cards had to start falling his way sometime. They certainly had been going against him all day.

It was the summer of 1957. Sarno was booked through the end of the following week at the Fontainebleau, Miami Beach's defining monument to modern luxury. He had a job to do there, but he didn't see why he couldn't have some fun playing cards in the meantime.

He glanced at the curving half-circle of the hotel tower, then behind him at the frolickers in swim trunks and flowered one-piece bathing suits jumping and splashing in the rectangular pool. Sunbathers soaked in the rays on neatly arranged navy blue deck chairs, waiters weaving among them with trays of drinks and snacks. Further out, past the carefully groomed trees, a swooping series of cabanas marked the boundary between the Fontainebleau and the wind-blown dunes that overlooked the sea.

It was just a quick look. Sarno didn't even let his eyes rest for more than an instant on the buxom blonde sunbathing just behind him. Refocusing, he stared at the man sitting across from him. Sammy Cohen, Sarno thought the name was. He owned a fur store in Philadelphia—or was it Boston? He kept looking, even after Cohen glanced up from his cards.

"You say you're in hotels?" Cohen asked, taking his time to decide whether to draw from the discard pile or stock.

"That's right," Sarno replied. "I'm a prominent hotel man in Atlanta. I've got almost a dozen apartment buildings there, too," he padded his resume considerably, "and quite a few motor hotels around Georgia. My partners and I have also built professional buildings across the South. But I'm proudest of the hotels."

Sarno's voice carried a little farther in the salt air when he mentioned hotels. Becoming a "hotel man" was about as high as a man in his circumstances and of his generation could hope to go. At a time when restrictive covenants still barred Jews from the tonier country clubs and neighborhoods, the hotel business, like the movie industry, was relatively open. Smart Jewish attorneys, bankers, and doctors were, of course, tearing down the barriers that had kept them out of old-money law firms and brokerage houses, but Sarno didn't want to work those hours. Owning a hotel seemed the quickest way to get rich, which was itself a means to an end. What it could buy— gambling, women, comfort—was worth hustling for.

As Cohen finally drew a card from stock, Sarno asked "Do you ever make it to Augusta?"

"No, not really."

"I built this fantastic motor inn there, just a few miles from the golf course." Sarno picked up one card and quickly dropped another. "You like to golf?"

"No, I don't. Old war injury. Burma-India-China theater." Cohen glanced involuntarily at his left leg, rubbed it just above the knee. "Had me laid up for months. Did you serve?"

"Yeah, Army Air Corps. Are you going to draw?"

"Oh, sorry," Cohen said, and they drew and discarded without speaking for a few minutes. Sarno started building up a nice heart run.

"You're here with family?" Cohen asked, seeming eager to make small talk. He must have even worse cards than me, Sarno thought, and couldn't completely suppress a grin.

"Maybe." Sarno drew a four to add to his hearts. "Last summer, I promised my mother that I'd get married within a year. I'm still a young man—thirty-six—but she wants me to settle down. You know how it is."

"You're here with your mother?" Cohen asked.

"No, she's up in Long Beach. Actually, since I've got to get married and my year's almost up, I figured I'd try to wrap it up this week. I've got two real prospects, but I can't decide which one I want to go with." Sarno watched while Cohen wiped the sweat from his brow. It was hot, but not that hot, he thought.

"I flew them both down here," Sarno continued, "with their mothers to chaperone, of course—and I'm seeing them both until I make up my mind."

Cohen looked at him.

"It's all perfectly respectable," Sarno added quickly. "Neither one knows about the other." He picked up his half-finished corned beef special, dabbed it in some Russian dressing that had dripped onto the plate, took three bites in quick succession. He didn't waste much time chewing. Wiping his mouth with his hand, he gulped down the rest of his iced tea. Almost as an afterthought, he dropped a stray ace on the discard pile then, as Cohen's eyes flicked from one end of his cards to the other, finished off the rest of the sandwich. Cohen's pastrami and tongue, with only a single bite eaten, lay tantalizingly out of reach. If the game went on much longer, Sarno thought, he had have to have a waiter bring him some chocolate cake from the coffee shop, or maybe some of the knishes.

Cohen laid down a three of hearts. Sarno snapped it up, dropped a seven of spades, and ginned.

"That puts me over the top!" he declared. "Well, Sammy, you've had the honor of losing to one of the best gin players in the world. How about one more game—maybe ten dollars a point just to keep it interesting?"

Stunned for a moment, Cohen began to appreciate just how much money was about to change hands. No, he said quietly, he wasn't interested in another game. After some polite figuring, they agreed on the total. Cohen opened up his wallet and handed over several hundred dollars—much of it originally Sarno's, but that was beside the point.

Jay Sarno stood up, pocketed the thick roll of bills without counting it, and shook Cohen's hand. Sarno had nothing straight or narrow about him. His slightly bowed legs supported a full belly. He flashed a broad smile over a plump chin as his wide, deep-set eyes gleamed beneath a sharply receding hairline. For a second, he stood, splay-footed and rooted to the ground. Then he sauntered away from the table with an athletic grace that belied his girth.

"Morrie," Cohen said weakly to one of the men behind him. "Don't ever let me play for five dollars a point again. What was I thinking?"

"That Sarno'll keep coming back until he wins, or until he can't borrow any more," Morrie said. "If he had lost this game, he woulda talked you into ten dollars a point for the next one. You'd have agreed, too. A guy like that, he'll never quit. Trust me, you got off easy."

With a lingering look at the blonde sunbather, Sarno started toward the lobby. He had a date with Francine and her mother tonight, and he wanted to get in some time on the putting green before he freshened up and changed into one of his new suits. He paused as his eyes adjusted to the darkened interior. God, he thought, this place is perfect. Antique statues gave the room real class, and the sofas were so plump you could get lost in them.

This was no accident. Morris Lapidus, the Fontainebleau's architect, had started his career as a store designer, liberally using bold decoration, sweeping curves, and bright light to draw people into shops. People needed stimulation, he stressed to clients. Buildings should look and feel welcoming, make their guests feel better about themselves. Though the architectural orthodoxy excoriated the young architect for pandering to the base emotions of the rabble, store owners found that their customers enjoyed shopping in Lapidus-designed boutiques. They spent more money. Pragmatism beat theory—he built what people liked, not what his professors had said they should like.

When extrapolated to hotels, the result was the Fontainebleau, a Miami modern classic filled with imported chic and paying customers. In this, his first ground-up commission, Lapidus planned an overarching French modern provincial theme, marking the bathrooms for *dames* and *messieurs* and tricking out the hotel rooms with Louis XIV fixtures. Sarno, like most of the guests, liked it here: it made him feel like he was far from home. He got a kick out of the restaurant names: the Fleur de Lis Dining Room, the Poodle Lounge, the La Ronde Nightclub. The buffet plates piled too high, the lobbies crammed with ornament, were plush, comforting.

As a budding hotel man, Sarno noted the tricks Lapidus used to make the guest feel like a million bucks. All the hotel was a stage; the famous staircase to nowhere (actually to the coat check) was just one example. Lapidus consciously designed platforms where people could be seen. To enter the hotel's main restaurant, guests walked up three steps, stood on a dais lit by soft pink floodlights, then descended three steps. It was an egotist's delight, an exhibitionist's parade.

Looking at the curved staircase that dominated the lobby, he imagined each of his two potential wives walking down it, wearing a fur he had bought her, glittering with his diamonds, while everyone gazed in envy. He still couldn't choose.

Then the most beautiful woman he had ever seen walked through the front doors.

Jay actually gasped as she paused for a second before walking across the black and white marble floor like it was a fashion runway, her back straight, each step perfectly measured. She glided past him. Before he could put it into words, Jay could see it. This was the woman who'd wear his diamonds as she descended into the Fontainebleau lobby. She had to be. He hustled after her.

"Miss, miss!" he almost shouted as he caught up with her. Behind the reception desk, a clerk looked up in alarm. The blonde turned around.

"My name's Jay Sarno. I'm a big hotel man in Atlanta, one of the top guys at the Standard Town and Country Club." He looked down at her left hand, thanking God for the bare ring finger. She stared back at the stocky, balding, but not entirely unhandsome man in front of her.

"I know you've got plans tonight," he said before she had the chance to say a word, "but please break them for me." Sarno had been using this line since his college days; it worked about a third of the time. This, he knew instantly, probably wasn't one of those times, but it was worth a shot.

"Why should I do that?" she wanted to know.

"Because I'm going to marry you."

"You don't even know my name."

"That'll give us something to talk about then, won't it? Just be down here at seven. I'll pick you up in my new Cadillac. You ever ride in a Cadillac? We'll grab something to eat, maybe see Eddie Fisher at the Newport."

"I'm not going anywhere with you," the blonde said, though she allowed him to walk with her. "I've got to meet my parents."

"That's fine! Bring them too! I won't take no for an answer. Let me meet them. You'll see—they'll love me. You'll love me! Come on, tell me that you'll have dinner with me."

"No, I've already got plans with my parents," she replied, but as they walked, she kept talking.

Her name was Joyce Cooper. Her parents were Jack and Bertha of Brooklyn, Michigan, a little town in the south of the state. She lived in San Francisco, where she owned the Patricia Stevens College, a finishing school and modeling agency.

"That sounds great," he offered, "but I can give you everything you've ever wanted. Just give me a chance."

He meant it, too. Jay was generous with everyone, starting with himself. He felt no guilt at all about the four sandwiches he had eaten since breakfast, or the hundreds of dollars he had nearly lost at gin. He was smart, he was sometimes lucky, and he deserved to have fun. As they stepped into the late afternoon sun, Jay started considering what he would say to her parents.

A few minutes shy of 7:30, Jack, Bertha, and Joyce Cooper piled into Sarno's Cadillac. They were starving, and so was Jay, but he didn't seem to be in much of a hurry.

Jack, Sarno learned over dinner, owned Cooper's Department Store, which was *the* department store in tiny Brooklyn. Joyce was twenty-four and had bought her Patricia Stevens franchise with Jack's money after she had been a student there.

"What does your family do?" Jack asked.

Sarno shared a bit, hitting the positives. His oldest brother,

Herman, was a successful lawyer and real estate investor in New York City, second-oldest Sam was a doctor in Morehouse, Missouri. Brother Louis, well, his brothers made sure he always had a job. Then there were his sisters Sara, Hannah, and Phyllis. Most of his family now lived in New York. They were not exceptionally wealthy, but were respectable enough.

Jay didn't want to waste time talking about his parents, who still preferred to speak Yiddish, or his childhood in St. Joseph. His best asset was his future.

"I want to build more hotels—lots of them," he volunteered. "I'm looking for the perfect piece of land in Atlanta right now. I want to build something that's geared towards the businessman, but with some style: as glamorous as Miami Beach, but as convenient as a regular motor inn."

That made sense, Jack agreed between bites of his filet. Bertha looked on appreciatively. Joyce appeared to be counting the tiles on the far wall.

"So how did you get into hotels?" Jack asked.

This was something Jay wanted to talk about. "After I finished up at the University of Missouri, I went into business laying tile with one of my friends, Stan Mallin. I found a guy in Indiana who gave me a great deal on tile, so all we needed was to hire day laborers to install it. We started right here, in Miami, where my cousin Sidney was already running a tile company of his own. He said there was plenty of work to go around, so he didn't mind a little friendly competition.

"We called the company Tilecraft of America, and at first we didn't do too badly. There was plenty of work with all of the hotels going up, but if an owner didn't have a good tourist season it was hard to get paid. So we weren't doing as well as we should have been. Then we ran into a fraternity brother of ours who had moved to Atlanta and married a girl whose father was in construction. He said they needed good tile guys up there, and after looking into it Stan and I relocated to Atlanta.

"We're making a pretty good living, and I notice that these guys we're doing jobs for are complete *schlubs*. I wondered how a guy who wears overalls and blue jeans can afford to build a hundred-unit apartment building."

Jack was listening but Joyce wasn't.

"It turns out there were government programs that practically gave away money to builders."

This was true. In order to encourage new housing after the war, the Federal Housing Administration underwrote the liberal 608 program, which advanced substantial loans to those willing to risk new construction. From its inception in 1948 until its demise in 1954, the 608 program financed the construction of nearly a half-million apartment units nationwide. If builders could get an option on a piece of land, the federal government would practically pay them to build an apartment building.

"So, getting a loan wouldn't be a problem, but we didn't want to build something that was just like what everyone else was doing. Having just moved to town, I knew that there really wasn't anywhere for a single man to live. You can only live in a hotel or boarding house for so long, and it's such a *schlep* buying furniture and all that when you don't know if you're going to be putting down roots. So I said, why not build a place that's fully furnished?"

He explained that they had snatched up a piece of land in the Brookwood section of town and, 608 loan in hand, built a small building with only efficiency apartments. Sarno and Mallin named it, with no great imagination, the Brookwood North Apartments. The one-room units rented fully furnished for $75 a month—a perfect setup for a young, single man who didn't yet know whether he would be staying in his new city. Sarno and Mallin each moved into a Brookwood North unit. They never had a shortage of tenants.

After a while, the developers got tired of living in their efficiencies. As nice as the rooms were, sleeping next to the kitchen table lost its charm after a while. He didn't mention this to Jack.

"The Brookwood was so successful that we started looking for a bigger challenge, so we decided to build something with one-bedroom units, all furnished, too."

The Barbizon Towers was an eight-story, 80-unit building on Lombardy Way. Mallin, who'd just gotten married, moved into a penthouse unit, which was two regular apartments knocked together, while Sarno chose a regular one-bedroom.

It was an even bigger success than the Brookwood: units filled up almost immediately. After telling the waitress he would take just one slice of the key lime pie for dessert, Jay explained to Jack why the Barbizon had worked so well.

"I would say 90 percent of the tenants were guys getting a divorce. We had doctors, we had lawyers, because when a guy got kicked out of the house, he needed a place to go. The Barbizon was respectable, and a guy didn't have to worry about all the little things. We made it very uncomplicated. You've got to know how people think."

Jack agreed that Jay had a point.

"After that, Stan and I worked on other projects. He built a few more apartments, and I built the motor inns—Augusta in 1953, Atlanta in 1955. Then we teamed up to build a few doctors' buildings. But I'm really excited about getting us back into hotels. That's where I'm going to make my mark."

By this point, Jay was speaking with such conviction that Jack didn't register that the hotel man who was trying to sweep his daughter off her feet hadn't yet opened a real hotel.

Dessert came. Watching Jay systematically demolish his oversized slice of pie, leaving not a crumb behind, Jack noted that this was a man who seemed to get what he wanted.

After dinner, Jay returned the Coopers to the hotel and, with a promise to drop by the next day, said goodnight. That Joyce hadn't shown much interest didn't really bother him; he knew that it was just a matter of finding the right approach. No doubt about it, she was the one. He sent his two would-be brides back home with two phone calls and no regrets. That loose end wrapped up, he dove headlong into the courtship of Joyce.

Sarno had a deadline: the Coopers were leaving Miami in less than a week. It would take longer than that, he thought, to get through to Joyce. After two weeks of dinners and gifts, maybe she would agree to go on a solo date with him, but he didn't have time for that. Her parents, he knew, would be more immediately receptive.

He showed up at the Coopers' room the next day and casually invited Jack and Bertha to join him for lunch while Joyce met up with some friends from school. He gave Bertha a small diamond pin—it was nothing really—that he had picked up that morning. He asked Jack about how he had built up the store over so many years, complimented Bertha on her hair and clothes. He was as charming a man as they'd ever met, though they still didn't know much about him.

"What did you do during the war?" Jack asked after they'd finished eating.

"I was an aviation flight line technician in the Pacific," Jay answered.

"Really? Where were you stationed?"

"A few places. New Caledonia, then Guadalcanal, then Biak."

"Did you see any action?"

"Not on the front lines. I was support. When the planes got back from flying missions, they'd tell the chief mechanic what was on the fritz—a radio, the radar unit, what have you. Then I'd unscrew whatever was broken and put a new one in."

"That sounds interesting. I hear electronics is a great field. Did you ever think about going back into it?"

"Nah, I didn't know a thing about how anything worked, I just knew how to use a screwdriver. It was the most tedious job I ever had. But I had a sideline that made it worthwhile." Jay looked at his guests. This wasn't a story he told often, but he was enjoying himself.

"You figure a guy who's out there fighting in the jungle has to blow off some steam, right? I mean, he could get killed at any moment, he's thousands of miles away from home, he hasn't even seen a girl in months. He's going to need some relief, right?"

Jack nodded. Jay continued.

"We didn't have just fighter pilots landing at the base. There were cargo jockeys too, guys who were hauling freight from the mainland or Australia—sky truckers, really. They were good guys, for the most part, and once I got to know them they didn't mind carrying a little extra weight if they could make a few bucks on the side.

"So a couple of the pilots brought me a few cases of booze each week and I took care of them. I had a guaranteed market with the marines who were rotating back to base, and pretty soon I was pulling down a couple of hundred dollars a week.

"Not bad, right? But this was just the start. I bankrolled a craps game and really cleaned up. It helped to pay for my rummy games with the officers."

"Sounds like you did all right for yourself."

"Oh, it gets better than that." Jay was swimming in memories now. "After a few weeks, I got my own personal Jeep. This was something that most officers, even, didn't get. What I did was I paid the mechanics in the motor pool to snag a spare part here, a spare part there. Then they built me a Jeep, all out of spare parts. The best part is, because they built it from the ground up, officially it wasn't even there, so no one could do anything about it."

This fellow Jay could land on his feet, Jack thought.

At dinner that night, Jack and Bertha sang Jay's praises to Joyce. If they'd have known that he was out looking for a dice game, they might have thought twice, but they could only judge him by what he had told them that afternoon.

Sarno accepted that Joyce was out of his league, but divined from a few of Bertha's offhand comments that she was under just as much pressure to marry as he was. This, he decided, could only benefit him. He didn't know that her problems ran deeper than over-eager parents. Joyce's polished exterior concealed some deep insecurities. She had been overweight as a girl, but since losing the weight had discovered that she was interesting to men. Still, Joyce never quite shook her adolescent lack of confidence, though she aspired to a bigger world than her parents; that's why when her father insisted she go to college, she went to Patricia Stevens, which was then an old-fashioned finishing school.

Once she bought the school, there was no turning back; after living in San Francisco, the boys of rural Michigan weren't good enough for her. As a result, Joyce turned down several marriage proposals. She was hoping for someone who would share a big city's culture and class with her. An ambitious hustler from Atlanta wasn't really him. But her parents were anxious about her prospects. She was their only child, and they were desperate for a grandchild. At twenty-four, Joyce teetered on spinsterhood.

The Sarno charm offensive convinced Joyce's parents their son-in-law had arrived at last: this was no unsophisticated Michigan boy, but a suave, well-connected, big-city developer. He could make a fine husband. They now began pressing the issue, though Joyce remained unconvinced.

"Where are you going to get a guy better than this?" Jack asked Joyce. "And look how badly he's after you."

Joyce still wasn't interested.

"He's like a maniac for you," Bertha persisted. "Imagine how well he'll take care of you. You'll never get a better deal than this."

Joyce had many strong points, but sticking to her guns was not one of them. Until late in life, she tended to wilt next to more dominating personalities, and her parents were so insistent. Maybe this wasn't such a bad idea. After all, Jay was promising her so much.

Four days after he first saw her walk through the doors of the Fontainebleau, Joyce agreed to become Mrs. Jay Sarno.

Jay immediately jumped on the phone to order a flawless four-carat diamond ring from his brother Herman's connection in New York; he got a good deal.

Jay's mother was over the moon, as were Jack and Bertha. Even Joyce was optimistic, though getting married would mean selling her Patricia Stevens franchise and moving from San Francisco to Atlanta; life with this free-wheeling entrepreneur might be exciting. He was no Cary Grant, but he was handsome in his own way, especially when he was excited about something. His eyes sparkled with a sheer love of living that touched something in her.

With both sets of parents eager for a quick marriage, the wedding was set for three months hence, in Windsor, Ontario. This was close to the Coopers' Michigan home, but more importantly, Herman Sarno happened to own a hotel there, which meant that no one would be paying for a room. It was just another benefit, Jay told Jack and Bertha, of their only daughter becoming a Sarno.

With the Coopers safely dispatched, Sarno celebrated. He practiced his swing on the putting green and had no trouble finding high-stakes gin rummy games. He enjoyed the action, but he got just as much pleasure simply soaking in the Fontainebleau.

Jay Sarno had come to the Fontainebleau to choose his wife, and he had known he wouldn't leave until he had a fiancé. A little bit of luck, a little hustling, and he had gotten the girl of his dreams. In a hotel like the Fontainebleau, he thought, a man could do anything. Someday, he would own a hotel like that.

TWO

The Windsor Knot

Jay Sarno arrived in Windsor two days before the wedding, unsure of everything. Driving up from Atlanta, he had begun to wonder if he was ready to settle down after all. When he got to the hotel, his brothers and sisters were everywhere, offering advice about everything from china patterns to diaper services. His one-bedroom apartment at the Barbizon Towers suddenly didn't seem quite so empty.

Worse yet, his in-laws were about to meet his father.

Alexander Sarno looked like an older version of Jay—short and balding—but they didn't have much in common besides a short temper. Alex had never quite adjusted to life in the United States, and Jay had never quite adjusted to his father. Jack Cooper seemed so confident, so at ease, even among strangers. Alex, on the other hand, still spoke with a heavy Eastern European accent and had a tendency to shout when people didn't understand him. He seemed to be under a perpetual cloud.

The old man hadn't had an easy life. Like his father, his grandfather, and his grandfather's grandfather, he had been born in Szczuczyn (pronounced "shtoot-chin"), a small settlement of about five thousand, of whom three-quarters were Jewish. Today part of Poland, the town was then within the bounds of the Russian Empire, about five miles from the Prussian border. It was a place where survival was difficult, tradition an anchor, and upward mobility unthinkable: the grocer's son became a grocer, the cobbler's son learned to repair shoes, and the best the tanner's daughter could hope for was to marry someone who sold leather goods.

Even the town's name was ridiculous. Names, Jay reflected, were not something they put a lot of thought into over there. He and his brothers didn't even know the correct English spelling of the last name their father had been born with: it was probably Sarneivicj, but it might have been Sarnovicj or even Sarnovitch. In later years, Alex's grandchildren would joke that however it was spelled, it rhymed with "sonofabitch." But Jay expected as much from people who lived in a town like Szczuczyn, so bleak that it verged on parody. As Jay's parents described it (though they didn't often speak about the old country), Szczuczyn was a town of perpetual bitter cold and hardship, where even simple pleasures were nothing more than rumors, things that happened to other people in other towns.

Over the years, Jay had learned only a little about his father's life before he came to America but could surmise that his childhood had been monotonously unpleasant. As a teenager, Alexander was drafted into the Russian military, where he learned the trade of woodworking, though he never revealed how or why the tsar's army had given him this skill. On his release from the army, which might or might not have been entirely official, he returned to Szczuczyn to marry Nellie, the bright daughter of a small-time grain dealer.

Jay's parents never spoke of any great romance that led to the union, but it was fruitful from the start. Almost immediately, they had Herman, then about a year later Samuel. Nellie and Alexander seemed to be settling into lives similar to those of their parents and grandparents, dominated by large families, tiring work, and modest religious devotion. But as the Russian Empire loomed on the verge of collapse, antisemitism and hard times mounted, and the villagers slowly began to realize that to survive they might have to abandon the land they'd hugged for so many generations.

Not wanting to take his chances on being recalled to the army, in 1909 Alexander decided to try his luck in America, leaving Nellie and the children temporarily behind. He booked passage on a ship out of Rotterdam sailing for New York, where he met a confusing arrival. An Ellis Island immigration inspector, his ears attuned to the thousands of Southern Italians he had processed, wrote "Sarno" on Alexander's papers after Alexander mumbled his name. Just like that, a name that had been his father's and his father's father's was erased. He registered no regrets.

The newly-christened Alex Sarno ended up in a woodworking shop in Kansas, where within two years he had saved up enough money to send for his wife and sons. Nellie, however, almost immediately found life in Kansas intolerable and demanded that the family move. Nellie and Alexander settled on St. Joseph, Missouri, as their new home. Alexander found a job at the cabinet-maker Ehrlich and Sons, and the family moved into a largish house on Indiana Street in South St. Joseph. They let out most of the rooms to boarders.

Jay cringed just thinking about that house. God, it stank. His parents had moved into the shadow of a meatpacking plant. He remembered a classmate covering his mouth and nose with his sleeve blocks away because of the stench. Not that he had a great many visitors. Born squarely in middle America, Sarno grew up an outsider. At the time, St. Joseph had a Jewish community of perhaps 750 men, women, and children, of whom the Sarnos were the poorest, with a correspondingly low place on the social register.

Nor was there comfort outside of the small Jewish community. At Hosea grade school, in the heart of South St. Joseph, young Jay was a frequent target for bullying by the children of the Poles, Lithuanians, and Latvians who dominated the packing plants. He won his share of fights, but lost his share too. Brute force counted for much, as did animal cunning, but appeals to justice fell on deaf ears.

No one in the Sarno household shielded him from life's hardships; certainly not his father. Nellie had long ago established herself as the family's chief, settling any uncertainties with a word. Alex groused and found fault, but became an increasingly ineffectual autocrat. His sons and daughters still acknowledged him as titular patriarch, but when they really needed something, they asked their mother.

At a very young age Sarno internalized the Darwinian imperatives that he saw all around him. Power mattered. Those who didn't have it were condemned to humiliation. But smarts made a difference: if he could figure a way around the bullies, he could make it to school and back in one piece. There was no place for empathy or compassion; that words could hurt just as badly as fists did not mean he had to choose them carefully. In his Depression childhood, there was no courage for the meek, no mercy for the miserable, no nourishment for the hungry. He learned only that if you couldn't feed yourself, you'd starve, both physically and spiritually.

N o one was going hungry in Windsor, Herman made sure. In fact, things were going better than Jay had hoped. Their father hadn't embarrassed him too badly. And Joyce had utterly captivated his sisters.

"My god, look at her," they cooed after she left the room. "Gorgeous, just gorgeous. We'll be getting some looks mixed into the family tree. And so classy."

It had been a long journey from St. Joseph to Windsor for all of them. Jay had been born at a time of transition, when Alex had saved enough to become a small-time capitalist. He quit his job with Ehrlich and opened Sarno's Hardware, a small store in southeastern St. Joseph. Nellie, who didn't share Alex's confidence in his entrepreneurial acumen, took a job as a saleswoman at Feldenstein's, a dry goods store, as a precaution. Eventually she ran a small grocery store. The children worked as well, washing dishes at local restaurants, delivering papers, and serving as runners for stores, including their mother's.

Amid the change, the family celebrated the birth of another son, given the Hebrew name Jacob but loosely called Jay, Jake, or Jack, on July 2, 1921. For much of his childhood, he remained the baby of the family, though another sister, Phyllis, would be born seven years later.

Eight days after his birth, Jay had a traditional Jewish *brit*, or circumcision. This was the last religious ceremony he would willingly participate in. His family was of two minds when it came to religion. Alex attended synagogue at least weekly, chanting the Hebrew prayers and keeping up with Torah readings better than most of the other congregants, but he didn't communicate any of the awe or passion of his faith to his children. Outside of the temple, he didn't try especially hard to observe the Sabbath, a major mark of an observant Jew. The family kept kosher casually: Alex and Nellie wouldn't think of eating pork and shellfish, though they went to non-kosher restaurants, and their children for the most part ate as they liked, considering their parents' food taboos an old-country superstition. And though Alex taught his children Hebrew and Yiddish, none of them became particularly religious as adults.

Jay pushed that skepticism a step further. His brothers had dutifully been bar mitzvahed when they turned thirteen, chanting a Torah reading from their synagogue's pulpit. But Jay refused to submit to the ritual, which requires months of preparation. Over twenty years later, no one was surprised that he didn't consider having a traditional religious wedding ceremony with a rabbi presiding.

Meanwhile, Herman was in his element. Everyone had arrived and checked in on time. He even had time for some cards with his brothers. It wasn't as much fun as playing with the *machers* in New York, but it was a way to pass the time.

He was now calling the shots for the Sarno clan—to the extent that Nellie let him. It had been that way for nearly twenty years. Herman had worked hard to get to where he was. He had started early; by the time he was ten, he had read every book at his level in the local Carnegie library, and by the time Jay was old enough to get his first job Herman had already worked his way through New York University law school. After that, he didn't practice law, but instead started on a career as a real estate developer, buying properties on the cheap and selling them at a profit. When Jay went off to the University of Missouri in 1939, Herman was in the process of resettling his parents in New York City, having become the acknowledged leader of the family.

He was not always a benevolent despot. Herman insisted on telling his siblings, their children, and his own parents, where to live, where to work, and where to invest. Herman helped his brother Sam through medical school—a favor he never let Sam forget when he needed to borrow money—and got his sister Sara a job at a New York department store, even though she had gone to school to become a teacher and had just received her teacher's certificate from the state of Missouri.

Herman had done well during World War II, buying hotels and converting them into temporary housing for war workers. He made well-placed friends, counting Laurance Rockefeller as one of his investors, and even owned the parking concession beneath Rockefeller Center for a time. At war's end, he was a middling New York deal-maker with a foot in the door of the city's elite.

Despite his success, Herman had flaws: he was as abrasive as his father, and he gambled too much. He swelled with pride when prominent New York businessmen asked him to play gin rummy, never realizing that it was just because he was a lousy card player with deep pockets.

Herman's businesses suffered as a result of his gambling problems. Typically, Herman would need money to pay off a bookie; he would call Sam in Missouri for help, offering him a small interest in one of his properties. When Sam's wife, Rosalind, got wind of the new "investment," she would launch into her husband, sparking a bitter argument. There were allegations that things weren't completely kosher with Herman's books. Eventually, Sam started talking back to his older brother, leading to furious fights.

Herman, still, was used to getting his way. Jay frustrated him. It wasn't right that a man should work so hard at avoiding responsibility.

As one of the youngest children in the family, Jay grew up more quickly than his classmates. Before any of them, he was introduced to cards, cigarettes, girls, and drinking. He also picked up bits and pieces of his older siblings' schoolwork, so when his class finally got to the topics he remembered, he had the feeling of learning nothing more than what he already knew, so naturally he felt intellectually superior to his peers and got used to knowing a bit more about the world than those around him. Most of the time he really did.

Jay had always refused to play it straight. For all the Sarno children, each day meant work and not much else. Up before dawn, they'd help out at their mother's store then head off to school. After classes, it was back to the store or off to a job outside the home, then homework, then bed.

This was the world he knew: no time for child's play, only work, hardship, and self-denial.

"We were a poor family," he said years later, after he had become one of Las Vegas' wealthiest men. "We were all taught to be self-sustaining."

They toiled with a somber devotion: their daily labor was a sacrifice to be made, something to be taken very seriously. Jay took a different approach, refusing to plod along making mere pennies when he could risk everything for a few dollars. By the time he had started earning money outside the house, he had already been introduced to the wonders of cards. His father and older brothers played often, for nickels and dimes mostly, and he noticed that the players became more animated as the stakes got higher. He had started playing kids games—hearts and war—but soon graduated to pinochle and gin rummy. Cards taught him that the more money you had, the more action you'd find. Before he was even shaving, he was constantly on the prowl for money-making opportunities, delivering newspapers, running errands, and sweeping up stores, then trying to push his fortunes by gambling his tiny wages. He didn't always win.

Jay, Herman thought, was infuriating. Here he was in his mid-thirties, still not married, and he was talking about wriggling out again. He had done it once before. When he was fresh out of college—the second time, after the war—he had talked one of his brother's sisters-in-law into bed. Gotten her pregnant, too, then refused to do the right thing and marry her. Herman fumed just thinking about it. To leave a woman in a position like that was bad enough, but to disgrace the family, to defy *him*…it was unthinkable.

This was worse. Jay had promised to marry this Cooper woman, gotten him to make all the arrangements, and now he had cold feet? It was ridiculous. And he had the nerve to beat him for three hundred dollars at rummy the night before, and smile about it.

With the hours ticking down, Jay was getting more and more uneasy. "I'm just not sure," he complained to his sisters.

"But you can't disappoint mother," came the reply. "You promised. Isn't she good looking enough?"

"She's beautiful, of course—even an idiot could see that. But I'm just not ready."

"Right, she's beautiful, and she comes from a fine family. She even plays golf, Jay. What more could you ask for? She's perfect for you."

"I know, I know, but I'm just not sure anymore." Jay could never tell his sisters this, but he was afraid of being trapped by marriage to anyone: he enjoyed playing the field, savoring his conquests in his one-bedroom apartment at the Barbizon. Trading that in for one woman, no matter how attractive, didn't seem right.

At the Saturday night rehearsal dinner, he looked like a man about to explode, talking a mile a minute and eating even more than usual. Several of his siblings went to bed that night unsure if there would be a wedding the next day.

The Sarno and Cooper families rose on Sunday morning and dressed for the wedding as the tension grew. Jay flitted from room to room, talking with a brother, then a sister, still undecided.

"Is she pregnant?" Herman asked again and again, ready to argue that this time Jay wouldn't skirt his duty. But, to the best of everyone's knowledge, Joyce wasn't pregnant.

The Coopers sensed that something was amiss but kept quiet. The Sarnos, on the other hand, began arguing with Jay, then each other. Nellie and Alex broke into Yiddish, as they often did when the talk got passionate. This was not a family to discuss anything quietly: the traditional Passover *seder* dinner was often ruined when a disagreement over a minor point of the ceremony sparked a shouting match. Jay leaving a woman at the altar took even this well-practiced group of arguers to a new level of fury.

"For God's sake, it's just not right! We flew up here to see him get married! And the cake's already been paid for!" They were all angry at him, but somehow they ended up screaming at each other while Jay slunk off.

Then they saw through a window that he was outside, walking toward his car. Someone threw a chunk of ice at him. It fell short, skidding away harmlessly as he closed the car door and drove off. The Sarno/Cooper union was broken.

Jay knew that it would take a long time for him to live this down: to his sisters, he would always be their cherubic little brother, but Herman would see this stunt as an affront against morality, and his mother would be devastated. He didn't know how he could make this right to them. Joyce was almost an afterthought. It wasn't her that he was abandoning; it was the entire idea of making a choice. She wouldn't take it personally.

But Joyce was livid. She had only reluctantly agreed to marry this man and *he* was the one pulling out? Still, she was more than a little relieved as she returned to her parents' house in Brooklyn and began planning to put her life back together.

On the long drive back to Atlanta, Sarno began to have second thoughts about his second thoughts. He *had* promised his mother he would get married. He probably wouldn't find anyone better than Joyce, and he thought that he could really love her. She had already spoken about children, and he wanted children. He just couldn't see it happening to him yet. But, he thought as the miles clicked by, he couldn't wait much longer. He turned the car around.

There was a knock on the Cooper's front door.

"Please let me in," Sarno begged Jack from the doorstep. "I've got to talk to your daughter."

"I think you said plenty up in Windsor," Jack replied.

"I didn't say enough. I couldn't. I was nervous. Don't you ever get nervous, Jack? Just let me in to talk to Joyce—that's all I ask. I made a mistake, I know that. But if she doesn't forgive me, I don't know what I'll do."

With a glance at Bertha, who slowly nodded, Jack opened the door. Seeing Jay standing there, his tie askew and his pants covered with crumbs, Jack could no longer hate the man who'd abandoned his daughter at the altar. He looked so pitiful.

"I'm so sorry. I'm so sorry," Jay said to Jack and Bertha, and he looked sincere. "I don't know what I was thinking. I've made some big mistakes in my life, but this is the biggest. But I still care for Joyce. If you give me a chance, I know I can make it right."

With Jack and Bertha's assent, Jay walked to Joyce's bedroom. He rapped lightly on the door. Hearing no response, he started talking.

"You've got every right to hate me, I know that, but just let me talk to you. Give me ten minutes. If you still want me to leave after that, I'll go. But you owe it to yourself to hear me out, Joyce. I don't want you to make the same kind of mistake I did. I know I could make you so happy. Please talk to me."

Joyce opened her door and let her lost fiancé in, closing it behind him.

No one knows exactly what he told her in the bedroom; she never confided anything to her children, and Jay was mum, as usual, about his past. Whatever it was, it must have been good enough to make her forget her humiliation at Windsor. When she opened the door, she announced that she planned to elope with him.

Joyce quickly packed and said goodbye to her parents. Their honeymoon was the drive from Michigan down to Atlanta. Along the way, they stopped at a justice of the peace to be married, with no fanfare and no family.

Despite his heartfelt return to woo his bride, Sarno wasn't entirely focused on his new wife as they drove toward a new life together. When they stopped to visit Jay's brother Sam and his family in Morehouse, Missouri, Joyce confessed to her new in-laws that the drive was taking longer than expected because of her new husband's wandering eye. Whenever he saw a golf course, she explained, he insisted that they stop and play a round. She couldn't talk him out of it. But she found that, if she spotted a course on the right side of the road first and then squared her shoulder into the car window, she could prevent Jay from seeing it, and he would blissfully drive past.

From the start, she knew that a certain measure of creativity would be the key to this marriage.

THREE

Jimmy Lends a Hand

The newly-married Jay and Joyce Sarno moved into a single-family home on Westover Drive in suburban Atlanta in early 1958.

Now a family man, Jay committed himself to seriously building his name in Atlanta by building a real hotel. As he had told the Coopers, Sarno had found some success in Atlanta, though he hadn't told the whole truth. His motels in Atlanta and near Augusta had flopped, draining most of his capital and much of his reputation.

And Stan Mallin was more important to him than he had told Jack or even Joyce. They'd met at the University of Missouri, where both were business majors and members of the small Jewish community there. They had shared the good times at Zeta Beta Tau, dressing up for nightly dinners under the watchful eye of the fraternity's house mother. Like Sarno, Mallin had interrupted his time at college to serve his country during World War II; he left the armed forces as a respectable second lieutenant.

Mallin's father had grown up in Russia, like Alexander Sarno. Like Nellie's father, he sold produce for a living. He came to America just in time to serve in the U.S. Army during World War I. Following his demobilization, he settled in Kansas City, Missouri, selling fruits and vegetables door to door from a horse-drawn cart. After years of strenuous work, he opened a produce wholesaling concern. After prospering for a while as a distributor, he sold his business and purchased several apple orchards. By the time Stan was born, the family was living in a comfortable house with a swimming pool—an uncommon luxury at the time—in the nicest part of southwestern Kansas City.

With impeccable manners, the good-looking, well-dressed Mallin was everything that Jay Sarno wasn't. While Sarno had scrapped and fought in the slaughterhouse district of St. Joseph, then braved Central High School, Mallin attended Kansas City's Southwest High School, the best school in the city. Where Sarno was plump, Mallin was slender. Sarno was brash, outspoken; Mallin was almost painfully reticent. Sarno gloried in high-stakes gambling; Mallin made it a point to avoid risk.

Still, Stan Mallin had reasons for wanting to partner with Sarno. His older brother was the heir apparent of his father's produce business; he was sick of apples and pears anyway. So when his fraternity brother called him up with a proposition, he listened. With some money left over from Jay's wartime profits and generous help from Mallin's father, Tilecraft of America was born. In Miami, then Atlanta, Mallin had been content to follow his confident friend's lead, though he was aghast at his gambling. At Missouri, Sarno had been the biggest gambler on campus; Mallin remembered that more than once Jay had begged money from his brother Sam after he had pawned his clothes to pay his debts. Back then he had just thought Jay was a kid from St. Joseph trying to act like a big shot, something he would grow out of.

But God, he could gamble. One of Stan's ZBT brothers, Al Einbender, had told him just how serious it got. Sarno had talked him into accompanying him to a sizzling crap game at the Lake of the Woods motel, a small dive on the edge of town.

"But I don't want to play," Einbender protested as they pulled up. "I don't have that kind of money."

"No, kid, you can play for small stakes. Here's a hundred bucks. Pay me back after you win."

Einbender lost. Sarno loaned him more money. Einbender lost again, and again, until he was down three hundred dollars—enough money to pay for his room and board for half the year. Jay was down several thousand dollars, an unimaginable sum for young Einbender.

Al was out the door, agonizing over how he could repay his older friend, when Jay stopped him.

"Come on, kid," he said. "Let's go back in for one more try."

They did, and incredibly enough started to win. Once Jay felt the dice getting hot, he wouldn't dream of leaving. They stayed until they had won all the chips on the table. This was the stuff that gamblers' dreams were made of.

Al won enough to repay Jay and keep a windfall that lasted him the rest of the summer. Still, the dread of nearly being in debt nauseated him, and he didn't relish the thought of ever doing it again.

Jay lived for it.

Already Sarno displayed the hallmarks of the problem gambler. He needed to bet escalating amounts of cash to get the same thrill. After losing, he gambled more to get back on top, chasing his losses. He gambled because he was bored; he gambled because he was stressed; he gambled because he couldn't find a date; he gambled to celebrate getting lucky. Like most problem gamblers, he ignored his frequent losses and celebrated his long-shot wins.

Stan had figured that eventually he would lose interest, but adulthood hadn't tamed his partner, and it became clear that the risks of starting up and nurturing a new business weren't enough for Sarno. He continued to gamble heavily, particularly on golf, but also on cards, dice, and sports.

Trying to stop Sarno from gambling, Mallin learned, was like trying to bail out a lifeboat with a sieve. Once, he returned from a short trip to discover that Sarno had lost a thousand dollars on a Georgia Tech game. It was the partners' last remaining cash reserve, and it almost ruined both of them.

Now his friend was, at last, a married man, and he was consumed by his latest obsession, the elegant conference hotel. This might change him, Stan thought.

Inspired by his new domestic situation, perhaps, Sarno began promoting his latest venture as the "very special marriage of the hotel and motel." In Sarno's words, this meant combining the self-service and convenience of the motel with "the ultimate in luxurious pampering." He might not have the budget to build a real Miami Beach hotel, but something catering to businessmen might work.

He would call it the Atlanta Cabana—a nod, at least subconsciously, to the landmark cabanas of the Fontainebleau.

It wasn't a bad idea; in the coming decades, hotels built along similar lines by major chains would drive many mom-and-pop roadside motor inns out of business. But he and Mallin faced a problem: it was nearly impossible to borrow money to build a motel. With the Eisenhower recession limiting credit, banks weren't lending much, particularly for risky projects. So it was a stroke of luck when Mallin's attorney, Morris Abram, recommended a possible lender.

Abram was not just another Atlanta lawyer. As a student he had been part of the prosecution staff at the Nuremberg tribunal. Upon his return to the United States, he took up the cause of civil rights, eventually advising presidents Kennedy and Johnson and garnering an impressive array of accomplishments and accolades, having variously served as a university president, United Nations ambassador, chairman of the United Negro College Fund, and president of the Field Foundation. Through his wife, he was a small investor in Stan Mallin's Standish Apartments, and hearing of plans for the Cabana, suggested that Mallin get in touch with another one of his clients, rising Teamsters union power Jimmy Hoffa, who had money to lend and was willing to give a decent guy a chance.

James Riddle Hoffa was just becoming well known, having recently been elevated to the presidency of the International Brotherhood of Teamsters. Hoffa worked his way up from stockboy to union organizer to local president to national chieftain of the country's toughest union with little more than his native intelligence and determination. He made enemies along the way: first, rival union organizers and trucking bosses, then bigger fish, like a young attorney working as counsel to the McClellan Committee, a Congressional body then investigating labor corruption. Hoffa became known to this lawyer when he attempted to bribe a commission staffer; the staffer reported the incident, and Hoffa was tried for the crime. That Hoffa was acquitted by a jury didn't wipe the slate clean; it only earned him the undying enmity of Robert F. Kennedy, a hatred that would be repaid with interest when Kennedy's brother named him attorney general.

Sarno shared with Hoffa an essentially amoral worldview; neither cared much for abstractions like God and country, truth and justice. Both were willing to get their hands dirty to further their aims, though Hoffa was an ascetic in contrast to Sarno. He didn't have much use for fancy clothes or jewelry. "I don't need to impress anybody," he said when a well-meaning friend suggested he visit a men's store. He was almost prudish when it came to sex, not even tolerating dirty jokes. Of course, Hoffa went about his daily work with a stream of blistering profanity, but to him that wasn't the same thing at all. He looked askance at any distractions—other than his wife and family—from work, and refused to play golf, claiming that twenty pushups each morning was all the exercise a man needed.

Despite their differences, Hoffa surmised that the Atlanta Cabana offered the union a good deal: though inexperienced, Sarno talked a decent game and would probably run a good operation. While he was paying back the loan, the union would have a well-situated Atlanta hotel for conferences and business travel. In these years, Hoffa was extending his negotiating authority from the Midwest to the South and East, en route to signing the comprehensive 1964 National Master Freight Agreement, so this was a definite consideration. It didn't hurt either that Sarno had been referred by Abram, a lawyer with influence in Washington. He decided to give him the loan. The approval of the pension fund's trustees was a mere formality.

Money in hand at last, Sarno bought two adjacent parcels—one a former undertaker's establishment—at the intersection of Seventh and Peachtree streets in downtown Atlanta. He wanted to hire Morris Lapidus to design the Cabana, but quickly learned that the architect was out of his price range. So instead he hired Melvin Grossman, a Miami Beach-based architect who'd begun his career as an engineer in Lapidus's firm before hanging his own shingle. His two biggest commissions to date had been the Seville, a 1955 Miami Beach hotel whose eggcrate façade and screen block parapets anticipated the Cabanas and Caesars Palace, and the 1957 Deauville. These two major hotels, along with the Dunes and International Inn motels, established Grossman's reputation as a solid resort architect who could pull off Lapidus' sweeping baroque style on a budget.

Settled on his architect, Sarno then began looking for someone to execute his vision of the Cabana's interior design. He found that factotum in Jo Harris. From a young age, Harris had wanted to be an architect, and she began working as an unpaid assistant in a small architect's office at the age of fourteen. After attending Georgia Tech's architecture school, she had done commercial design work in Tulsa, Miami, and Atlanta before answering an ad Sarno had placed for a designer.

"You've got great stuff," Sarno said after he glanced at her portfolio, "But I don't hire any woman unless she's going to be my girl."

"I'm a married woman," she replied.

"I'm a married man."

"Anyway, I've been to Miami…I've heard the stories. If I wanted to do *that* kind of work, I could make six times what you're offering. You hire me as your designer on my abilities alone, or you find yourself someone else."

Sarno wasn't used to being told no, but he liked Harris's work. He hired her, and she stayed with him for the next twenty-five years.

Harris executed Sarno's ideas better than he could imagine. With Teamster money finally giving him the springboard he needed, Sarno had few brakes on his imagination. By the time that the mirrors had been hung and the bedspreads fluffed in preparation for the first guests, he was as giddy as a little boy.

The Atlanta Cabana debuted on December 5, 1958, with an open house and flower show. The latter was a bit unusual for a motel geared to business travelers, but it was a sop to the best genteel Atlanta traditions—garden clubs had long been popular in the city. More than 2,000 Atlantans streamed through the building, marveling at the opulence. Not even the birth of his first son, Jay Cameron, six months earlier, had given Sarno this kind of thrill.

A specially-commissioned mural called "Transcendence," which symbolically illustrated the life of Venus, watched over a lobby flooded by light from floor to ceiling windows. The natural light cut down on electric bills, Sarno noted approvingly. A gigantic chandelier hanging near the mural was designed especially for that space by Harris. The terrazzo staircase that connected the lobby to the mezzanine level was said to be the largest of its kind. At its foot, a hand-woven rug from Puerto Rico, said to cost $3,000 (about $25,000 in today's dollars), decorated the lobby floor.

The bar and grill, called the King's Inn, was done up as ye olde English tavern, with strolling violinists thrown in for good measure. Furthering the eclectic mood, the conference center, called the Gaucho Room, was meant to evoke the South American Pampas. The 201 guest rooms had three motifs: Italian Provincial, French Provincial (pale blue carpet with a bit of lace stuck on the wall) and "Modern Mandarin" (a bronze comforter, tan carpet, and Chinese ideograms above the bed).

From the street, screen block cladding gave the hotel tower a Moorish look, while out back antique-looking statues of Venus de Milo, Apollo, Minerva, and Canova's two dancers, newly fashioned from real marble quarried in Carrara, Italy, gazed down into reflecting pools that dotted a formal garden. Beyond that lay the pool, which Sarno claimed was "the most beautiful and modern in the South." Not only was it heated, it had underwater lights and music. Next to it sprawled the putting green, a necessary component, Sarno insisted, of any business hotel.

The Cabana's international flair jibed with the current vogue in American popular culture. With the United States comfortably astride the world stage since World War II, its citizens were becoming more curious about the rest of the world. Tiki bars and a growing fascination with the primitive provided a counterpoint to atomic age modernism. Earlier in the decade, several hotels— including Lapidus's Fontainebleau—had skimmed an eclectic array of influences. It was a fashionable internationalism.

A few weeks after its opening, an *Atlanta Constitution* caption crowed, "Italian Statuary on Peachtree Street," ecstatic over the classical exhibition in the heart of Dixie. Sarno carried the clipping with him until it became tattered. The *Atlanta Journal* called the Cabana "plush" and "pampering," and in a caption reported that the "$3,000,000 Structure Boasts Swim Pool, Steam Room, and Foreign Air," three apparently equally important elements of a modern business hotel.

Yet all was not peaches and cream. Though it wasn't mentioned in any of the opening press accounts, it was common knowledge that Teamster loans had financed the Cabana. This gave it a slightly unsavory repute. But it also gave Sarno and Mallin reputations as men to be reckoned with; Sarno in particular fell into the habit of mentioning that he would soon be seeing "Jimmy" when he felt it would have an appropriate effect on his audience.

A man with such friends, Sarno thought, shouldn't work, so much as reign. Fittingly, his office at the Cabana was an out-sized modern emperor's court with a soaring ceiling, the latest in contemporary wood paneling, and a few carefully placed abstract sculptures on the walls. At the center stood a custom-built desk. An elongated oval that stretched nearly fifteen feet, it had two grand stations: one for Jay, one for Stan.

That Sarno, between golf and his travels, was seldom around to use the office didn't make it any less impressive as far as he was concerned. If someone wanted to see his desk, he could take them into a Danish Modern cathedral.

He hadn't inherited a feel for that kind of joyful abandon or ostentation from his family. Herman had only taught him that a good building was one that threw off plenty of ready cash he could apply to his gambling debts. Then there was his cabinetmaker father: surely a man who molded wood into a work of practical beauty, whose craftsmanship might have inspired Sarno to see graceful lines and beautiful forms where others saw a dirt lot. But Alexander got paid to make cabinets, so he made cabinets the way the tsar's army had taught him. Even his work for his family, which should have been a labor of love, was solid and unremarkable, with no hint of originality. His son would take the opposite approach, always making things seem grander than they really were.

Looks meant everything because class was in the eye of the beholder, and that eye could be easily fooled. By covering a hotel room's wall with a mirror, you automatically doubled the size of the room, so you could actually make it just large enough to fit a bed and nightstand. You made sure the lamps were larger than customary: they cost the same and gave off the same light, but they looked classier. Since the bed was the biggest thing in the room, if you covered it with an expensive-looking bedspread, a guest would conclude that he was basking in luxury.

And it worked. Every story about the Cabana's opening lavished praise on the genuine reproduction of statues found in the Vatican, the Capitoline Museum, and the Louvre, right there in Atlanta, the $150 bedspreads, and the $95 lamps. None remarked on the motel's convenience for travelers, the quality of the accommodations, or the soundness of its construction.

"You know," he told Harris after reading an especially enthusiastic press report, "I think we're on to something here." Already, he was thinking how to build something better—and riskier.

If you really wanted to find Jay, you didn't call his office; you stopped by the Standard Town and Country Club, Atlanta's Jewish country club. Many country clubs throughout the nation still refused to admit Jewish members, so most major cities had at least one predominantly Jewish club. Like their Protestant brethren, these clubs featured golf courses and leisurely camaraderie among the local elite. But they had a little something else: in Atlanta, as elsewhere, the Jewish country club was a serious gambling joint. Sarno was in heaven there.

In addition to winning and losing at the card table, Sarno played some better-than-average golf, being crowned the Standard club champion. He aspired for more, and was a serious contender for the 1958 City Amateur Championship...about as serious a contender as he could make himself.

He made a name for himself in the quarterfinals. Sarno liked to sight his putts by dropping prone for "a sniper's view," which was surely more for show than anything else. But early in the match against Jerry Greenbaum at the Standard, he stooped a bit too emphatically and split his pants.

A more modest man might have slunk off the greens, but Sarno steamed boldly ahead with one concession to propriety: on subsequent putts, he checked if there were any ladies behind him before dropping to his customary position. He changed pants on the back nine and birdied his way into the semifinals in one of the most talked-about games in city championship history.

Thus the legend of Jay Sarno was born.

He was a joker, to be sure, he looked wider than he was tall, but there was no denying his will to win. Atlanta's best amateurs weren't sure if they should take him seriously—how could you?—but losing to him would make them the butt of jokes for years to come.

Sarno knew he needed to up his game, and he wasn't too proud to ask for help. So he recruited Ray Gunkel, a former National Wrestling Association Texas Heavyweight Champion with no golfing experience.

"But he's an *athlete*," Sarno said when one of his Standard friends objected. "I just need someone to get me in shape. Golf, I know."

A good-natured blond giant, Gunkel sized up his portly new protégé and decided an intense training program wasn't in the cards. Instead, he turned to the latest performance-enhancing supplement: honey.

"Honey's the best," he told Sarno. "It assimilates very rapidly and gives quick energy."

Gunkel's training got Sarno through a tough semifinal match against R. L. Straughan, Jr., and into the finals against Gene "Dolly" Dahlbender, Jr., the three-time defending champion. Despite the tough competition, Sarno was already looking ahead.

"If I should win this tournament," he told a reporter, "I'm going to enter the National Amateur."

It was a misplaced optimism. Sarno didn't beat Dahlbender.

And that ended Jay's career as a competitive amateur golfer. He never made it that far in the City Amateur tournament again. He still enjoyed playing, of course, and remained a fixture at the Standard—both on the links and in the clubhouse, when it was time to deal the cards. But it wasn't the game itself that drew him—it was the gambling. Who wanted to spend hours out in the hot sun chasing a little ball? Not him, unless he could bet a few thousand dollars per hole on it. That made golf his passion.

But Sarno never systematically tried to improve at golf. He blamed his losses on a poor selection of clubs—he bought new sets compulsively, so he had plenty to choose from—instead of failure to improve his technique. Others might have built on Sarno's early amateur success and, through diligent practice and coaching, moved up in the ranks, challenging Dahlbender's Atlanta dominance, maybe even going further. Sarno just wasn't wired that way: after all, he hired a professional wrestler, not one of the many skilled golfers who lived in Atlanta, to train him for his big match. It wasn't about the game at all—it was about having fun. If he happened to win, so much the better, but if not, it was action.

With the Atlanta Cabana operational, Sarno planned a chain of Cabanas, stretching from coast to coast to cater to weary businessmen. With travel booming nationwide thanks to cheaper airfares and highway construction, it made sense to expand as aggressively as possible. You could, after all, stretch construction dollars pretty far. Having built a luxury hotel on a budget, he tirelessly explored cost-cutting possibilities. What about a hotel with no windows? Glass was expensive to purchase and install, and he was catering to business travelers who'd be spending all day at conferences and meetings. By the time they got back to the room, they'd be dog tired and it would be pitch black outside anyway. Why would they want to stare at a dark street? Sarno was at first perplexed when those he shared the idea with expressed their misgivings—no one, not even businessmen, wanted to stay in a room that felt like a bunker—but finally gave up on the idea.

Even with the cost of windows factored in, Sarno felt that he had hit a winning formula with the hotel/motel Cabanas.

"But we haven't really made any money yet," Mallin protested. "And we don't have any collateral. Nobody in their right mind would lend us money."

"That's not a problem, Stan. If I can convince Jimmy to help us, we're practically home free."

Sarno had become close to Hoffa. Even though the union boss abhorred the nonproductive waste of gambling, he was a risk-taker at heart. Sarno admired Hoffa's drive, his pride, and his unswaying dedication to his Teamsters.

"This is a guy," Sarno told his son Jay years later, "who doesn't care so much about money and doesn't care about dressing up or having a fancy car. He had rather drive a bulldozer and clear land. But," he paused for emphasis, "he cares about power and he really does care about the people in the union."

This was high praise from Sarno, who usually had no time for idealists. For his part, Hoffa appreciated the hotel man's creativity and his ability to get projects done. It didn't hurt that the Cabanas had the potential to be good investments for the Central States Pension Fund.

So Sarno was expectant as he and Mallin proposed a loan for a new Cabana hotel at the September 1959 Teamsters Central States Pension Fund trustees meeting, which just happened to be held at the Atlanta Cabana. Though Sarno was willing to concede ultimate ownership of the property to the Fund in return for the loan, they received a discount loan with no such preconditions—more generosity from Jimmy. With $3.6 million promised, Sarno planned to build his next Cabana in Dallas, on Stemmons Expressway at Continental Avenue.

For a while after the hotel opened in 1961, the Dallas Cabana had one of the top nightspots in town, at least in certain circles. The motel even earned a footnote in history.

In reconstructing Jack Ruby's movements prior to the Kennedy assassination, the Warren Commission placed him in the Cabana's nightclub, the Bon Vivant Room, on the fateful night before the assassination. According to the official records, he drove over from his own Carousel Club around midnight and had a "brief visit" with Lawrence Meyers, a Chicago businessman. Some conspiracy buffs, convinced that the Cabana's Teamster financing was proof of a direct link to the Mafia, spent years poring over the Cabana's guest book, scrutinizing each visitor for hidden connections to the assassination.

Sarno had his own reasons for hanging around the Bon Vivant. A young Raquel Welch was one of the waitresses, working there nights and modeling for Neiman Marcus during the day. Sarno thought she was one of the most gorgeous women he had ever seen. He wasted no time trying to bed her, but her mother made it a point to never allow Raquel unescorted within arm's reach of Sarno.

The Dallas Cabana was just a dalliance for Jay. He was working on something bigger before construction started: another Cabana in Palo Alto, about 35 miles south of San Francisco, that opened a few months after the Dallas Cabana in 1962. At 4290 El Camino Real, in a part of town that had long catered to business travelers, the Palo Alto Cabana carried on the classical motif that had become Sarno's trademark with a cocktail lounge named Nero's Nook. At the head of the drive-through fountain stood a replica of the Nike of Samothrace, a now-headless 3rd century B.C. statue depicting "winged victory." The original could be found in the Louvre. In the middle of the fountain, a replica of Michaelangelo's David calmly surveyed the arriving Buicks and Corvairs. Inside, a sweeping staircase in the Lapidus tradition gave the lobby a dramatic feel and became a favored setting for local wedding photographs.

Yet all that wasn't enough. Sarno knew he had to do something to really make the hotel stand out. "We're not the biggest, and we're not the tallest," he said, "So it's got to be something else. It's got to make people stand up and say, 'Wow!'

"Now, we can't do much with the bellhops or the desk clerks, but I've got some ideas about how we can make the cocktail waitresses something people will never forget."

Inspired by the Roman theme, Sarno declared that his lounge wouldn't have waitresses at all: men would be served by goddesses.

Beauties chosen by Sarno himself would do more than deliver drinks: they would create a fantasy. He didn't hold interviews; he held auditions. The girls had to sing, dance, or play a musical instrument: being able to jump onstage and perform the Twist was just as important as memorizing drink orders.

In their too-short toga-inspired skirts and stiff theatrical wigs, the goddesses were alluring, but unattainable for mere mortals. And it worked—the goddesses became minor celebrities, giving their autographs to awestruck locals. But there were limits. Sarno issued a strict edict that under no circumstances were goddesses ever to venture an inch above the first floor. The cheap hustling that went on in lounges across the country wouldn't be happening in *his* class joint.

"Do this in good taste," he lectured the goddesses before the opening, "or you're fired."

Sarno also made sure the drinks made an impression. The signature cocktail of the purple-and-gold lounge was called "Caesar's Seizure," and it lived up to its name: two-dollar pink champagne in a white goblet with grapes spilling over the sides, and an orange filled with heavy rum floating in the center. A goddess would light the rum and, flambé held aloft for all to see, sway through the room to the customer's table.

The drink often got a round of applause. After the first performance of the night, everyone else wanted one.

Sarno had even gotten a famous celebrity spokeswoman for free—in fact, she paid him to be part of the hotel. Doris Day had been a quiet investor in the Atlanta and Dallas motels, but her role in the Palo Alto was widely promoted.

She hadn't gotten involved willingly. Her husband and manager, Marty Melcher, placed too much trust in Hollywood attorney Jerome Rosenthal's can't-miss prospects, and he invested much of Day's money in Rosenthal's schemes, from cattle ranching to oil wells. Rosenthal had somehow hit on the Cabana chain as a sure-fire investment, and he began to worm his way into Sarno's confidence. Day had more at stake in the hotel than Sarno himself, who hadn't invested any of his own money in Palo Alto or Dallas. He didn't lack confidence; he simply didn't have any money to invest. Sarno had completely over-extended himself, hoping that each succeeding motel, built with other people's money, would create enough cash to let him pay off his previous investors. Atlanta and Dallas were doing tolerably well, but he wasn't seeing any of the profits.

Day could be forgiven for her apprehensions about the prospects of a partnership with Sarno. Yet *Life* magazine praised the Cabana as one of the finest hotels on the West Coast, and it had a brief run of fame in the 1960s.

With three Cabana successes, Sarno felt he could afford to be picky about his next project. Preferably, it would be someplace with a mild climate that afforded many good golf days. Birmingham, Alabama, looked promising, and in 1962 he announced plans to build what he called the "Bama Cabana" in that city. The future looked bright.

Jay continued to put down roots in Atlanta. In 1959, Joyce gave birth to a daughter, September Joy. Their three-story suburban set piece on Westover Drive had a huge front yard, a driveway leading to a covered carport on the side, and a small deck in the backyard that overlooked a field filled with daffodils. Beyond the flowers ran a creek where their son, Jay, caught water moccasins and small fish with his friends.

Joyce settled into a comfortable life as a homemaker with plenty of hired help around the house, and her husband, when he wasn't golfing or traveling for business, made a few trips to his office at the Cabana. Not that Sarno's presence was essential to the daily operations of his empire. He had mastered the art of delegating and trusted his office manager, Michael Rosenstein, with most major decisions, including hiring and firing the office staff, and thought nothing of leaving him in charge for days, even weeks, with only the vaguest hint of direction.

When Sarno was traveling extensively for the Dallas and Palo Alto projects in 1961, Rosenstein decided that he needed more help around the office. He saw a classified ad for a typist who needed to make extra money. He called the typist, Evelyn Spinks, who needed something she could do around her regular job at Georgia Tech, and invited her to the office.

She agreed, although she was a little scared of the Cabana because of the hotel's Teamster link. She found that Rosenstein was a complete gentleman. He showed her the tiny office where she and the rest of the staff worked, then allowed her a glimpse into Sarno's sanctuary. To her, the executive office looked like a movie set.

Retreating into their own cramped warren, Rosenstein and Spinks talked salary, then he put her right to work typing letters and invoices. For the next few weeks, she came in when the other typists left at five p.m., apparently on a trial basis. The closest Spinks got to seeing the real boss was handling his mail.

Several weeks later, Rosenstein hired Spinks permanently, and she quit her Georgia Tech job to work regular business hours at the Cabana. Soon after, she finally met Sarno. It was a momentous day at the Cabana. Real Hollywood stars Jayne Mansfield and Mickey Hargitay had stayed at the hotel. Mansfield had autographed a bust-spilling publicity photo for Sarno, which Spinks had placed in his inbox.

Rosenstein called Spinks into Sarno's palatial office, made the introductions, then returned to his cubbyhole. Sarno gestured absentmindedly for Spinks to remain while he glanced through his mail. Thinking she was to take a letter, Spinks stood stiffly, steno pad at the ready. She watched as this balding, rotund man, who'd been an imposing rumor for so many weeks, picked his way through the envelopes, grimacing with annoyance at this one, carefully opening that one. Then, suddenly, he stopped. His eyes lit up.

"Boy, oh boy," he said. Spinks watched him devour the Mansfield photograph. "I'd sure like to give her a good schooling."

"Am I supposed to write that down?" she wondered.

Inexplicably, the reserved Southern girl and the skirt-chasing businessman hit it off. Spinks soon became his personal secretary, and she worked with him for the rest of his life. She became his rock, and was, for him, beyond reproach, perhaps the only woman he never propositioned. Though he had a notably foul mouth, he became furious if one of his associates told an off-color joke in her presence.

During these years Sarno met another woman who'd stick with him, off and on, for the next two decades, exercising quite a different influence: Carol Freeman.

Like his wife Joyce, Freeman was blonde. She was also beautiful, which was essential to a man for whom beautiful things and beautiful people meant so much. But where the statuesque Joyce saw eye to eye with her husband, he looked down at the petite Freeman.

And he found he could talk with her, for hours at a time, about anything: his buildings, his hopes, his fears. She was, after Evelyn Spinks, the only woman he really confided in. Carol shuttled between Dallas and Palo Alto with Jay while Joyce stayed at home with the kids.

Carol was the love of Jay's life. That didn't stop him from running a parade of girlfriends in and out of the Cabana, but after his conquest of the day, he invariably returned to Carol.

Joyce knew what was going on. More than once, she called the office looking for Jay when she suspected he was with another woman. Out of loyalty to her boss, Spinks would offer a lame cover story.

"He's out playing golf…I don't think he'll be back in the office today."

Joyce knew Sarno's girl Friday was lying to her, but she didn't seem to hold it against her.

Still, Carol tested Joyce's forbearance. Sarno, with the cruelty of a Caesar, flaunted her in front of his wife, even demanding that Joyce teach his mistress how to play golf. This was particularly heartless, since unlike gambling, food, and adultery, this was one part of his life that Joyce shared with him. Now he wouldn't allow her even that.

So life on Westover Drive wasn't necessarily happy once the kids were put to sleep, but Sarno wasn't interested in domestic bliss. He needed action. Life, as far as he was concerned, was good. Even though the money wasn't rolling in yet, he was convinced that the Cabana gamble was about to pay off. Once the Birmingham hotel was complete, he would have a solid base of hotels in the South and a beachhead in California. As Hoffa's power over the union grew, he was sure to keep on getting loans. It seemed likely that, within ten years, he might invite his brother Herman to the grand opening of the New York Cabana. Sarno hadn't made a name for himself with bachelor apartments or the Terrace motels, but he seemed to have punched his ticket with the Cabanas.

But then Jay Sarno visited Las Vegas. Both he and the city would be forever changed.

FOUR

Las Vegas Comes to Jay Sarno

With his almost biological need to gamble, it's amazing that Jay Sarno didn't discover Las Vegas until he was over forty.

In later years he insisted that gambling had nothing to do with it, that he had happened across the city almost by accident.

"I had traveled to San Francisco by way of Las Vegas from Texas," he claimed in 1979, "and I noticed that when the plane left Las Vegas it was almost empty. That prompted me to investigate building a hotel here."

In fact, Sarno first came to Las Vegas for one reason: to gamble.

In February 1963, Sarno and Stan Mallin were recruited for a junket to the Flamingo hotel on the strength of Sarno's reputation as a wild gambler. The charter flight and hotel stay—a common marketing tool for mid-level gamblers in those days—was set up by Morris Lansburgh, who'd made his name operating six Miami Beach hotels with partner Sam Cohen. Three years earlier, they'd bought the Flamingo. Later it came out that Lansburgh was merely the latest in a series of fronts for underworld kingmaker Meyer Lansky (he would one day do jail time for it), but for now he was an eminently respectable hotel man. As an experienced hotelier, he had a good read on leisure travelers. His Miami Beach "Cavalcade of Stars" program allowed his guests to see performers at each of his hotels for no extra fee. He introduced a flight/hotel vacation package at the Flamingo that was modeled on his successful promotions, and even offered a combined Las Vegas/Los Angeles/Hawaii tour.

Lansburgh knew the hotel business in and out. But, despite his association with Lansky, he didn't know the first thing about casino management. Day-to-day operations remained under the charge of casino manager Chester Simms, who'd worked for Lansky in Havana and Kentucky.

Sarno lost some money playing gin on the flight, but this only increased his expectations for Las Vegas. The last hour was agony. He fidgeted and made small talk, trying to keep from exploding.

The plane touched down at McCarran Airport, a few miles south of the Flamingo. Finally the door was open. With Mallin following closely, Sarno stepped out into desert air.

It was chilly—not beach weather, not even good golf weather. In the distance, brown mountains ringed the flattest, widest stretch of land Sarno had ever seen. Porters lugged their bags out of the plane as Sarno and his fellow junketeers were steered into a set of station wagons.

Sarno nudged Mallin. "Station wagons? I thought this was a class joint."

As they pulled out of the airport, Sarno got a ground-level view of the casinos that he had heard so much about. In those years, the Las Vegas Strip started across from the expanding McCarran Airport. A little north of the iconic "Welcome to Las Vegas" sign stood the Hacienda, a casino that relied on package tourists and middling conventioneers. "Hayseed Heaven," the locals called it derisively. Further north lay the Tropicana, which boasted a reputation as the "Tiffany of the Strip." It was one of the newer Strip hotels, just five years old, and was doing well enough, though the original owners had been forced to step aside after it was learned that they were fronts for notorious underworld chieftain Frank Costello.

North of the Tropicana Sarno saw a few gas stations and motels, and then, nearly a mile away, on the west side of the street, the Dunes. The Dunes was in the middle of an expansion that raised a high-rise— the Diamond of the Dunes—over the lowly casino. It had yet to show much of a profit for its owners, but was still sending decent enough packages of skimmed money back to those who really counted.

Catty-corner to the Dunes lay the Flamingo. It had been thoroughly remodeled ten years earlier, its original Damon Runyon

Provincial style replaced by a modern green quartzite façade with "Flamingo" floating in pink neon above the entrance, the sixty-foot-tall "Champagne Tower" blowing electronic bubbles up its sides.

If they had continued toward downtown, he would have seen the Sands, which Frank Sinatra and his Rat Pack turned into their personal clubhouse with each nightclub stint; the New Frontier, whose 1955 space fantasia foreshadowed the post-Sputnik space race and the Kennedy White House; the Desert Inn, where former Cleveland bootlegger Moe Dalitz called the shots; the Stardust, which further carried Las Vegas into the space age; the Thunderbird, the Riviera, and the Sahara. The El Rancho Vegas, where the Strip had started in 1941, had recently burned to the ground as the result of a suspicious fire. It was never rebuilt.

These casinos were exciting inside. Outside, they were unremarkable, mostly cheaply-built motels whose wings converged on a low-rise casino/nightclub building. Only their neon signs showed any flash. When Sarno arrived, there were only two bona-fide high-rises on the Strip: the Riviera, which had opened in 1955 with nine stories and the Strip's first elevator, and the Sahara, which in 1959 added a fourteen-story tower. To a guy who'd already built three buildings with elevators, it wasn't impressive.

Sarno and his group entered the clean, modern main building of the Flamingo and got checked in. Most of the men helped themselves to a cocktail or two and then went to their rooms to freshen up. A pit boss arched an eyebrow as he saw the junketeers slipping off; they were there to gamble, not relax. But Sarno made friends quickly, installing himself at a craps table, and not leaving until he was near collapse.

This was a big week for the hotel. Lansburgh had made several changes to the Flamingo, particularly to its entertainment policy, and was beginning to reap the rewards. The previous year, he had stirred controversy when he fired the showroom's chorus girls and canned its production numbers: before, headliners had appeared in vaudeville-derived shows, alternating with dancers, jugglers, comedians, and even animal acts. Lansburgh stripped the Flamingo's shows down to the basics: a singer, a backing band, maybe a comedian to warm the crowd up, and little else. With this policy, which made the headliner more a star than an entertainer, he lured several new acts, including Mitzi Gaynor, Ethel Merman, Juliet Prowse, Dick Gregory, and Arlene Dahl. Soon, Bobby Darin would record a landmark live album at the hotel, which would cement its name as a mecca of popular music.

This weekend was no less exciting: Robert Goulet, fresh off his star turn as Sir Lancelot in the Broadway smash *Camelot,* was making his Las Vegas debut. It was only his second nightclub appearance, and a triumph for Lansburgh and Las Vegas. A local radio station declared a "Goulet Day" to celebrate his arrival, and his fan club turned out in force to meet his plane. Still, it was a station wagon and not a nobleman's carriage that took him to the hotel.

Sarno enjoyed the show, though it cut into his gambling time, but was more impressed when Goulet joined him and his fellow Atlantans for a while, eating, drinking, and socializing with them. In Las Vegas, maybe anything really *was* possible.

But he wasn't in Las Vegas to hang out with singers. Playing dice for $100 a throw without looking over your shoulder for a cop or a stickup artist was the only attraction that mattered. Many Las Vegas visitors in these years recoiled from the open gambling, the easy promiscuity, the complete disregard for any social marker but wealth. But others loved that what they could do only in secret elsewhere could be done openly here. Card and dice dealers were the city's lesser aristocracy, showgirls the flower of its womanhood, and former racket guys its undisputed lords. For a gambling hound, Las Vegas was an air-conditioned heaven.

At least it was supposed to be. Sarno was more impressed by the potential than the reality. At first he couldn't put his finger on it, but something about the whole set-up felt wrong. Then he realized it. Outside of his group's escapades with Goulet and his rounds at the crap tables, the Flamingo wasn't that fabulous.

"This isn't even close to a real first-class hotel," he told Mallin.

The whole experience was mundane. Guests pulled off the highway, hopped out of their cars, and maybe waited for a bellhop to unload their bags. Half of them schlepped their stuff to the front desk themselves. There was nothing special about it at all. They might as well have been going down to the Piggly Wiggly for bread and milk.

Inside wasn't much better. Sarno didn't have any complaints about the girls in cocktail dresses hanging by the bar, but he didn't understand why the place had to be so…tawdry. Sure, the advertising raved about how fantastic the hotel was, but outside the neon it wasn't anything special. Neither was anyplace else in Vegas. They all looked like cheap Western knockoffs, dressing their dealers in vests and string ties. Their cocktail waitresses showed slightly less skin than Arctic explorers. The owners, he convinced himself, had missed the point. The desert resort suffered from a visual drought. There was nothing special to *see*.

Sarno wasn't the only one who wasn't impressed. The first thing many visitors noticed about Las Vegas weren't its sights, but its sounds. "Loud, loud, loud," said *The Saturday Evening Post* in 1961. "A community of sin, din, and gin." The following year, a *New York Times* writer parenthetically mentioned the action in the "gaudy, ear-shattering casinos."

Sarno didn't mind raising his voice to be heard over the crash of slot machines and shouts of frenzied gamblers, but he took the lack of first-class accommodations as an invitation to do better.

"They don't have one good hotel here," he told Mallin. "If I could build one, we'd make a fortune."

Mallin put it down to Sarno's usual big talk, expecting it to go nowhere. But it became an obsession. Sarno left the group and toured the other casinos of the Strip, looking at them as a builder, not a gambler. Satisfied that he had correctly assessed the market, he returned to the Flamingo.

While walking through the gardens, Sarno became even more convinced he was right. The hotel promoted its acres of greenery, but didn't do anything to make them special. Hell, he had brought some of the most famous statues in the world into that postage stamp of a garden at the Atlanta Cabana. The fountains in front of the Palo Alto Cabana would put anything here to shame. There just wasn't any imagination in Las Vegas.

Sarno, walking through the casinos of Las Vegas, had a consuming thought: why wasn't there a place where a guy could get away from it all and live his fantasies?

And he was convinced that it could be done, and that he was the man to do it.

While Sarno was dreaming about the future, Las Vegas was at a crossroads. The old regime, represented by Lansburgh and his cronies, was living on borrowed time, but no one really knew who the new masters of Las Vegas would be.

On the surface, it looked like a golden age: Frank Sinatra and his chums Dean, Sammy, Joey, and Peter were packing them in at the Sands' Copa Room. Racial segregation was crumbling as an informal pact between the local NAACP and the big guns on the Strip, called the Moulin Rouge agreement, ended Jim Crow in the hotels and showrooms of Las Vegas. Casino owners no longer saw the world in black and white; they only cared about green. Business was booming everywhere: the futuristic saucer-shaped Las Vegas Convention Center held out the possibility of new directions, and with the nation rejuvenated by its youthful president, the space age lay ahead, filled with promise.

Yet beneath the glitz lay an undercurrent of anxiety. Many Nevadans feared that, as prosperous as gambling had proven, it was an unreliable basis for their state's economy. So in the early 1960s Governor Grant Sawyer led a very public push to lure industry to Nevada. Citing a low tax rate and favorable incorporation laws, Sawyer nonetheless got few takers. So the anxiety continued.

Indeed, many visitors found the city's appeal elusive. Writing in the August 1961 *Esquire*, Arthur Steuer found that in Las Vegas, the grotesque and absurd were considered normal, and even virtuous. "Behold," he wrote, "a city of temples devoted to gods long since discredited from our pantheon (Moloch and Mammon)." The downtown gambling halls were mere factories, with everyone, from the $10 a day shill to the $50 pit boss, merely punching the clock. On the Strip, "Ranch Rococo" and "Miami Baroque" filigree barely disguised that every square inch existed only to strip visitors of their cash, and leave them begging for more.

"We are standing at the end of the world," legendary gambler Nick "the Greek" Dandalos told Steuer, and readers could almost hear the desert wind whipping past them, "desolate as a crater of the moon, right where it should be: quarantined from the rest of civilization."

Dandalos was right to be wary; despite having had an estimated $500 million pass through his hands in gambling wins and losses, within six years he would die penniless, with his gambling cronies chipping in for his funeral. Though Las Vegas custom said that a man's past could, in Dandalos's words, be "whisked away like a stage set," no man could ever outrun his own nature.

Yet the longer Sarno stayed in Las Vegas, the more he convinced himself that he could remake both himself and the city. The past few years of hustling loans and arguing with contractors would be forgotten. He would be the city's top hotel man, a civic benefactor, a force to be reckoned with.

Las Vegas, too, was reaching higher: the Dunes, Desert Inn, Sands, and Stardust would complete expansions by the middle of the decade, adding hundreds of rooms. This was another stroke of luck for Sarno; much of the money to pay for those rooms came from the Teamsters. The union's Central States Pension Fund made its first foray into Las Vegas in 1958, with a loan that helped build the Paradise Valley Golf Course. Over the next few years, the fund loaned over $7 million to various Las Vegas enterprises connected with Moe Dalitz. These ranged from an even million for Sunrise Hospital, a for-profit medical center, to $4 million for the Fremont casino hotel in downtown Las Vegas.

Sarno was practically guaranteed the chance to build a Vegas hotel; if Jimmy was loaning money to everyone else, he would surely help his friend Jay out.

But Teamster money's low interest rate had a high price. Las Vegas itself was just getting the bill. With Robert F. Kennedy's ascension to the post of Attorney General in 1961, Jimmy Hoffa became public enemy number one. Kennedy set up a "Get Hoffa" squad, staffed with twenty young, ambitious attorneys augmented by a platoon of investigators and auditors, with virtually unlimited resources. It wasn't a good time to be a friend of Hoffa, and the labor leader's Vegas largess only confirmed Kennedy's fears that Nevada's casinos, though legal, were at best retirement homes for former hoodlums and, at worst, active sources of income for ongoing criminal organizations.

Jay Sarno knew firsthand the price that Hoffa's associates paid in the Kennedy years.

"Federal people have practically lived in my office for three or four days at a time," he told the *Los Angeles Times* in October 1962. "I've opened up my files to them."

Now Nevada faced a similar prospect. With the Attorney General taking a closer look at the "undesirable" element in Nevada, the onus shifted to Governor Sawyer to prove, in the court of public opinion if not law, that the state was not dominated by gangsters. The Sawyer administration had already ratcheted up the pressure on the Mob: in 1960, the governor directed the Gaming Control Board to compile and distribute a list of the most notorious "known hoodlums" who frequented the state. A printer bound the eleven pages of names, aliases, and photographs in a black binder; thus was born the "Black Book." The Gaming Control Board declared that the men in the book were so disreputable that their very presence in a state-regulated casino could undermine the state's legitimacy. Casinos were instructed to remove them, bodily if need be, and reminded that holding a gaming license was a privilege that could be revoked at the Gaming Commission's discretion.

One of the men on the list, Chicago's Marshall "John Marshall" Caifano, unsuccessfully challenged the Black Book's legitimacy; the United States Supreme Court tacitly endorsed it when it refused to hear his appeal in 1967. Frank Sinatra ran into trouble when, in 1963, Gaming Control Board chief Edward Olsen learned that the singer had been hosting Sam Giancana, a notorious Chicago mobster and charter member of the Black Book, at the Cal-Neva, a small Lake Tahoe casino in which Sinatra held an interest. Rather than defend himself against Olsen's accusation, Sinatra abandoned his casino license and sold his interests in the Cal-Neva and the Sands.

Thus the climb towards respectability began. Nevada regulators hoped that they could keep their house clean enough—or at least looking clean enough—to hold off the Justice Department. It wasn't easy, chasing Frank Sinatra out of the owner's suite, but Nevada has always been more practical than sentimental, particularly about business. In the showroom, Frank was a blessing, bringing in deep-pocketed gamblers. As an owner, he had the potential to bring down the wrath of the federal government. So, politely, he was asked to leave. With the potential of greater federal scrutiny of owners who had been grandfathered in to the Gaming Commission's licensing requirements, the state was looking for new blood—and new capital—in its chief industry.

Jay Sarno had never been arrested. He was a model citizen. Sure, he had been investigated by the feds for his relationship with Hoffa, but in Las Vegas a run-in with the federal government was practically a badge of honor. Any other city would have been suspicious of a developer with such close ties to a suspect union and unorthodox financial and architectural methods.

Las Vegas opened its arms.

Jay Sarno as a teenager. Always one to go his own way, he's wearing a white jacket and dark pants. *Courtesy UNLV Special Collections.*

An undated Sarno family portrait; Jay is the second standing from the right. *Courtesy UNLV Special Collections.*

Jay looking respectable for the camera. *Courtesy UNLV Special Collections.*

Joyce and Jay during their whirlwind courtship at the Fontainebleau, August, 1957. Within a week of meeting her, Jay convinced Joyce to marry him. *Courtesy UNLV Special Collections.*

Joyce and Jay pose with Jay's parents, Nellie and Alexander, in April 1958. *Courtesy UNLV Special Collections.*

Sarno's first major hotel had two elements in common with the later Caesars Palace: the screen block facade and a generous loan from Jimmy Hoffa's Teamsters Union. *Courtesy UNLV Special Collections.*

The Palo Alto Cabana's sweeping entry drive, lined with cypresses and centered by a fountain, was a dry run for Caesars Palace. *Courtesy UNLV Special Collections.*

This Nero's Nook goddess, lofting the signature Caesar's Seizure cocktail, wears another early iteration of a Caesars Palace staple, the short toga-dress. *Courtesy UNLV Special Collections.*

FIVE

From St. Peter's Square
to Flamingo Road

Even after Las Vegas had disappeared beneath the plane carrying them back to Atlanta, Sarno couldn't stop talking about possibilities.

"Think of what we can do here," he said to Stan Mallin. "Everything we've put into the Cabanas, plus the casino—it's guaranteed to win."

Mallin cautiously remarked that it might be a good market to get into.

"Don't worry about the money. I can get the money. I just need someone to co-sign the mortgage, when I get it, and the bank loans. You won't have to put a cent in."

Mallin wasn't sure that Sarno would ever get that far, so he agreed, not entirely because it was the only way he could get Sarno to stop bugging him. Before they'd crossed the Rockies, Sarno had a co-signer. When they got back to Atlanta, he scuttled his Birmingham plans and started sketching for Las Vegas. Given the level of competition, with a few tweaks to the Cabana formula, Sarno thought, he would become the top hotel man in Las Vegas. The key was to stand out.

To do that Sarno decided to take the thing that turned heads most in Palo Alto—Nero's Nook—and push it front and center. The country was in the middle of a Greco-Roman revival. Movies like *Quo Vadis* and *Ben Hur* had stoked an appetite for all things classical over the past decade. Sarno was right to do as the Romans did—the following year, *Cleopatra* would become one of the biggest movies ever, and a Broadway comedy, *A Funny Thing Happened on the Way to the Forum*, was making audiences laugh. People would flock to a Roman-themed hotel.

With a concept for what he called the Desert Cabana, Sarno started looking for a place to build. Land on the three miles of the Strip was plentiful and relatively cheap. For years, people had been buying, selling, and leasing land to be used for hotel developments. By luck or fate, the land that Sarno wanted to build on—right across from the disappointing Flamingo—was owned by a man who would become one of the city's towering figures, building the world's biggest hotel-casino three times: Kirk Kerkorian.

Kerkorian had just entered the Vegas real estate game. He had parlayed a World War II stint as a pilot into an aviation career, starting with the Los Angeles Air Service, a small charter airline whose chief route was Los Angeles to Las Vegas, in 1947. Kerkorian expanded the carrier, adding numerous civilian and military routes and renamed it Trans International Airlines in 1960. Two years later he sold it to the Studebaker company, though he remained as president. He used a share of the proceeds from the sale to buy a parcel from Fred and William Backer, who'd owned a section of land across from the Flamingo since 1950. Kerkorian's Tracy Lease and Finance Corporation took title to the land on June 17, 1963. By the time Sarno came calling, he was ready to start earning some income from his investment. They arranged a business dinner to talk general principles.

Sarno was eager to impress his potential landlord that night. And he did: Kerkorian could hardly believe how much food Sarno wolfed down before they started talking business. His appetite almost matched his enthusiasm for his new project.

"This is going to be the greatest hotel-casino in the world," Sarno said. "Everything is going to be top-notch. We'll have the finest restaurant, the best entertainers, the most luxurious rooms… people won't want to stay anywhere else. It can't lose."

Kerkorian wanted to hear more. They made a date to play golf on the Dunes course. Kerkorian expected Sarno to be a pushover on the links, and he was astonished by Sarno's no-handicap game. A man with the kind of drive to play golf that well, he thought, had to be taken seriously.

Still, what he was proposing—an ultra-luxury hotel in a market that had never seen one—seemed risky.

"I've done this before, Kirk," Sarno said. "Doris Day thinks enough of me that she's invested three times."

They were close to a deal, but there was one sticking point: Kerkorian wanted a straight lease of the land, with money upfront each month regardless of how well the casino performed. Sarno wanted Kerkorian instead to accept a share of the profits. In the end, he proposed a compromise: monthly rent plus a share of the profits, when they came. Though he would rather have had a bigger monthly rent and not have had to tether his fortunes to the profits of the casino, Kerkorian agreed. By early 1964, Sarno had a parcel to build on.

With a site in hand, getting a ten-million dollar loan commitment from the Teamsters seemed easy. It was, however, a stupendous accomplishment: the kid from St. Joe, on the strength of his imagination alone, had secured an eight-figure loan.

But there was no time to gloat; this only got him a little more than halfway to the nineteen million he would need to build the casino of his dreams. Building a casino of lesser stuff, naturally, was out of the question.

Unfortunately, investors working with their own money were not nearly as generous as Sarno's friend Jimmy. No one in Atlanta wanted to loan him money to build in Las Vegas, and no one in Las Vegas knew who he was. So Jay talked to his brother Herman about approaching a few of his friends in New York real estate. Herman was happy to help, he assured him, but there just wasn't money in New York to be had for something as speculative as a casino.

At Herman's suggestion, Jay and Stan drove up to Washington, D.C., to talk with Morris Seidelbaum, who'd done well for himself in the laundry business and was looking for investments. As it turned out, the laundry king wasn't quite ready to loan money to a casino, but he thought he knew someone who might be.

"Why don't you give my insurance guy a call? He lives in Baltimore."

That insurance guy was Nathan "Nate" Jacobson, a well-dressed businessman who was, on paper at least, a model citizen. He had been the president of the Maryland Chapter of the Charter Life Underwriters Society, a commissioner of the Baltimore Civic Center, and founder and chairman of the United Small Business Investment Corporation. He was even one of the original owners of the Baltimore Bullets basketball team. After hearing their pitch he was as enthusiastic about Sarno's Las Vegas plans as Sarno himself.

Sarno and Mallin agreed to farm out the money-raising to Jacobson. In return, for getting them the nine million dollars, Jacobson would be named the president of the resort. Seeing his chance to make the big time, Jacobson quit the insurance business, married himself to Sarno's dream without hesitation, and ultimately moved to Las Vegas.

Jacobson, like Sarno, loved to gamble; by the time the casino was open, it was clear that he had a gambling problem almost as big as Sarno's. Entrusting a pathological gambler with your finances was not the most prudent business decision; yet compared to some of the partnerships Sarno would strike to get his casino built, this one was almost sensible.

On February 6, 1964, Sarno and Jacobson flew to Las Vegas to hash out details of the lease agreement with Kerkorian, and more importantly pay obeisance to the men who really mattered—the power brokers. Since the 1930s, Nevadans had welcomed outside money into their state, but there was a right way and wrong way to do business there. First and foremost, you had to take care of the locals. There were plenty of ways that county and state authorities could trip up a would-be hotel man, and it paid to make friends with the well-connected locals who could keep those officials at bay.

So Sarno and Jacobson were a little nervous as they caught a cab to downtown Las Vegas, where they'd been told attorney Clifford Jones kept his offices.

Getting to know Jones was a big step in establishing themselves as Las Vegas players. In a town built on "juice," or connections, Jones's nickname was "the Big Juice." He had moved to Las Vegas in the 1930s, and by the end of the decade had established himself as a deal-making lawyer. After two California businessmen gave him a share in their casino in exchange for help getting a license, Jones learned that this business made money for almost everyone. He soon had shares in over a dozen casinos and, as his influence grew, was elected to a judgeship and then the lieutenant governorship of the state. According to some, he was the model for Vegas Vic, the over-sized neon cowboy who waved to visitors from the roof of the Pioneer Club on Fremont Street.

The Big Juice's influence was felt in more subtle, though no less significant, ways. He was at the center of an ecosystem in which mob money guys, state officials, and earnest gamblers moved with ease, building a better future for Las Vegas—and for themselves. This made for strange bedfellows. In 1954, for example, Jones was caught on tape telling an undercover operative that he could procure a reputed East Coast thug a gaming license despite a criminal record. And in the following year, a local newspaper linked the Thunderbird, a Strip casino in which Jones was a major partner, to underworld financier Meyer Lansky. Three years later, he sold all his Nevada casino interests under a cloud.

Still he remained the most influential man in the state. He continued to practice law in Las Vegas and owned shares in several casinos outside the state, including the Havana Hilton in Batista's Cuba. It was rumored that he continued to secretly hold stakes in Nevada casinos as well. Governor Sawyer called him "an absolute deal-maker without peer." You needed to talk to Cliff Jones before you even thought about breaking ground in Las Vegas.

And if the Big Juice made time to see you, you didn't keep him waiting.

The cab dropped Sarno and Jacobson off at the address they'd been given and left. The building was a drug store. Maybe they'd gotten the digits mixed up? They walked down the street, looking for a law office. But no one on either side of the street knew anything about any lawyers.

Finally, someone remembered that yes, Jones had once had an office in the area, but that he had moved to a building miles away.

There was no way they'd make it. Jones was a busy man, and he wouldn't look kindly on strangers who wasted his time. Sarno and Jacobson started looking for another cab, each trying to hide how frantic he was getting.

Meanwhile, FBI Special Agent James Ford was approaching his bureau car, parked near the corner of Gass and Las Vegas Boulevard, about a half-mile south of Fremont Street's neon cavalcade. He was running through a few bank robbery leads as he passed two shortish men, one whisper-thin and the other bulging out of his tailored suit. As they moved slowly past him, the larger one said, "Hello."

Ford grumbled in response, continued down the street, and got into his car. Tracking down these leads was boring, usually unrewarding work, and grunts like him ended up getting the worst of it.

Before Ford could put his key in the ignition, a sudden rapping on the window startled him. It was the heavyset man from down the street. Ford rolled down his window.

"My name is Jay Sarno." He spoke quickly and forcefully. "I'm a hotel man—I've built several hotels around the country with Doris Day. My friend and I got our addresses mixed up, and we're running late. We can't find a cab down here. Is there any way you could give us a ride to our lawyer's office?" He gave him the address. "You'd be doing me a real favor."

You've got no idea, Ford thought. He had heard the name Sarno before. Though the Bureau didn't have any idea the hotel builder had set his eyes on Las Vegas, the Detroit office had reported rumors that "hoodlum money" was planning to finance a major new hotel there. Sarno had been mentioned in connection with Hoffa in previous briefings, and Ford clicked the pieces together. This might be an opportunity to gather some intelligence, maybe get off bank robbery details for good. He decided to take a chance on Sarno. The worst that can happen, he thought, is that I waste a half-hour driving a citizen to a meeting.

"Get in," Ford said. He didn't say much else; he didn't have to. Ever the showman, Sarno launched into a detailed pitch for the Desert Cabana.

"It's going to be the best hotel in town," he said. "It's going to cost about $25 million. Whaddya think of that? That's going to be good for business, huh? And we'll get plenty of celebrities to promote the place. It's too bad Doris won't get involved. She says she can't have her name associated with Las Vegas, because of the movie studios.

"I don't have any problems with your city," Sarno continued. "In fact, I'm planning to move to town to oversee my investment. The prospects here are just unbelievable."

"So where are you going to get twenty five million to build a hotel?" the agent asked when Sarno paused to take a breath.

"The Teamsters," Sarno replied. As Jacobson shot him a look he added, "I'm never too concerned who I borrow money from, it's who I loan it to that concerns me."

This seemed to satisfy the driver.

"I've talked to a few of the hotel men in town here," Sarno went on. "Like Moe Dalitz at the Desert Inn. I just wanted to let them know they'd be getting some competition." Ford tried to hide his interest; the FBI had been investigating Dalitz for years, but couldn't pin anything on him. "And it's the strangest thing. I thought they'd be upset about seeing someone with this kind of money moving in. But Moe patted me on the back and said he welcomed my group to Las Vegas.

"That's just strange. I never met a man who welcomed competition."

"I think they're straight shooters out here, at least," Jacobson chimed in. "I've been writing insurance for Morris Lansburgh at the Flamingo and I've found him 100 percent honest."

Finally they were at Jones's office. As he got out of the car, Sarno leaned back in, feeling magnanimous.

"Say, kid," he said, "I never asked you what your line is."

"I'm Special Agent James Ford with the Federal Bureau of Investigation, in the Las Vegas field office," the driver replied. He didn't show a badge, but it sounded like he had. Sarno promptly got back in and closed the door, waving Jacobson, who hadn't heard the exchange, into the office.

"I'm actually glad that I got the chance to talk with you, as a matter of fact," he said as quickly as he could. "I just read that book *The Green Felt Jungle* and I was talking about it with some of my partners." This was Ed Reid and Ovid Demaris' expose of corruption, vice, and mob influence in Las Vegas, which had a chapter called "Hoffa's Fountain of Pension Juice," that Sarno must've missed, along with a lengthy discussion of Cliff Jones's role as a Las Vegas fixer in great detail. "We were worried about coming in contact with that hoodlum element here."

"If you're worried about getting involved with hoodlums," Ford said, "There's only one thing you can do. Cooperate completely with us. If someone approaches you and makes representations that he's working for hoodlum elements, let us know. We can protect you. They won't.

"You seem like an honest man, Mr. Sarno. I'd hate to see you get in trouble because you got mixed up with the wrong element out here."

"Thank you for leveling with me," Sarno said. "I appreciate that. I'm leaving town tomorrow, but I'll be coming back soon, and I'll touch base with you as soon as I return."

Sarno left the car and hurried into Jones's office. He didn't tell Jones or Jacobson about his chauffeur.

Little did Sarno know that Ford came to regret the chance encounter almost as much as him. Like any good agent, Ford promptly put the conversation on paper and reported it to his higher-ups. This set off a furious round of airtels and letterhead memoranda between FBI headquarters and the Las Vegas field office. The investigation of Jimmy Hoffa was still one of the Justice Department's highest-profile inquiries. In 1962, he had been indicted by a federal grand jury in Nashville, Tennessee, for receiving kickbacks from employers in violation of federal law. The trial ended in a hung jury and allegations of witness tampering. In January 1964, just before Sarno came back out to Las Vegas, Hoffa was convicted of jury tampering in Chattanooga. The FBI was continuing to help Justice Department attorneys build a case against Hoffa for misuse of union funds, and was still examining the union pension fund's investments with a fine-toothed comb.

So in February 1964, anything having to do with Hoffa was a potential departmental hot potato. After debriefing Ford, Dean Elson, the Special Agent in Charge (SAC) of the Las Vegas office, decided to send Ford's version of the meeting to Washington, just to cover themselves.

Elson was right to be concerned. Washington immediately wrote back, demanding to know why agents had interrogated two Hoffa associates, when a previous memo had specified that "no open inquiry is to be conducted."

Sarno, according to a General Investigative Division memo, had been "generally uncooperative" during earlier inquiries into Hoffa's influence in the Atlanta and Dallas Cabanas; he had even threatened to sue Attorney General Kennedy after one audit. Those inquiries, by the FBI's own admission, had uncovered no evidence of kickbacks, hidden interests, or other improprieties, which only convinced the FBI that something so well concealed must be incredibly well-organized. They would have loved nothing more than to nail Hoffa and Sarno. Still, the brass demanded to know why a Bureau agent had apparently detained and questioned Sarno, who as a Hoffa associate was off limits.

SAC Elson sent a teletype marked "urgent" back to Washington that same day, stressing again that Ford had acted properly. "He was only carrying on a conversation which was initiated by Sarno and Jacobson."

In a final petition for leniency, the SAC acknowledged just how bizarre the whole thing sounded, but insisted that Ford had done nothing wrong: "Although this accidental meeting is almost unbelievable," he pled, "it nevertheless occurred exactly as set forth above."

Sarno had frustrated one of the world's premier intelligence-gathering organizations just by being himself.

"This whole thing sounds fantastic," a General Investigative Division covering memo concluded in disbelief. Ultimately, Ford avoided discipline, and even got a quiet atta-boy from Elson, who didn't think Sarno would have any more surprises for his office. He was wrong.

Despite Sarno's late arrival, the meeting with Jones went as hoped. With Jones's approval, Sarno finalized his deal with Kerkorian.

Sarno then made the rounds of the casinos, spreading his money around, losing more than he won. Jacobson wasn't much luckier. "It's an investment," Sarno rationalized. "We're going to be part of the community here, we need to show these schmucks we can afford to lose a few bucks at the tables."

Though the old hands who'd been running Vegas casinos since the 1940s never really liked Sarno, they were convinced that he wouldn't be bad for business—probably the most important barometer of civic approval in the desert city.

Sarno and Jacobson also took care of business in more traditional ways: they started paying rent to their new landlord. Kerkorian formed a new subsidiary, Tracy Leasing Corporation, which took title to the parcel on February 21, 1964 and leased it to Sarno. The initial rent was $10,000 a month. Once the hotel opened, the rent would become $15,000 a month plus 15% of the profits. Sarno, who didn't have nearly that much to his name, borrowed the first month's rent from his Atlanta factotum Michael Rosenstein. Sarno didn't have the financing to continue leasing the land past the first month, much less build a resort on it, but Rosenstein had a hunch that he would get his money back.

Rosenstein bet right. When the Teamster loan went through Sarno paid Rosenstein back and hired Melvin Grossman to turn his and Jo Harris's sketches into architectural plans.

Sarno had modeled the Atlanta, Dallas, and Palo Alto Cabanas almost entirely on Miami modern hotels like the Fontainebleau and Eden Roc. His Las Vegas project was so important, though, that he took the unprecedented step of making an Italian reconnaissance trip to get a better read on this whole Roman architecture thing.

The Las Vegas hotel was to be nothing less than a palace, and Sarno decided that he would have to crib from the greats: Michelangelo, Borromini, and other Renaissance icons who'd given Rome its grandeur.

It didn't matter that these artists had lived more than a millennium after the heights of Imperial Rome because, Sarno reasoned, nobody cared; no one, at least, who'd be coming to his hotel. For him, and for them, Rome was a city of ivory columns and fluttering togas, now and forever.

Jay and Joyce made the rounds of the Coliseum and the Forum. It didn't look like the movies, Jay thought. They walked across the site of the Circus Maximus. This was where the crowds had packed in to watch the chariot races, he learned from the tour guide.

"And some of them probably lost a bundle betting on them," he said to Joyce under his breath. He hadn't gambled in more than a week, and he was getting irritable.

But the real inspiration for his casino hotel didn't come from ruins haunted by Julius Caesar or Octavian Augustus—or even Nero.

After nearly dozing off while the tour guide pontificated on the apparently quite long history of the hulking Castel Sant'Angelo, Jay dutifully trudged alongside Joyce down the Via della Conciliazione as the guide expounded on the glories they would see at St. Peter's Basilica. He had remembered a few snatches from his college art history class about Michelangelo's work on the church and was looking forward to being able to tell people that he had been there.

The group had just crossed into St. Peter's Square when he finally looked up.

He saw Bernini's colonnades sweeping outward, welcoming everyone in, past the massive obelisk and fountains at the square's center, focusing attention on the basilica's façade behind them. In the distance he could barely make out Christ and the apostles perched on the roof, but the dome looming beyond was unmistakable.

It put the Fontainebleau to shame. *This* was how you built classy.

"Joyce, this is it! This is what my hotel is going to look like!"

It didn't really occur to him that, for millions of Roman Catholics, this was one of the holiest sites in the world, a square shaded by saints and martyrs. The architecture, the buildings and columns in front of him, were all that mattered. They made everything look majestic, larger than life. It didn't matter whether you had the pope or a craps table inside—the effect was everything.

"See how those colonnades draw you in? I thought I had a great building in Palo Alto, but I knew there was something missing. Here it is! I'll build two low-rise wings off of the hotel tower and cover them with columns. It'll be perfect!"

This was the worldly home of the Church, a Renaissance set piece designed to awe and humble with temporal might and spiritual majesty. And to Sarno it was the perfect model for a luxury hotel and casino that would uplift a man, let him be the gambler, the gourmet, the lover he had always yearned to be. He would take what he saw in Rome and turn it towards something sweeter than sin: indulgence.

After Sarno's epiphany at St. Peter's, the trip slowly wound down. Jay and Joyce went shopping at marble quarries, looking for statues and their replicas. On the flight home, he was more excited than ever. He had found what he was looking for.

B ack on terra firma, Sarno spent a few days with his sister Sara Corash in eastern Long Island. Sara's son Larry, a junior in college who had just taken an art history course, walked in as his uncle was waxing eloquent on the glories of the statues he would be importing from Italy, how they'd give his hotel that regal touch. Real glamour for everyone, for twenty bucks a night! He showed off photos of the statues and sketches he had drawn on the plane. Sara looked adoringly at her brother, a real hotel man. Her son was less impressed.

"How can you possibly do this?" Larry asked after looking at the drawings. "This has got to be the tackiest thing I've ever seen!"

"Oh no," Sarno assured him. "It's all going to be very elegant."

"But who's going to stay in a place with all this fake crap? No one who knows anything about real Roman ruins is going to take this seriously."

"You ever been to Vegas, kid?" Sarno asked. "I've thought this all out. This is exactly what that town needs. It can't lose."

Sarno made frequent trips down to Miami Beach to visit Melvin Grossman's office, swapping his sketches for finished renderings. On one sortie, he stopped by his cousin Marian King Portman's house. Here, no smart-aleck nephew dimmed his enthusiasm. Spreading drawings across her living room, he scribbled in new ideas as they came to him.

"The thing about Las Vegas is, it's so goddamned flat out there," he said. "The land, the casinos—most of them are simple two-story wood-frame buildings. The way they talk—flat, flat and boring.

"I'm going to do something they've never seen before, Marian," he said. "Look at this pool—the biggest in the world." He showed her a sketch.

"But out front, we'll need to make a statement, grab those people driving past at forty-five miles an hour, say, 'This is different.'"

He took an old drawing of the front elevation and sketched the colonnaded wings.

"You need something in the middle to make those columns look really grand," he said. "Something that'll put the Dallas and Palo Alto hotels to shame. Something that'll put the Trevi fountain to shame. Something like this."

Working the pen, an unbroken line of fountains, extending from the boulevard nearly to the casino's front step, took shape.

"Imagine it, water shooting a hundred feet in the air! An oasis in the middle of the desert!" He put down the pen and stood up.

"We're going to have fountains, fountains!" he exclaimed, skipping around his cousin's living room, seeing only cascading water and gently-lit masonry around him.

Scratching out plans was one thing; paying for the resort was another. Sarno was learning he couldn't rely on Jacobson to deliver everything, so he started looking for investors again. Sarno didn't have any real money of his own, and as supportive as his sisters were, they didn't either. His brothers, well, Jay thought they could have afforded it, but they said they were broke.

Having exhausted his own contacts, Sarno began going farther afield. Somehow, he arranged a meeting with Marshall Logan, a wealthy Floridian looking for investment opportunities. Logan directed Sarno to make his presentation to his attorney, Burton Cohen. The lawyer was no stranger to hotels; he had been raised in the business, working his way from bellhop to desk clerk while in high school, and had represented hotels since receiving his law degree from the University of Miami in 1948.

Cohen was reviewing a particularly complicated contract when his secretary buzzed him.

"A Mr. Jay Sarno to see you, Mr. Cohen."

"Send him in."

Sarno walked through the door, carrying a roll of architectural plans. He looks like a penguin, Cohen thought, as they exchanged pleasantries.

With little more than a hello, Sarno charged into his pitch.

"I'm building the most fantastic hotel ever out in Las Vegas," he began. "I've got a lease on land across from the Flamingo from the airline guy who owns it, and a ten million dollar loan commitment with the Teamsters Central States Pension Fund. This'll be the fourth hotel I've built with the Teamsters, and it's going to be even more successful than the others."

Sarno unrolled the drawings, explaining the significance of the fountains. To Cohen, who was familiar with Sarno's Atlanta hotel, it looked like a glorified Cabana.

"It's going to be a unique concept," Sarno assured Cohen. "No one in Las Vegas is doing what we're going to do. It can't miss. Would you like to look at the paperwork?"

Cohen spent the next five minutes reviewing the lease, the plans, the short prospectus, and the loan commitment. He thanked Sarno, who hurried out of the office with his plans barely rolled up.

Confident of his assessment, Cohen called in his secretary and began dictating a memo.

"Mr. Logan. This afternoon I met with Jay Sarno and reviewed his plans for the Las Vegas hotel. I examined the terms of his lease, his loan commitment, and his business plan.

"If you put one penny into this deal, I promise I'll have you committed to a mental institution."

Years later, Cohen would work for Sarno as he built and opened Circus Circus, and he would later become the president of Caesars Palace in a career that would see him helm the Strip's most illustrious casinos—the Frontier, Flamingo, Dunes, Thunderbird, and Desert Inn among them—and, in 2010, be named to MGM Resorts' board of directors.

"Caesars Palace," he admitted in that year, "turned out to be one of the most successful hotel casinos in the world." He kept his memo to Logan in a file for decades after he rebuffed Sarno.

"I open it up periodically when I start thinking I'm too smart, just to show how stupid I can be."

Cohen wasn't the only one the Desert Cabana underwhelmed. Jacobson kept assuring Sarno and Mallin he could get investors, but he was having trouble producing gamblers willing to sink $50,000 into a casino. They'd happily sign a marker for that much if they'd lost the money fair and square at the tables, but *investing* that much… it was just too risky. Non-gamblers, for the most part, frowned on putting their money into a Las Vegas gambling hall, no matter how persuasively Jacobson argued its merits.

So when Sol Silberman, president of Coral Gables' Tropical Park racetrack, demanded that strings be attached to his investment, the partners were willing to listen. In return for a quarter-million dollars—less than three percent of the $9 million Jacobson had to raise—he insisted that a former bookie turned casino manager named Jerry Zarowitz be put in charge of Sarno's casino.

Zarowitz's spotty past didn't disqualify him from enjoying a long career in Las Vegas casinos as long as he kept a low profile. He had gone to prison for attempting to fix the 1946 New York Giants-Chicago Bears National Football League championship game and allegations of organized crime ties followed him before and after his conviction.

"Mister Z," as casino employees reverentially called him, was typical of his generation: he had learned the business in the illegal gambling underworld and was now going legit, or at least appearing to go legit. But it was impossible for a man to put his past completely behind him. After all, it was never easy getting the money to build these places, even though they were completely legal, and it usually fell to men like Zarowitz to get that money, often from men with continuing illicit enterprises.

To get that money, the owners had to make promises; it was up to men like Zarowitz to see that these promises were kept. Typically, this required nothing more sinister than making sure that a small portion of the winnings were skimmed off the top and sent to illicit investors back east. But a man like Zarowitz spoke with the weight of many dangerous men behind him.

Certainly Zarowitz hadn't been alone in trying to fix football games, and a man didn't get and maintain a top position as a bookmaker or running a Las Vegas casino without friends who could keep the heat off him and make things tough for his enemies.

"Who's this guy representing?" Mallin asked Sarno.

"I don't care," was the answer. "We need the money. We've got to make some concessions."

"He's a crook," Mallin said more bluntly. "He went to jail for fixing games."

"We're not going to be betting against him," Sarno said. "Relax."

Indeed, Zarowitz would play the part of casino boss perfectly. He cut a fine figure, walking through the casino in an expensive new suit, and laying the charm on gamblers. He strode past the craps tables like a wiseguy colossus, perfect posture, not a hair out of place. His friends nicknamed him "the Quarterback."

Through his connections with the East Coast bookmaking and gambling fraternity, Zarowitz was able to get many investors for the casino; more importantly, he would be a bridge to the big gamblers who could steer junkets and big players to Las Vegas—a key piece of the puzzle. On paper, Silberman never came up with the money, though his accountant, Harry Lewis, borrowed a large enough sum from a Swiss bank to become the project's single largest stockholder. Wherever that money came from, Zarowitz stayed, and he was worth his weight in casino chips. He didn't invest a cent of his own money, and was never officially licensed, but he became the de facto one-third owner of the casino.

Sarno was still managing director of the casino hotel they were planning, but he was starting to understand that he wouldn't be running it. Still, he thought, he would win in the end, just like he had done so many times at gin rummy. No one else in the game could keep up with him.

Not yet, anyway.

SIX

Building a Palace for Caesars

Sarno was his usual energetic self at the ground-breaking for his Las Vegas hotel just a few months later. He had gotten one of the Miami Beach legends to build the place: Miami's Taylor Construction. Owner Morey Mason had built more than forty Miami Beach hotels, including the Saxony, Eden Roc, Americana, and, notably, the Fontainebleau. Better yet, Taylor was already a Las Vegas veteran, having built the Riviera in 1955 and the Tropicana two years later.

On his own, Mason couldn't post a performance bond for the $10.5 million hard-money contract, which required him to deliver the hotel as promised, no matter what his final costs were. Unlike his client, he didn't like these kinds of risk, so he turned to a former employee, Rob Johnson, who'd worked on the Riviera and Tropicana for Mason before starting his own Las Vegas-based company, and Mort Crane, a Chicago contractor, to split the bond. They started building before the ink on the paperwork was dry.

The job started slowly, with grading, digging, and foundation work. Despite his experience in Florida, Mason found some new challenges in Las Vegas. Like sand. Miami's sand knew its place: for the most part, it remained on the beach. But not so in Las Vegas: when the wind kicked up, massive sandstorms tore across the desert scrub and through the job site, threatening to shut work down. Superintendents learned to pass out goggles on windy days so workers wouldn't be blinded by the grit.

As construction began, Sarno kept planning. Michael Rosenstein didn't come out to Las Vegas to manage the construction, even though he owned a small share of it and eventually moved to Las Vegas to become the hotel's director of purchasing. Instead Sarno asked Harry Wald, who had done the interiors of the Palo Alto Cabana, to become project coordinator.

Wald, born Hans Eichenwald in Rheine, Germany, fled his homeland with his sister as a teenager; the rest of his family perished in the Holocaust. During World War II, he served with the U.S. Army's counter-intelligence division. Tormented by fears for his family's safety, personally driven to defeat Hitler's armies as quickly as possible, Wald's war experience could not have been more different from Sarno's bootlegging vacation from college. After the war, Wald remained with the army and ultimately became a brigadier general in the Nevada Army National Guard.

With Wald tending to the administrative details, Sarno was free to sketch and tweak his hotel's design. He soon decided the name of the hotel itself would have to go. "Desert Cabana" wasn't grandiose enough, but "Desert Palace" might be. That's the name he gave the holding company that, to this day, still owns the casino that he built.

After a while, even "Desert Palace" sounded too pedestrian to Sarno. A hotel this unique had to have a one-of-a-kind name. In an inspired moment, he decreed the hotel would be known henceforth as Caesars Palace.

A grammarian reminded him that a Palace belonging to Caesar would properly be Caesar's Palace.

"It's not a palace for one Caesar," he insisted, "It's a palace for all the Caesars, for all the people. Everyone who steps through these doors is going to be a Caesar." Didn't everyone want to be the center of attention? Why not let the guest believe that this entire palace had been built to service him and only him?

He wasn't too clear about what women could expect at his hotel; later apologists claimed that guests could be "Caesar or Cleopatra," but Sarno wanted Caesars to be a place where men had most of the fun: they shot the dice, had their shoulders rubbed and temples massaged while waiting for dinner, and took cleansing steam baths. Women—whether their job title was goddess or change girl—

were to serve men. Caesars Palace might have been the last gasp of unabashed male chauvinism.

But the fantasy wasn't just in the service. It was in the entire building. Jo Harris convinced Sarno to make the Caesars theme so all-encompassing.

"If this is going to be a Roman hotel, it's going to be the most Roman hotel in the world. Every aspect of it, from the uniforms to the stationery, has to reflect back on that theme," she insisted. Sarno listened, and he opened his checkbook.

She started with the temporary facilities that customers would never see. The two sets of double-wide trailers that housed the construction offices were elaborate affairs with white gabled roofs, fronted by a whimsical copy of a tetrastyle Greek temple: four columns supported a triangular top, under which were two windows and an unpainted wooden door, with a copy of the triangular upperworks crowning it.

There was nothing remotely Roman about the craps table they'd installed in one of the trailers, which helped Sarno and Jacobson blow off steam, though it didn't prevent them from shouting at subordinates—and each other—when things didn't go their way.

Despite the Roman theme, Sarno borrowed elements of the Miami Modern style just as unselfconsciously as he cribbed from the Italian greats. Screen block, for example, was a practical adaptation of modernist forms to the South Florida sun: it shielded glass walls from direct sun but still admitted plenty of light. Sarno had used it in Atlanta and Dallas, but was dissatisfied with commercially available blocks.

"None of these look very good," he complained to architect Melvin Grossman as they assessed samples. "The coverage dents are too high. They don't let in enough light. The guests are going to feel like they're in a cave."

Grossman insisted that these were the best products available.

"They're not good enough." Sarno didn't think it was Grossman's fault, but he made it sound that way.

"Why don't you make your own, then?"

"That's just what I'm going to do," Sarno said, and set himself to designing the ultimate concrete block. It took some experimentation.

He had model after model made, then tested them in various windows of the Atlanta Cabana.

The gigantic desk that he and Mallin shared was soon surrounded by stacks of Styrofoam mock blocks. His son Jay, now six years old, delighted in these new toys; every day, he would stack them up, construct a sofa cushion roof and climb inside his fort.

He was building, and having fun, just like his father. Except little Jay didn't have to borrow money from the Teamsters, or beg it from bookies, to build his palaces.

With construction moving along, Sarno decided that, like Caesar campaigning against the Gauls, he must move his seat of power to the front lines. He prepared to relocate his family to Las Vegas.

When the emperor's court travels, his personal retinue follows. So he took it as a given that his secretary Evelyn Spinks would join him.

"We're going to move," he said to her one day, a definitive statement, not a request.

"Well, you may be moving to Las Vegas, but I'm not," she replied. "I'm a Georgia girl, and I'm going to stay right here."

"If you don't go, you'll never know what you missed," Sarno replied. He thought for a moment and spoke again. "You should really think about going. It would be good for you." He didn't need to add that it would also be good for him.

Spinks did think about it on her way to her parents' house, where she still lived. She didn't know anything about the desert town except what she had picked up from Sarno's stories. It didn't sound inviting. That night, she told her parents about it, expecting them to forbid her to go. She was surprised when they said that it was a wonderful opportunity. Sarno was pleased but not surprised the next day when she told him she would be going.

Moving was an opportunity for Sarno's family as well. Joyce had grown tired of Jay's running around and began dropping hints that she would take the kids and leave him. But as much as Jay wanted the freedom to chase girls, he couldn't bear the thought of being separated from the children—he adored Jay, September, and Freddie, who had been born in 1961. Time and again he convinced her to stay with him. And he had allies: Joyce's parents didn't relish the idea of their daughter getting a divorce, and her mother usually counseled her to work things out.

"He'll change, he'll change," she would say. "And with three kids, where are you going to go?"

So when Sarno broached the subject of moving, he spoke convincingly of a new life, a fresh start, a prominent place in local society for Joyce—anything she wanted was waiting for her in Las Vegas. More importantly, it would be a life without Carol: Jay promised to devote himself fully to the mother of his children. She would be at his side at the big social occasions, and he would come home to her at night. It might be late, of course, since hotel men didn't keep banker's hours, but he would come home.

Joyce agreed and arranged the details of the move in the summer of 1965. Jay announced that he was needed at the job site and moved himself out to Las Vegas several weeks before his family. He took a suite in the Dunes hotel, from which he could watch his hotel beginning to take shape across Flamingo Road. He found he liked waking up a short walk from the dice tables. Maybe he could convince Joyce to let them live in a suite at his hotel once it opened.

Joyce didn't see it quite that way. She insisted Jay buy a proper home for the family. He did, though it wouldn't be ready until a few weeks after they arrived, and she agreed to stay with him at the Dunes until then. At last moving day came: the children were giddy at the prospect of cross-country travel. Even Joyce was optimistic. Jay had flown back into town to shepherd his family on the flight to their new home. There was still plenty to do in Las Vegas, but a man had responsibilities.

It was a three-leg flight: from Atlanta to New Orleans, then to Dallas, and finally home to Las Vegas.

The children had never flown before. So as Joyce readied her kids for the flight, she was not as cheerful as her husband, who predicted smooth sailing and star treatment all the way. But Jay started getting fidgety while they were still over Georgia. Though he traveled often, Sarno never liked planes. He would sketch and doodle, but the boredom—no real food, no phone, no golf, no gambling—drove him nuts. While the kids were models of decorum, their father was climbing the walls as they touched down in New Orleans. He announced that he was going to get a candy bar and insisted that the family deplane with him.

"But we don't have time," Joyce argued. "They'll leave without us. Then what will we do?"

"No way," Jay assured her. "They'd never take off without us. We'll just be a minute."

The family trudged after Sarno to the newsstand. He didn't walk like a man with a plane to catch. As Joyce looked anxiously at her watch, he browsed through the newspapers. "Just another minute," he said more than once as she gestured down the terminal. A story in the paper had caught his eye.

After a slow and meandering trek back to the gate, Sarno was positively shocked to learn that the plane had taken off on time and without him. After a parley with the gate agent, he told his family they'd be staying in New Orleans that night. Their luggage was en route to Dallas and then Las Vegas, but that didn't seem to bother Jay at all. Joyce, who would be presented with the actual mechanics of caring for three youngsters with no change of clothes or toiletries, wasn't as blasé about the change in plans. All over a candy bar.

Late in the afternoon on the next day, the Sarno family finally touched down in Las Vegas. When they stepped out of the plane, even Joyce's eyes widened.

It was hot—burning hot. The mountains loomed in the distance. Beyond the tarmac, they couldn't see any trees, any sign of life. "My god, Dad's taken us to the moon," Sarno's son Jay thought.

Luckily, there was a familiar face waiting for them. Evelyn Spinks had driven out on schedule and met the family at the gate, not surprised that they were a day late.

This was reassuring to the kids; she meant that the world they'd known wasn't totally gone.

Evelyn drove the Sarnos to their future home, which was in the final stages of construction. Young Jay, used to the endless woody backyard of Westover Drive, was perplexed by the dry, white caliche yard that surrounded the house. This wasn't the backyard he was used to. After a quick look, the family drove to the Dunes.

Three weeks later the Sarno family moved into their home at 3541 Maricopa Way, a small cul-de-sac in the Paradise Palms subdivision—a housing development that, not so coincidentally, had been built by Moe Dalitz and financed by a Teamster loan. The back fence butted up to the grounds of Ruby S. Thomas Elementary School, which the Sarno children attended. It was a short walk, and the kids could shout to Joyce from the playground, and she would dutifully appear.

There was also a new world to explore: Paradise Palms was then surrounded by barren desert, and the kids delighted in riding their bikes through the sage brush and into washes. Back in Georgia young Jay had caught water moccasins, and he learned to hunt for lizards in the sagebrush. Stuart Mason, Morey's son who came to Las Vegas as assistant project manager on Caesars, had moved his family down the street from the Sarnos. With other families joining them, more than two dozen kids soon lived on the cul-de-sac, spending their afternoons playing together in the street, making their street a neighborhood.

It was a suburban idyll, a far cry from the "City of Sin" that muckrakers like Ed Reid and Ovid Demaris, or confirmed gamblers like Jay Sarno, imagined in Las Vegas. But it was part of the growing city that was adding thousands of new residents for each casino that opened as the metropolitan region nearly doubled in size, to 125,000 inhabitants, many of them living in new subdivisions like Paradise Palms.

The Sarnos and Masons became friends, even though Stuart and his wife Flora didn't enjoy the nightlife like Jay. One night, the Sarnos came to the Masons' for a family dinner. After stowing the Sarnos' coats in his daughter Debbie's room, Stuart steered his guests to the dining room.

Flora had prepared a dish she called "Jewish hamburgers," small meatloafs really, seasoned, pan-fried, and slathered in onions. She served them on a big Lazy Susan in the middle of the dinner table, and everyone took as they wished. They were delicious, and the adults indulged in two or three a piece, and felt guilty afterward.

After the children had been excused, the adults stayed around the table, talking shop and gossiping about their new hometown. Six Jewish hamburgers remained on the Lazy Susan, and Flora thought the leftovers might make a good lunch for the kids the next day. The two couples sat and talked, everyone enjoying the moment too much to start cleaning up.

"Hey, let's go sit on the couch," Stuart finally suggested, and his guests rose to follow him. Flora started to clear the table.

The Lazy Susan was empty now; Jay had polished off tomorrow's lunch as a casual after-dinner nosh.

The kids were chasing each other from room to room. Flora and Joyce talked about Ruby Thomas Elementary, while Sarno snoozed on the sofa beside his wife, seemingly dead to the world.

Just then the Masons' daughter Debbie walked in.

"Daddy, look what I found on the floor in my room!" she said. She waved a three-inch wad of hundred-dollar bills, still wrapped in a currency band that said "$10,000."

Stuart didn't have time to react before Jay popped up, suddenly wide awake.

"Oh, it must have fallen out of my jacket pocket," he said, and skipped over to Debbie, quickly pocketing the bills.

Stuart had never seen anyone so casual with so much money. "There's a whole other side to this guy," he thought.

That was an understatement.

The family settled into life in Las Vegas over the next few months, and by time the calendar turned to 1966 things didn't seem so new or strange anymore.

Jay spent most of his time down at the job site. With Stuart Mason running things in the field and project manager Alex Dalton keeping track of the money back at the office, the building began to take shape. Harry Wald was setting up everything the hotel would need—from bellmen to seafood vendors—once the doors opened.

Joyce settled into a routine, waking up hours before her husband, getting the kids fed, washed, dressed, and out the door for school. Though someone came in once a week to help with the heavy cleaning, she did most of the housework and ironed all of Jay's shirts (he insisted that only she could get them perfect).

Everything seemed to be going well, until Joyce learned that her husband hadn't left everything in Atlanta behind. Carol, she discovered, was now living in Las Vegas, and she had been seen around town with her husband.

"How could you?" she screamed at Jay. "You said we would be starting over. I never should have let you drag me out here with the kids."

"It just happened," Sarno responded. "But you're the one who matters most. Don't I give you everything you need?"

Joyce wasn't able to convince Jay to break it off with Carol, but she still couldn't bring herself to leave him. Carol became almost part of the family. Within two years, Jay had bought her a 4-bedroom house with a pool in Desert Park, an older but still stylish subdivision near Maryland Parkway and Charleston Boulevard. He gave her money to pay off the mortgage so she could own the house free and clear, and a car as well.

His girlfriend was happy, but Sarno's wife stopped trying to hide her heartbreak. Living in a strange city, with a husband who sometimes didn't come home for days, was too much.

Joyce wasn't the only one who felt that Las Vegas wasn't the land of milk and honey Jay had promised.

Evelyn was also increasingly unhappy with her new hometown. It was her first time living away from her parents. To make matters worse, paying for her own apartment meant that her salary wasn't going as far.

One day, upset at the prospect of returning home to an empty refrigerator, she complained to Jo Harris that she was seriously thinking about leaving Las Vegas; she was going to ask her parents to wire her money for the trip home. Later that afternoon, Harris collared Sarno.

"If you don't do something about Evelyn, she's going to go home."

"Why?" countered Sarno.

"She's not at all happy here," she explained. "She doesn't like it here and she's finding it hard to survive on her paycheck."

"Is that all?" Sarno seemed relieved. "I'll take care of that."

Harris assumed that Sarno was going to give Spinks a raise. But he had an even better idea. He walked over to Evelyn's desk and patted her shoulder.

"Don't worry about a thing, Evie."

"I'm sorry, Mr. Sarno," Spinks replied. "It's not that I don't like you or the work, but I hardly have enough money for food."

"Everything's going to be fine. Joyce and I are going to take you out to dinner tonight."

They had an excellent dinner at the Dunes. Sarno didn't mention a raise, and it became clear that this was his solution to the problem: if his secretary didn't have money for food, he would take her out to dinner.

After the meal, he sauntered down to the craps table and, while Spinks and his wife watched, lost about three thousand dollars in a half hour.

The next morning, she had told Jo, "I really feel a lot better now. Here's a guy throwing away three thousand dollars on a game and I can't buy groceries."

Still, she stayed with Sarno, who relented and gave her a raise.

As construction continued, Sarno couldn't help but see a million things he should do differently: the stage for the dinner theater raised two feet higher; the stage lowered three feet; a higher ceiling in the casino.

Nate Jacobson talked him out of most of the changes. A simple, "I can tell you exactly how much that would cost, Jay," from Stuart Mason was usually enough to get him onto the next subject. Caesars Palace went through about a million dollars of change orders—not chump change by any means, but not exorbitant for a $10.5 million contract.

Sarno was making better progress at publicizing the resort. As early as March 1966 *Los Angeles Times* writer John L. Scott was eagerly anticipating its planned mid-July opening. He led his weekly Las Vegas column by listing the "stellar" entertainment options the hotel would deliver. Caesars had signed a range of performers, including Anthony Newley, Woody Allen, Petula Clark, Tony Bennett, Joey

Heatherton, and Andy Griffith into the Circus Maximus dinner theater. Xavier Cugat, Damita Jo, Mongo Santamaria, and the Checkmates had been inked for the Nero's Nook lounge. The hotel itself, though far from finished, was described as "spectacular."

This wasn't standard-issue hype: the Aladdin, scheduled to open in April, was buried at the end of the column, with no superlatives. This was for good reason: the Aladdin's entertainment lineup featured two anonymous production shows (one starring the Three Cheers, the other the song-and-dance-heavy "Jet Set Revue") and the Jackie Mason Show, each playing twice a night in a round-robin format. This was low-wattage next to the Caesars parade of stars.

A month before the opening Scott devoted an entire article to a "Palace really fit for Caesar," based mostly on a tour conducted by Nate Jacobson. When asked if it had been his idea to "bring the glories and luxuries" of Rome to the Strip, an uncharacteristically smiling Jacobson credited Jay Sarno with introducing the "Classic architectural motif." More importantly, Jacobson said, they would do something that had never been done before: make money.

"We intend to run our hotel (rooms, food and beverage, etc.) efficiently and at a profit," Jacobson told him. "In the old days Vegas spots depended on gaming to pull the entire load. Not any more."

This shift in emphasis deserved more than a brief mention in a travel column. Sarno was going to turn the business on its head. He had been appalled by the "loss leader" mentality during his stay at the Flamingo in 1963. The hotel, dining, and entertainment departments were not expected to show a profit. Cheap accommodations, food, and shows would funnel gamblers into the property, where they'd lose far more than the value of the free or discounted fare. Cost control was the key: if designers made the hotels too elaborate, they couldn't afford to give rooms away. So mediocrity reigned.

Sarno had no problem doing things on the cheap, but he understood there was a right way and a wrong way to keep your costs down. He had built his career on selling bargain-built rooms as luxurious ones. Caesars Palace was to be the same, only more so.

Steve Wynn, a man who knows the tricks of casino hotel design better than anyone alive today, says: "Jay figured out a way to make this Roman orgy, bacchanalian kind of motel look expensive by using a concrete block that you could see through. And that would allow you to do the cheapest possible construction but hide it because it was the entire facade. And you laid behind the block a neon tube and it gave it a sexy glow. You put a couple of phony statues and a fountain in front of it. And customers thought they were driving up to the Taj Mahal."

The least expensive rooms slated for Caesars Palace were fourteen dollars a night; the average on the Strip in 1966 was about nine dollars. Caesars was in its own league, even before it opened.

Before they could open Caesars, Sarno and Jacobson had to endure the rigors of licensing by the Nevada Gaming Commission. This was more daunting than wrangling with punchlists and dickering with subcontractors.

In preparation for the hearing, Gaming Control Board investigators looked into each of nearly sixty shareholder applicants, some of whom owned less than half of a percentage point in the casino. This was consistent with the Board's directive to investigate all investors, no matter how small, to keep out even the rumor of organized crime. But there was an eight-hundred pound gorilla in the room: Jimmy Hoffa. He wasn't even mentioned during the Gaming Commission meeting on May 18, when most of the Desert Palace, Inc. stockholders were licensed. There were a few questions raised about Harry Lewis, on paper the second largest stockholder after Sarno himself. Investigators had learned that he had gotten the money to buy his casino stock from a Swiss bank, but were satisfied that he was suitable for licensing, despite rumors that he was involved with Silberman's Tropical Park race track. Only one applicant was denied a license: Dr. Abe Konick, a Pittsburgh dentist who was rumored to have been involved in bookmaking.

They may not have looked too closely at the hotel's lenders, but the regulators went over the project's financial structure and cash reserves with a fine-toothed comb, quizzing Nate Jacobson on the hotel's solvency. Like Sarno, they didn't seem to care much about where the money came from: they were only concerned that there was more than enough of it to go around.

"We know from experience," Gaming Commission member James Hotchkiss lectured Jacobson, "that inadequate capital to start with can cause a very serious difficulty and result in a serious problem for the community."

Jacobson retorted that all of his "business people" had decades of experience in manufacturing and retail, which were basically the same thing as the casino business, and were up to any challenge.

Without knowing it, Jacobson had thrown down the gauntlet. The regulators thundered back that the gambling business was unique; they'd better be prepared for anything.

"We have had casinos lose as much as $300,000 the first night to complimentary neighbors who come over to pay their respects and walk away with your bankroll, and this can happen legitimately," Commission chair Milton Keefer explained.

The only solution, they told Jacobson, was to raise at least $350,000 more to have on hand opening night, should the gamblers get lucky. With Jacobson's solemn vow to do just that, the commission unanimously approved that Caesars Palace be allowed to open, pursuant to getting the additional capital.

Jacobson's promises satisfied the Gaming Commission, but there were serious questions about exactly where the money was coming from. Allegations that the licensed managers were fronting for a coalition of mobsters found their way into print on August 1, but Nevada's regulators publicly insisted that, having done their due diligence, they were satisfied the project was free of undesirables. Nevadans were not particularly suspicious of Greeks bearing gifts, and they certainly weren't going to scrutinize mock Romans spending millions.

As July approached, it became clear that the opening would have to be pushed back. Too much work remained to be done. Newspaper advertisements placed in likely feeder markets, particularly Los Angeles, began trumpeting the "Gala August Premier" of the casino. Like the invitation sent to special VIP guests, the news ad featured Caesars inviting guests to an "orgy of excitement." But there was much more:

"What's going on? Everything! High-powered action that'll jolt you into a new lease on life! Excitement that never quits! Luscious food! Feast…play…caper and cavort in Bacchanalian raptures of revelry! Join the lively ones…rub shoulders with the Jet-set, in the newest, most magnificent headquarters for the action faction!"

But early in July, Sarno had a new worry: the jet set might not be making it to his hotel. On July 8, talks between the International Association of Machinists and five major airlines broke down. More than 35,000 mechanics walked off the job. Many other airline workers joined the picket lines, effectively grounding most commercial flights throughout the United States.

There was nothing he and Jacobson could do about this but fume. They hoped that management and labor would reach a compromise before the hotel opened, but it didn't look good. This was a problem that no Caesar ever had to deal with.

In the construction trailers, the mood was closer to anxiety than anticipation by late July. The building wasn't close to being done. Sarno, Wald, Mason, and a few others moved into the hotel as getting it finished on time became a twenty-four hour a day job.

They ran into a few problems. The loan covenants and other materials specified that the hotel was to have 680 hotel rooms. But try as they might Nate and Jay just couldn't squeeze 680 rooms out of their budget. Between the curving high-rise and wood-frame rooms that swept around the pool, they were still short.

"Wait a minute. This says 'keys,' not 'rooms,'" Sarno said as he, Jacobson, and Mason examined the loan agreement.

"Yeah, it does. So?" asked Jacobson.

"If we take a few of the suites on the upper floors and give the rooms keys—say, a key for the bedroom and a key for the living room—we might just make it, right?"

"That's right," said Jacobson. Sarno noticed that Mason wasn't quite nodding.

"Hey, we're not trying to cheat anyone here," he said. "We could have given them 680 cheap rooms. Instead, we've got some of the finest suites in the country. You know that. We're not cheating anyone."

"If they want to walk around and count keys," Jacobson added, "this is how many keys we'll have. Go and make it work."

Mason did just that.

Sarno was right: the rooms, no matter how many they actually built, were like nothing the town had ever seen. His crews faced plenty of problems they hadn't before: for example, what's the best way to secure the mirror above the bed? More than once, he saw one of his workers lying on a circular bed, looking up at the mirror and laughing.

"Just make sure it doesn't fall down once the guests are in," he usually said. "That would be…inconvenient, I'm sure."

This wasn't the worst problem, though. The company that was supposed to furnish the hotel went bankrupt just as the rooms were ready to be fitted out. Jacobson willed the furniture, still packed in shipping crates, out of the warehouses, but the guys who delivered it were just truck drivers; they weren't about to start arranging furniture. They stacked it, floor to ceiling, wherever there was room, and that was that.

"Do something," Sarno said to no one in particular.

"You've got workers out there," Jacobson told Mason. "Have them get to work, dammit!"

Mason didn't care to answer that they'd been working feverishly just to get the place built. Instead, he pressed a crew that was just going off duty into carrying the crates out of the hotel, where they were no good to anyone, and lining them up in the finished parking lot. All red chairs went in one line, all blue sofas went in another, and so on. Once they were in order, Mason ordered the guys to start uncrating.

When they started cracking open the boxes that held lampshades and other breakables, they saw that they'd been packed in popcorn—real popcorn. Since they were missing breakfast and lunch, many of them snacked on the piles of popcorn that grew in the parking lot. Meanwhile, under Mason's direction, they started hauling the furniture into its correct rooms—at least those rooms that were finished.

That many of them weren't, Mason knew, was a problem for tomorrow.

"Looking good," Sarno told Mason as he watched the workers carrying furniture into his hotel. "What's going on with that?" He pointed to one of the mounds.

"It's just popcorn," Mason said.

"And it's okay to eat it?" Sarno asked.

"Well, no one's died yet."

Sarno walked down the rows of uncrated furniture, munching on handfuls of popcorn as he did.

It wasn't exactly manna from heaven, but to him, every bit of good luck was a small miracle. And he would need more than a few miracles to get his hotel open on time, and to fill it with gamblers.

SEVEN

The Triumphs of Caesar

Jay Sarno was used to bad luck, but this was ridiculous.

He had gone home to Joyce and the kids to get one last night's sleep before the opening but he had spent most of the night tossing and turning, sick over what was going on across town at his hotel. More than two years of planning, and so much was still up in the air. As he lay in bed on the morning of Friday, August 5, 1966, he ran through some of his problems.

First, there was the money: there wasn't enough of it. Although the Gaming Control Board had warned them about having a sufficient bankroll on hand before the place was ready to take bets, they had only $100,000 behind the cashier's window, not $350,000. This was a gamble: with a run of luck, winners could break the bank. The casino would have to close.

Then there was the airline strike. Virtually all commercial airline traffic had been grounded for nearly a month now. With the rates he was charging, Sarno needed to draw a wealthier visitor than Las Vegas had seen before, the kind of jet-setters who wouldn't drive or take a train, let alone a bus. The downtown places were booming despite the strike, and the other Strip casinos that relied heavily on weekenders driving up from Los Angeles were limping along. None of them were as vulnerable to the airline strike as he was. Even if they bused people from Los Angeles and filled the hotel, it wouldn't help in the casino. Without the East Coast high rollers, without the *machers*, this might be a big bust.

Third, he and Nate Jacobson weren't getting along. They had an arrangement: Jay would be the idea man, and Nate would be the money man. But each wanted to be the boss. Jacobson infuriated Sarno with his penny-pinching; Sarno's disregard for the bottom line drove Jacobson nuts. Sensible adults who respected each other could see past these differences, but the tension between the two would-be bosses grew. Maybe it was because they were both self-described degenerate gamblers who figured that one of them winning meant the other was losing, but fundamentally, they just didn't like each other.

Fourth, the place just wasn't ready to open. The night before, Stuart Mason had given him an honest assessment of how much work remained. The casino was mostly done, but guys were still laying carpet in the lobby. Half of the rooms wouldn't be ready for another three days; the first guests were due to arrive in three hours. Most of the rooms that overlooked the pool didn't have their plumbing hooked up. He lost track of how many rooms didn't have all their furniture; several thousands of dollars worth of beds and chairs were still sitting in the parking lot. At least it hadn't rained.

Then there were less immediate troubles. His friend Jimmy Hoffa had nearly exhausted his appeals and would probably be sitting in prison in a few months. Without his help at the Teamsters Union, Sarno might be cut off from the loans he would need to expand the hotel, and he would be without a powerful ally. Right now, declaring "Jimmy says so," ended more than one argument. A few months from now, who knew?

Plus there were rumors swirling in the papers that his casino was overrun by mobsters, that a crew of Mafiosi had already divvied up control in the joint. Had they? He knew that Jerry Zarowitz didn't answer to him or Jacobson, but he couldn't say whether this would be a problem.

There were plenty of reasons not to go ahead with the opening, to say that he had given the casino business his best shot and slink back to Atlanta, where the Cabana guaranteed a living. But Sarno never thought of backing down. The uncertainty was wonderfully excruciating.

He wasn't the only one holding his breath. Las Vegans await a casino opening the way Romans look for white smoke wafting from the Sistine Chapel. In a town built on an understanding of gambling odds and good public relations, each new resort is an act of civic affirmation, a reminder that as long as the hotels keep rising and the dice keep rolling, all will be well. Caesars Palace's debut promised to be one for the ages. It was the most expensive casino ever built, anywhere, costing about four times more than earlier casinos like the Sands or Dunes, even though he was a master of squeezing the most out of a dollar. They were getting a lot of bang for their buck—but would it be enough to draw the big gamblers?

The sun was shining as he waited for the driver to pick him up. He considered this a good omen, even though the sky was just as cloudless about 310 days a year in Las Vegas. In fact, as important as the day seemed to Sarno, it was shaping up like a normal day for nearly everyone else in Las Vegas. Like every other Friday it was the real start of the workweek for many. The sun had been up for hours by the time Sarno's car arrived and the mercury was already in the upper 90s: it would reach 111 degrees that day.

But this was no ordinary Friday. In place of an opening party, Sarno planned a three-day Roman debauch. Even the invitations were part of the gag. You didn't just get one in the mail: a centurion knocked on your door, his armor glittering over his taut abs, and unrolled a scroll with charred edges (to suggest fiddling while the world around you burned). Then he read the Roman script that formally invited you to "the gala preview of Las Vegas' newest and most exciting resort."

The invitation described the party as an "orgy of excitement" including "libations, feasting, casting of dice, spinning of wheels, turning of cards, and revelries of entertainment featuring the noblest Roman of them all…Mr. Andy Williams." The orgy would continue "on and on until the collapse of the participants…or sunrise, August 8, whichever event shall first occur."

Those who knew Sarno got a chuckle out of the cartoon logo at the top and bottom of the scroll: a chubby toga-wearing Caesar who looked suspiciously like Sarno reclining on a couch, with a scantily-clad blonde who bore a remarkable resemblance to Joyce draped across his lap, dangling a bunch of grapes over his open mouth. Sarno might not have his name on the hotel, but he would personally welcome guests to the property in a series of invitations, brochures, and guidebooks, in caricature at least.

Now the day was here, Sarno thought, the die was cast. As his driver approached Las Vegas Boulevard, he leaned forward.

"Drop me off in front," he commanded. Instead of being left off in the back, by the construction entrance, he would walk through the front door like a paying guest. No, better than that, like an emperor. At Las Vegas Boulevard, the driver made a right then a quick left, and Caesars Palace was upon them.

Sarno had visualized every brick before a shovel had been turned; then he had walked every inch of the property while it was being built. There were still pickup trucks and delivery vans surrounding the hotel. But seeing it on the day of the opening, Sarno felt like he was laying eyes on his casino for the first time.

The fountains were working just as he had imagined they would. Eighteen of them centered the 135-yard driveway from the Strip to the porte cochere, jetting water sixty feet in the air. Real Italian cypress trees lined either side of the drive, enclosing arrivals in a cocoon of forest and water.

As his driver eased the car towards the entrance, Sarno saw a phalanx of uniformed bellmen. Passing the water on one side and the slender cypresses on the other, he left the world where he was just another hustling developer and stepped into a Roman fantasy where he was the emperor.

Nate Jacobson and Jerry Zarowitz might have disagreed, but Sarno knew he really deserved the title: Caesars Palace was his idea, and if it was different from everything else in Las Vegas, he was the reason.

Sarno had fussed over every detail. Even the driveway he was moving down had a special purpose. Most of the Strip hotels were pushed behind large set-backs used as parking lots, practical but unglamorous.

"No one's going to drive three hundred miles and pull into something that looks like a simple parking lot," he reasoned. You could move the lots behind the casino, which meant that customers who parked themselves would have to schlep all the way across the pool to get to the casino, and those who valeted would have to wait longer for their cars.

Or, Sarno figured, you could make the parking lot into something special. In St. Peter's Square, Bernini had figured out a way to make the huge space in front of the Vatican a venue fit for a papal address; the colonnades made it look more dignified and imposing than a mere empty lot. Sarno built his own Bernini-inspired colonnades by shellacking a classical façade over the curving low-rise wings that concealed guest rooms, executive offices, and convention space.

Sarno's fountains centered the colonnades. As he insisted in including in press materials, there were more fountains in front of Caesars than there were in front of Versailles. By implication, the casino was more elegant than the royal French palace, its guests more regal.

The driveway was meant to do more than just guide cars from the Boulevard to the front doors; it was to transport the guest out of time, out of space, away from his workaday life and into a fantasy world—neither wholly real nor entirely imagined—that would let him be the man he had always dreamed he should be, with gratification only a throw of the dice or the flash of a smile away.

"It's perfect," Sarno said to himself.

Sarno's car pulled up to the canopied entrance. A bellman wearing an outfit that looked like a toga crossed with a jumpsuit opened the car door, and Sarno stepped out a new man. His wife and children on Maricopa Way, the debts still hanging over him from the Cabanas, the million delays and annoyances that kept him distracted from the real purpose of life—chasing action—disappeared.

Sarno looked at the marble reproduction of Giovanni Bologna's *Rape of the Sabine Women* that had been authentically handcrafted to his specifications in Florence a few months earlier.

"Is Harry here?" he asked a bellman, knowing that the project manager hadn't left the hotel for days.

"I haven't seen him leave."

Sarno pushed his way through the doors, held open by a guard of toga-wearing attendants, and saw the casino stretching in front of him. Under an oval dome which was supported by twenty columns of real Italian marble, more than two dozen games—craps, roulette, and blackjack—were ready for gamblers, their green felt brushed clean of construction dust. Spiral arms of slot machines—208 of them—reached across the remaining space. On the right, Nero's Nook had a stage for performers and tables and chairs for revelers. To the left, the registration desk was only a few steps away, with a custom-built sixty-six foot couch opposite.

Though construction workers and casino personnel, feverishly preparing for the coming hordes, were making an unholy racket, Sarno felt at peace. This was by design. "Over the years that I have been creating hotels," an expansive Sarno told a reporter in the late 1970s, "I've discovered that the oval is a magic shape conducive to relaxation. Because the casino is shaped in an oval, people tend to relax and play longer." The stately columns that ringed the room and a ninety-foot wide chandelier hanging at its center were the final proof that this room packed with gambling tables was elegant. How could you argue with that?

Sarno headed toward the front desk, walked behind it as the clerks paused from their work to watch one of the bosses go by, and took an elevator one story up to the executive suite.

Wald was in his office, on the phone wrangling with a seafood distributor about the lobsters that were being unloaded, Sarno surmised, in back of the hotel. Before going into his office, Sarno paused to look at a rendering of the hotel lying on a table.

He had designed the hotel to be as convenient as possible for the guests, as inexpensive as possible for the builders, and as ostentatious as possible for those who doubted that he could bring elegance to the Nevada desert.

To the sides of the driveway lay the colonnaded wings. The casino, officially called "Caesar's Forum," was directly in the center. Towards the back on the left side, the Circus Maximus supper club was getting ready to host that famous noble Roman Andy Williams in the "Rome Swings" revue. Past that lay the Noshorium, a Capitoline Hill-meets-Hester Street coffee shop, several small stores, and the tower elevators. Beyond the elevator lobby, guests found the Bacchanal gourmet restaurant, which was just far enough removed from the action to allow guests to savor their food and wine away from the sounds of gambling. The hotel tower rose fourteen stories high, its crescent shape screened in the block pattern Sarno had designed himself. By day it gleamed white and at night it glowed aquamarine thanks to lights carefully placed behind its screen block. Behind it, almost as an afterthought, more rooms in hexagonal two-story wings swept around the Garden of the Gods, the outdoor recreation area that featured a bar, a putting green, and an immense pool in the shape of a Roman shield. Sarno knew it couldn't miss.

If he could get everyone to the opening on time, that was.

"How's the plane coming?" he asked before Wald had hung up the phone. Sarno had arranged a high rollers-only charter flight for the opening. It would take off from New York, make one stop—in Baltimore, where much of the money for the casino had come from, thanks to Nate Jacobson—then fly nonstop until it touched down in Las Vegas.

"In the air," Wald answered. With a nod from Sarno, he got back on the phone, trying to reach another one of the vendors.

Sarno headed back down to the casino to make sure everything was going right. His casino was going to open, and no one could stop it.

Out on the floor, Stuart Mason wasn't so sure. He was exhausted, like everyone else on his crew. They'd been working around the clock for two weeks now, and as the first guests started to arrive, they weren't anywhere near ready to open.

Facing reality, Mason abandoned the system he had been using to get the furniture moved into the rooms—all the beds, all the sofas, all the chairs, all the tables, then all the lamps methodically brought up to each floor—and shifted into triage mode. Workers started bringing up whatever could fit in the elevator, and put it into whatever room looked like it needed it. Standing behind the front desk with a walkie-talkie in his hand, he kept an eye on who was checking in, and which room they were taking. Watching Mr. and Mrs. Archie Smith register for room 603, he got on the walkie-talkie.

"Room 603, what do we need in room 603?"

"Standby." Per his instructions, the clerk was taking his time with the Smiths, giving Mason time to contact his man in the tower.

"Room 603, we're short a sofa and a lamp."

Mason then called down to the guys in the parking lot. "Get a sofa and lamp, standard, up to 603 pronto."

"We're on our way."

The desk clerk finally gave the Smiths their keys. As they started toward the elevator, Mason decided this would be as good a time as any to check in with the guys in the tower. He got into the elevator with the Smiths. It was a tight fit.

"That's a very fine couch you've got there," Mrs. Smith said to the workers standing behind it.

"I'm glad you like it," Mason said and smiled. "It's going into your room."

He was starting to believe that maybe they'd pull this off.

A few hours and several furniture deliveries later, the hotel was as ready as it was going to be. Mason called Flora and told her to bring his tuxedo. As tired as he was, he wouldn't miss this party for anything. He also needed to be ready to fix any last-minute glitches the hotel—and his clients—might throw at him. Flora arrived, and Stuart got undressed to take his shower. When he peeled his socks off, they were sticky with blood. In his frenzy to deliver the hotel he had rubbed several holes in his skin.

Luckily, Flora had brought a fresh pair of black socks.

Meanwhile, Jay was running around the property with surprising grace for a man of his size. One minute, everything looked great. The next, everything looked awful. The lights were too bright—the place didn't look romantic at all, it looked like an operating room. The waitresses' skirts were too long, they looked like schoolmarms; their skirts were too short, the bluenoses on the Gaming Board would close him down. He was in agony. He was alive.

Then he saw an apparition. He had built ancient Rome, but a wizard—the image of Merlin himself—was walking the halls.

"Hey, you," Sarno called out, not sure if this was a man or a ghost.

"Yes?" It was definitely a man, a man wearing a floor-length black robe emblazoned with stars, and a conical wizard's hat.

"What are you doing in my hotel?"

"I'm the earthly representative of the Cult of the Good Father,"

Merlin replied. "I am sensing the vibrations and perturbations of this construction." He gestured obscurely toward the wall.

"And? What do you think?"

"There are very auspicious emanations in this spot!" Merlin said. "This is your hotel?"

"Yes, I'm Jay Sarno, the managing director. It's all my design."

"And a wonderful design it is. With your permission, kind sir, I would like to pronounce a profound benediction upon this magnificent temple." He began to raise his arms.

"Wait, wait!" Sarno said. He was pretty sure this guy was nuts, but who knew what kind of edge this could give him? "I'll take you up to my suite. We're having a little party before the party."

So they sauntered off toward the elevators, Jay Sarno and Merlin. And no one batted an eyelash.

Upstairs, the party was in full swing. Joyce was there, along with a few of the top executives and construction guys, with their wives, tastefully toasting the possibilities of the opening. Jay breezed in with Merlin, not interrupting the flow of conversation. He had to tap a champagne glass to get everyone's attention.

"We all know this is a first-class hotel. Well, we've got a real wizard here who's going to say a few words in favor of the place."

"To the gods and goddesses!" Merlin shouted, raising his arms. "Please look with favor, cherish, and bless the opening of this fine hotel. May its auspicious vibrations lead to a successful opening, and successful venture." He closed his eyes, maybe in prayer. Everyone watched him as he stood silently for five, ten seconds.

"The gods and goddesses have spoken," he declared. "This will be a singularly successful enterprise. Fortune will smile upon you."

With that, Sarno showed him the door, and Merlin walked off, running his hands over the wallpaper and babbling to himself.

Conversation inside the room picked up right where it had stopped.

Downstairs, the real Caesars Palace opening bash got started a little later than promised, but what it lacked in punctuality it made up for in excess. Nearly two thousand invited guests, including well-connected politicians, serious gamblers, and celebrities from Hollywood to Broadway came to pay their respects. Everyone who was anyone—or at least anyone who Sarno could get out to Vegas—was there. So you had Batman, or at least his current television actor Adam West, rubbing shoulders with Jimmy Hoffa and Eva Gabor, with Johnny Carson and Nevada governor Grant Sawyer along for the ride.

The fun started late in the afternoon, with the casino finally taking real bets while celebrants feasted on two tons of filet mignon, the single largest order of Ukrainian caviar ever purchased by a private organization, and more shrimp cocktail than anyone could measure, all washed down with 50,000 glasses of champagne.

Yet something was still missing, even while Merlin was giving his benediction: the real gamblers. But not for long. Groaning under the weight of the biggest assortment of rounders, plungers, and out-and-out suckers ever seen outside a Damon Runyon story (including a wide-eyed twenty-four year old Steve Wynn, even then not entirely out of place among the game's biggest players), Wald's chartered plane finally touched down on the tarmac at McCarran Airfield, solving that problem.

The new arrivals were ready to party.

"It was a riot. You should have seen these guys," Wynn recalled over forty years later. "They were so excited. It was the biggest event in the history of America, this opening of Caesars Palace."

Once the heavy hitters arrived, the bash started in earnest. With plentiful food and flowing champagne, they were willing to forget that they'd had to step over rolls of carpet to get to their rooms. Some of them laughed about it.

"I'm finally in the room," a smiling Wynn said to the man across from him, a bookmaker from Staten Island, "and a guy comes in without knocking and says, 'Excuse me, sir.' And he puts a shower curtain rod in, then he puts up the curtain."

"At least your toilet works," the bookie said. In fact, they weren't alone: some guests checked in to find carpenters and plumbers still hard at work, while others had to wait outside their rooms while crews laid down the carpet. One visiting starlet was surprised when a group of workers "accidentally" barged in on her as she was changing into her bikini.

But the fountains out front worked flawlessly, sending jets of water sixty feet into the August heat. The Roman-style employee uniforms were impeccable. Every single front of-the-house worker wore something inspired by ancient Rome. The first guests marveled at asking a centurion to take their luggage to the room. Only the casino executives wore twentieth century business attire. Being served a drink by a girl in a low-cut tunic was one thing, but not even Sarno would ask his customers to fill out credit applications for men wearing togas.

As the night wore on, invited guests started weaving their way to the dinner theater. The casino was the hotel's centerpiece, but the Circus Maximus was its crown jewel. It was modeled on the Coliseum. Each of its 800 seats had a clear view of the stage; it had been designed so that no support columns obstructed the sight lines. The walls were ringed by a colonnade bedecked with golden shields, standards of the legions of Rome. The predominant shade of blue was intended to suggest a calm evening.

The theater's first evening, however, was anything but calm. Sarno could only see that the area in front of the theater didn't look the way he thought it should. It was too damned bright.

"Mason!" he shouted, snagging Stuart as he headed towards his seat. "Get out here! Do something about these lights!"

Mason excused himself and followed Sarno out to the foyer.

"Get those goddamn lights down lower."

Mason found a ladder and, in his tuxedo, climbed up and unscrewed a few light bulbs.

"That's better," Sarno said as the lighting dimmed. He finally saw just how badly things were going. The lobby was filled with gawkers who prevented the invited guests from getting to their seats. No one could move, it was so crowded. It was pandemonium.

It was after midnight, and the big show hadn't started yet. But the guests didn't mind the delay. The champagne and scotch had been flowing freely since the afternoon. With everything—besides the gambling—on the house, the party-goers were giddy.

At last, everyone found their seats. The audience mingled Hollywood stars, Teamster aristocrats, and gambling maniacs. David Janssen, Maureen O'Hara, Andy Griffith, Paul Anka, Steve

Lawrence, Eydie Gorme, Gregory Peck, Anthony Quinn, John Wayne, and Ed Sullivan, along with a host of producers and power brokers, represented Tinseltown. A fair number of Nevada politicians enjoyed the Palace's hospitality.

Finally, the emcee introduced the principals. Governor Sawyer, who had vigorously defended his state from federal charges of mob corruption, said a few congratulatory words to the owners and welcomed the visitors to Nevada.

But the real star of the night was Jimmy Hoffa, who was hailed like a Caesar. Surrounded by a protective circle of associates, he sat at a ringside table. Sarno had reserved the hotel's finest suite, room 1066 for him. It was directly over the porte cochere, with a commanding view of the fountains and the empty desert that stretched beyond them to the east.

It meant nothing to Hoffa. He refused all drinks, quietly watching the drunken debauch around him. But Sarno, Jacobson, and the rest tripped over themselves to pay him homage.

"We needed a guy like Jimmy," Sarno declared from the stage, when it was his turn to speak. "Only someone with his class, his integrity, could have added a little Greco-Roman class to Vegas."

It should have been a triumph for organized labor. Instead, it felt more like a last hurrah. Unless Hoffa's lawyers could do the impossible, he would be heading to jail soon. Though he could still maintain control of the union by appointing a man he could trust to be president while he was away, Hoffa faced the prospect of officially being divorced from the Teamsters Union for the first time in his adult life. No wonder he wasn't in the mood for fun.

By the time Andy Williams waited in the wings for his cue, the crowd was oblivious to just about anything short of one of the atomic bombs that were still being detonated at the Nevada Test Site, a hundred miles to the north.

Revved up by the majestic surroundings, the aura of celebrity, and hours of free booze, the chatter was slightly less deafening than a jet engine. When the dimmed lights and orchestral cues failed to silence the din, Williams walked to the center of the stage and began performing an *a capella* rendition of the classic "Danny Boy." With that, he had the crowd in the palm of his hand. The rest of the show went off without a hitch.

After the show, the less hardy partiers crawled off to bed—assuming their room had a bed—while most of the revelers thronged the tables in the casino. Joyce went up to the suite and, with a peck on the cheek, wished Jay luck. She knew that this would be a late night. And it all seemed to be going so well.

But then the real trouble started, trouble that made Sarno wish the doors had never opened. It was just as those killjoys on the Gaming Control Board had predicted: the gamblers got lucky. If they all decided to cash out, the $100,000 bankroll couldn't cover the action. Gaming would close them down. Sure, the hotel would stay open, but the casino would stay closed until they could borrow even more money to make up an even bigger bankroll—money that, Jacobson had already convinced Sarno, just wasn't there.

Sarno and Jacobson gritted their teeth, too nervous even to scream at each other. It was an agony, seeing their entire future live or die with each throw of the dice. They had never thought that running a business could be so exhilarating. The only way it could have been better was if they were the ones throwing the dice.

An hour went by with no change.

"What is he doing down there?" Sarno asked Jacobson as they watched Jerry Zarowitz glide around the tables without a care in the world. "Doesn't he know that we're on the hook here?" Sarno fought the urge to go down there and tell Zarowitz to do his damned job.

After another hour, the tide seemed to shift. They began to hear tell of good omens and favorable prodigies: a dice thrower who'd been red hot all night had sevened out three times in a row, with plenty of the "smart" money backing him; the big slot jackpots had raised excitement to a fever pitch, and now the players thronged the machines, which helpfully kept most of their coin; and more than one blackjack player, now down for the evening, decided to call it a night.

To gamblers like them, such a sudden reversal wasn't that surprising. Luck turned, they knew, with little rhyme or reason. That's why you gambled.

But others said that luck had nothing to do with it. According to them, the real money in the casino—the money that Jerry Zarowitz listened to—wasn't willing to beg for scraps at the altar of chance.

"The craps table's caught on fire," a man said when he reached an extension at the Aladdin casino, which had some of the same hidden interests as Caesars. "Send down a fireman."

So a fireman, who'd helped turn the tide on more than one night when the gamblers got too lucky, headed down to Caesars.

Whatever the reason (and Sarno didn't care to know the details), by the early morning it was clear that the house was winning big. The festivities continued for two more days, but after the first night the casino's fate was never in doubt.

All told, the opening bash cost more than $1 million (about $7 million in today's dollars). It was a feast suitable for a coronation— or a debauched emperor's final spree. They didn't quite make it all back at the tables that weekend, but everyone was satisfied. By the end of the weekend, the hotel was already half-filled with repeat bookings for the next two months.

The word was out: Caesars Palace was a winner. And with the results in, few of the revelers failed to congratulate Sarno. He was elated, but there was still something missing.

Long after the well-wishers had left him alone, Sarno didn't feel like going up to his room to sleep. He was starving. He went down to Noshorium, hoping they could whip him up some steak and eggs.

Even when word of the house's remarkable run made it up to room 1066, it didn't lighten the mood. If Jimmy Hoffa enjoyed his stay, he kept it to himself. For him, every minute surrounded by slaves and goddesses was wasted. There was union business waiting, and of course his appeal. He wanted to spend as much time as possible with his wife Jo before he went to jail. She deserved it. Having put in his required appearance, he checked out the next morning.

The room didn't stay empty for long.

At the opening party, Steve Wynn had introduced himself to Jerry Zarowitz, explaining that he had married Sonny Pascal's daughter Elaine. Zarowitz knew Pascal from Miami. After Wynn told him that Nate and Eddie Jacobson had gotten him a room, Zarowitz invited him to sit down and have a drink. During the course of the conversation, Wynn let slip the tale of the shower curtain.

"Where are you?" Zarowitz asked.

"I'm in the back, by the pool."

"One of those dumps? Don't worry, we'll move you tomorrow," he said. The next morning, he received a phone call: a bellman was on his way to move him. That's fine, Wynn thought. One room's as good as another.

As he walked through the door opposite the center elevator on the top floor, he realized that he was now in the best room in the hotel.

"I can't believe it," he said to himself. The view was incredible. The bellman began hanging Wynn's clothes in the oversized closet.

Before he could even look around the room, the phone rang. With his wife pregnant at home, Wynn rushed to the phone.

"Hello, Mr. Hoffa, we have a long distance call for you," said the extremely polite voice on the other end.

"This is not Mr. Hoffa. I'm sorry. Is this his room, 1066?"

"This is not James Hoffa?"

"Operator, I think that Mr. Hoffa's gone. He must have checked out. I'm Mr. Wynn and I just moved in."

"Thank you, Mr., um, Wynn. I'm sorry to disturb you." The operator got off the line without another word.

"I'm in Jimmy Hoffa's room," Wynn realized. Three years earlier he had been impressing professors at the University of Pennsylvania. He was the youngest guest there, by at least a decade.

"Is there anything else, sir?" the bellman asked. Wynn realized that he was being attended to with a degree of respect he had never known before.

"Shit," he thought to himself, "these guys probably think I'm some hood's son. He reached into his pocket for a tip and, with a smile, the bellman shut the door behind him.

A day ago, he had been Mike Wynn's son, a small-time bingo hall operator laboring to pay off his dead father's debts. In Caesars Palace, they gave him the suite of a Teamster Prometheus. And the way they'd looked at him…it was intoxicating.

At that moment, Steve Wynn knew he would be coming back to Las Vegas.

In the end, Caesars Palace was a success in the only way that matters in Las Vegas: the place made money.

Others, less concerned with such commonplace tallies, had a good laugh at the expense of both winners and losers. The *New Yorker's* "Talk of the Town" wrote up the new casino, ecstatic that "what is surely the most preposterous example of this classical revival has manifested itself in the most preposterous setting: a gambling casino-nightclub-restaurant-hotel called Caesars Palace.

"We salute Caesars Palace with awe," the author concluded, "as perhaps the biggest and silliest architectural throwback of all time.

"For years, the big casino-hotels on the Strip—the Sands, the Flamingo, the Thunderbird, the Stardust—have vied with each other in degrees of opulence. Now comes Caesars Palace in an attempt to dominate them all—an enormous, fourteen-story confection of white stone and concrete set down in thirty-four acres of Vegas desert.

"We think of Nero in Hades, shaking his head in wonder and envy. Rome—his Rome, which he rebuilt with broad streets and splendid villas—was never a patch on Vegas."

To Sarno, any press was good press. He had Evie make Photostats of these clippings and pressed them on anyone who walked by his office. At last, people were paying attention.

Jay Sarno had finally built his dream. But he would soon find himself contending with more plots than any emperor could imagine, and though he didn't care for fiddling, he would be throwing the dice like there was no tomorrow while his new empire threatened to collapse around him.

EIGHT

A Palace Coup

Both Jay Sarno and Nate Jacobson thought they were the real boss of Caesars Palace. But neither was. Sure, Sarno had planned the place, and Jacobson haggled with the linen suppliers and kept the books. But they didn't run Caesars Palace.

Jerry Zarowitz did.

Even though he wasn't licensed by the state to run a casino, he had the final word on granting credit to players, raising betting limits, and hiring and firing dealers. Early on, Zarowitz explained to Sarno exactly how much input the "managing director" would have in running the casino.

"See this color carpet?" he asked, pointing to the hotel lobby. "That's where you walk." He pointed down. See *this* color carpet? This is the casino. That's where you don't walk."

Sarno started to say something, but thought better of it.

"If you ever step over that line," Zarowitz finished, "you'll never get back to the other side."

Sarno kept his feet on the hotel carpet.

With Jacobson holding the purse strings, Sarno, despite his business degree and twenty years in real estate development, still had to play second fiddle. Jacobson had gotten the money, which gave *him*, he thought, the last word on everything. Arguments ensued.

The trees, for example. He couldn't get Jay to be sensible about the trees. The managing director had insisted that the driveway be lined with Italian cypresses.

"They're perfect," he had said. "They've got an ideal shape. Since they're tall and thin they play off the columns in the wings. And you don't see anything like them anywhere else in town."

"You don't see anything like them anywhere else in town," Jacobson had responded, "because they can't live in the desert." The trees were already looking worse for wear. "According to the guy at the nursery, there's no way we'll get them to survive in this heat for more than a few months."

"So what? When they die, we'll just put new ones in."

"Do you know how much a fully-grown tree costs? Do you know how much it costs just to truck them in? We can't carry those kinds of costs on a regular basis. Why not just put in some palm trees in? You just need someone to trim them every few months."

"Palm trees?" Sarno was getting mad. "They don't have the character we want here. We don't want people to think they're in the desert. We want them to think they're in Ancient Rome."

As Jacobson fought a rearguard action against his excesses, Sarno found himself squeezed more and more into the role of special events coordinator, preferably throwing together events that didn't cost much but got plenty of press.

Celebrity weddings were absolutely made to order. Casinos could make a bundle in the wedding trade, but you had to land a big celebrity or two to make a name for yourself. Sure, Nevada had been celebrated as a divorce haven since the thirties, but by the time Caesars opened Las Vegas had logged more than eight times as many weddings as divorces. So Jay Sarno went into the wedding business.

He had a long tradition of celebrity weddings in Las Vegas to build on, going all the way back to Clara Bow and Rex Bell's 1931 nuptials. From then on, Las Vegas casinos competed to land Hollywood vow exchanges: Rita Hayworth and Dick Haymes got hitched at the Sands, Joan Crawford tied the knot with Alfred Steele at the Flamingo, and Paul Newman wed Joanne Woodward at the El Rancho Vegas. A few weeks before Caesars opened, Frank Sinatra kicked off his brief marriage to Mia Farrow at the Sands. Landing a big wedding was the *sine qua non* of a casino wedding chapel. The stakes were high: thousands of tourists were wed in Las Vegas each year, and many of them wanted to do as the stars did.

So Sarno was glad that he was able to make Caesars' first wedding a celebrity affair: bandleader Xavier Cugat, soon to perform in Nero's Nook, got married to a Spanish singer and dancer named Maria Rosario Pilar Martinez Molina Baeza. She would soon become world famous under her stage name, Charo. It wasn't exactly Elvis marrying Priscilla (the Aladdin would score that honor in a few months), but it was a start.

On the whole, Sarno didn't want to overemphasize the sanctity of marriage in his hotel. In fact, part of the attraction of the casino, in his eyes, was that it helped loosen—at least for a little while—the bonds of matrimony.

His own bonds were certainly loose. In addition to Joyce and Carol, Sarno chased a procession of "girlfriends" before the casino was even open.

"Hey miss, did you drop this?" he had say to a young woman who caught his eye, handing her a hundred-dollar bill. That usually broke the ice. If it didn't, well, it was only money. But that was small potatoes.

"Here's a couple of thousand dollars," he'd tell a cocktail waitress he had had his eye on but who'd been impervious to his charms. "I'm going out of town and I need you to hold it for me." A few weeks later, when the money had probably been spent, he would say, "Well, you don't have to give it back to me *if…*"

To Sarno, women were at Caesars mostly to please men simply by being beautiful. It was part of his overall sensualist orientation: above all, he wanted to be stimulated by pleasant sensations. Visually, this meant beautiful women in flattering, revealing clothes.

These were the years when Hugh Hefner was transforming a girlie magazine into an empire centering on the "Playboy lifestyle." *Playboy* held itself out as a magazine for men who appreciated women and wanted to live like properly hip swinging bachelors. Rounding out the latest Jayne Mansfield pictorial might be advice on which hi-fi set to purchase or a list of highball recipes. Like Caesars Palace, *Playboy* was about gratifying all the senses: the eyes, primarily, but also the palate and the ears. While Sarno was developing the Cabanas, Hefner opened a series of Playboy clubs that featured waitresses in skimpy bunny outfits and live entertainment up to *Playboy* audiophile standards. But in reality the magazine was essentially voyeuristic: it could instruct and it could depict, but it couldn't provide most of its devotees with any actual life experience. A few might be lucky enough to live in a city with a Playboy Club. Almost none could boast of having set foot in the Playboy Mansion, or knew closer than second-hand the delights of the Grotto. *Playboy* readers were on the outside looking in.

Sarno, on the other hand, created pleasures that any man could experience. He promised his guests endless gratification, starting with the building—dripping fountains set in sensuous curves; green-hued neon softly humming against the desert night, while inside laughter, passion, and action ran riot. It continued with the food—a gourmand's fantasy that never ended, and reached its culmination with the girls—the cocktail waitresses flitting by in skimpy togas, Roman fantasies not entirely out of reach.

Sarno, who loved to eat, made the Bacchanal gourmet restaurant the heart of the experience. He had spared no expense, giving executive chef Nat Hart carte blanche to create dishes that were richer and more sumptuous than anything else in town.

The restaurant was tucked around the side of the casino. To enter, guests passed a bubbling fountain, lit from below in red. Portraits of famous and infamous Romans adorned the walls.

The menu began with a pompous convocation: "Welcome to the most resplendent arena of gustatory delights. Here you shall embark upon an adventure of gourmet dining unparalleled outside my empire." Next came pithy quotations from twelve Caesars about food, in the original Latin with helpful translations. Nero's "Who is able to live without a snack?" might have been closest to Sarno's heart.

Indeed, in his quest for the ultimate Roman experience, Sarno contemplated Neronian cruelty. He had read somewhere that emperors kicked off their lavish feasts with an animal sacrifice, and eagerly sketched out his plans: a pool in the center of the restaurant would be filled with ravenous piranhas, which he heard could strip flesh from bone in seconds. Once all of the dinner guests had arrived, strapping centurions would file past the tables, carrying a live, struggling baby pig. After a brief invocation to the gods (in the vaguest sense, of course; no need to offend any religious sensitivities), they would dump the unfortunate porker into the water, which would erupt with the spectacle of a live animal being eaten to death.

It was inhumane; it was nearly inhuman. Oblivious to the logistics of importing piranhas (not an easy thing in the 1960s) and keeping their water clean, Sarno insisted it could be done. Might not the sight, sound, and smell put diners off their dinner? It didn't matter, he said, because it would be a show they'd never forget. It was only after it became clear that the health department would never sign off on such a stunt, that he dropped the plan.

The Bacchanal ended up being distinctive enough without nightly sacrifices. The food was exquisite, but the real attraction was the harem ambiance, provided by ever-present "wine goddesses." These were the goddesses of the Palo Alto Nero's Nook with the volume turned up. They welcomed customers to the Bacchanal room, brought them wine, peeled grapes for them, and massaged their temples; sex appeal in a classical robe.

Caesars Palace quickly became an icon. In November, when American Express, in conjunction with the Johnson Administration, flew 500 European travel agents and press writers to the States for a coast-to-coast tourism-promoting junket, they included a stop at Caesars. United Artists chose to publicize the 1966 opening of the movie version of *A Funny Thing Happened on the Way to the Forum* with a unique spectacle: a chariot race that began at Caesars Palace and ended at the Fine Arts Theater in Los Angeles, site of the premiere. Jay Sarno had done more than open a new casino in Las Vegas: he had brought Ancient Rome to America.

By its first autumn, Caesars Palace was drawing high rollers away from the former kings of the Strip, the Desert Inn and Sands hotels. Through their extensive connections in the gambling fraternity, Jerry Zarowitz and Elliot Paul Price, a Boston-area bookmaker later convicted in a national race-fixing case, made it known that Caesars was *the* place to gamble. Price, officially a casino host, was an omnibus ambassador to the gambling crowd and had a loosely-defined position in the casino.

"Every wise guy in the world, everybody was there," Steve Wynn remembered. "All the point holders [shareholders] were players. Cal and Irv Covens from Baltimore, all of Nate Jacobson's gambling buddies that were Flamingo customers and Sands customers, boom, right into Caesars.

"Good night, Sands. Good morning, Caesars. Suddenly you've got the Fontainebleau in Las Vegas. All the glamour and bullshit."

Sarno immediately began planning to expand: an elliptical conference hall, along with an arcade of restaurants to rival the Bacchanal. There seemed to be nowhere to go but up, and even those who hated him admitted that Jay Sarno might be the future of Las Vegas.

By all rights Sarno should be remembered as the man who transformed Las Vegas in 1966. But a few months after Caesars Palace opened a man more fantastic and flawed than him descended on the Strip. Through no design of his own, he completely stole Sarno's thunder.

When he arrived in Las Vegas on Thanksgiving weekend of 1966, Howard Hughes had been for decades one of the most famous men in the world. Orphaned as a young man, his inheritance, based on the profits of the Hughes Tool Company's oil drill patent, enabled him to try his hand at aviation, where he set several records, and film-making. His investments and achievements in both industries made him wealthy and famous.

In 1966, though, he was at a crossroads. He had sold his interest in the RKO movie studio and was forced, after a lawsuit, to sell his stake in TWA. Hughes was looking for a new place to live: tired of Los Angeles, he tried the Bahamas, then Boston, before deciding to give Las Vegas a chance.

He had been in Las Vegas numerous times over the previous three decades. He frequently visited the town's casinos, gambling moderately, and even rented a house close to the Strip in 1953. Though he lived there for only a few months, he ordered the house sealed upon his departure; it remained closed until 1976, and he never returned to it. At Hughes' direction, RKO had made a poorly-received Jane Russell vehicle in 1952, *The Las Vegas Story*. A frequent guest of the Flamingo in the 1950s, Hughes didn't share Sarno's assessment of the casino: as long as he had privacy, he thought it was just fine.

When Hughes returned to Las Vegas that Thanksgiving, the city had begun to change. Its hotels were taller and its casinos more crowded than they had been in the 1950s. It was brighter: the city's golden age of neon was in full flower, with massive sparkling signs at the Dunes, Flamingo, and Stardust. This was the city where Howard Hughes went to get away from it all.

Moving into the Desert Inn temporarily, Hughes took a liking to the place. He decided to buy it. In March 1967, the sale of the Desert Inn was official: for $13.2 million dollars, Howard Hughes had become Nevada's newest casino owner. But he didn't stop there, and embarked on a casino buying spree. By the time the dust had settled, he had bought the Sands, the Frontier, the Silver Slipper, the Castaways, Harolds Club in Reno, a television station, an airline, and thousands of acres of real estate, all of it from the air-conditioned comfort of his penthouse bedroom.

Jay Sarno wanted to make himself an emperor on borrowed money and big ideas; Howard Hughes simply crowned himself the king of Nevada, refusing to meet his public, or even to appear before the Gaming Control Board, as all other owners did.

While Hughes had been steadily losing touch with reality in the early 1960s Las Vegas had been changing: it was becoming a convention town, and casinos like the Stardust and Hacienda were reaching out to the mass market. Morris Lansburgh even ran package tours to the Flamingo. But to Hughes Las Vegas remained the small romantic getaway that he remembered from the 1940s. "I like to think of Las Vegas," he wrote in a memo to his chief executive, Robert Maheu, "in terms of a well dressed man in a dinner jacket, and a beautifully jeweled and furred female getting out of a an expensive car. I think that is what the public expects here—to rub shoulders with VIPs and Stars, etc.—possibly dressed in sport clothes, but if so, at least good sport clothes."

Jay Sarno's aggressive gambling, dime-store glamour, and fantastic architecture were unthinkable in Howard Hughes' Las Vegas.

"I don't think we should permit this place to degenerate into a freak, or amusement-park category, like Coney Island," he wrote to Maheu.

If he knew what Jay Sarno had up his sleeve, he would have left town without a glance back.

For the first time in his life, Sarno knew real freedom. Thanks to his standing at Caesars, he was treated like royalty everywhere he went. From the Strip to downtown, casino managers fawned over "Mister S," eager to have him play at their casino. Between them, Sarno and Nate Jacobson were losing thousands of dollars a night—and loving it.

Sarno had wrestled with his gambling problem since his adolescence; now, he abandoned himself to it completely. He could afford to. One night, he might drop $25,000 at the Frontier. No problem: a Frontier employee would stop by the cage at Caesars Palace the next day, present Sarno's marker, and be paid in cash. The following night, it might be $50,000 at the Horseshoe. Before the state forced stricter cash controls, it was more common than not for owners to treat their casino's cage as a personal piggy bank. The great thing was, no matter how often you broke it open, it kept refilling itself.

This was the worst possible position for a man with Sarno's gambling problem. At the same time the late nights and his constant womanizing put an even greater strain on his marriage. He didn't listen to Joyce anymore; he did what he wanted. For the time being, she tolerated it.

But that freedom came at a price. Like a playboy emperor held hostage by his own Praetorian guard, Sarno was in the thrall of men who'd come up harder—and even more cunningly—than he had.

"Zarowitz is taking over the place." he told Stanley Mallin. "What do we do?" Remembering Zarowitz's warning about the casino carpet, Sarno for once didn't want to make the first move. Mallin flew out to Las Vegas to check on his investment, and he didn't like what he found.

"Jay, the casino's full of mobsters—all those guys with big cigars. Why did you hire them?"

"I didn't. Zarowitz did."

Sarno suspected that he wasn't the only one with carte blanche at the cage. Caesars Palace had already become the latest Las Vegas casino to skim profits back to hidden interests, with well-placed managers diverting a flow of money to their friends back east.

When allegations about skimming became more serious and appeared in the papers, Sarno and Mallin hired a lawyer. Milton "Mickey" Rudin, who in his long career represented clients ranging from Marilyn Monroe to the Jackson Five, urged them to sell their interests in Caesars Palace before they were indicted on charges of abetting the ongoing skim.

They quietly began looking for a buyer, but Zarowitz didn't want to see him go. It wasn't sentiment on the former bookmaker's part, just a pragmatic assessment: with Sarno "in charge," he was free to take as much as he could from the casino's take provided he sent plenty back east. When the deck is hot, why reshuffle it?

"You sell this place," he told Sarno and Mallin, "you're both dead. Your families are dead. Don't even think about selling out. You're not going to fuck this up."

Mallin was able to convince Sarno that it was all bluster. They kept looking for a buyer. With a possible federal skimming investigation hanging over their heads, it was a delicate matter. Earlier in the decade, another Rudin client, Frank Sinatra, had faced a similar quandary and surrendered his gaming license rather than fight charges that he had abetted improper conduct at the Cal-Neva. Rudin thought that a similar strategy would work for Sarno and Mallin though they were in far different circumstances. Sinatra was a public figure for whom the bad publicity of a hearing would have been calamitous. Sarno and Mallin were, on the other hand, relatively anonymous businessmen whose chief business was Caesars Palace.

If he had dug his heels in, Sarno could have gotten rid of Zarowitz easily enough, provided that his talk of violence was just talk. They just had to put a call into the Gaming Control Board and ask why Zarowitz hadn't applied for a license. Because of his past convictions and continued associations, Zarowitz would never have gotten licensed by the state and would have been forced out of the casino. But for once Sarno didn't want to gamble. Leaving Rome in the possession of barbarians was starting to sound like a good idea.

Sarno couldn't have been so naïve as to have been unaware of his partners' notoriety. The FBI's informants were telling them that the "hoodlum element" secretly controlled the casino. Even the general public knew that something funny was going on at the casino. On August 1, days before the opening, the *Chicago Sun-Times* had alleged that a trio of mob bosses owned, between them, one-third of Caesars. These weren't cut-rate hoods, either; they were the notorious Sam "Momo" Giancana of Chicago, New England's Ray Patriarca, and Jerry Catena of New Jersey. In addition to these luminaries, several lower-level gangsters supposedly had hidden interests in the yet-to-open casino.

This was just the latest mob incursion, the newspaper charged. A range of mobsters from Meyer Lansky in Florida to the Eboli brothers of New York had long been siphoning profits from Las Vegas casinos. In 1963, their combined take was estimated at close to $6 million.

Yet responsible Nevadans insisted nothing was wrong. In response to the *Sun-Times* article, Governor Sawyer announced an investigation into the charges, while Gaming Control Board chairman Ed Olsen insisted that the state had no evidence to confirm the allegations. Olsen flew to Washington, DC, to confer with Attorney General Nicholas Katzenbach, but nothing that came of the talks was publicly announced.

Federal interest in Las Vegas was a carry-over from Camelot. Since 1961, the IRS and the FBI had been listening to, via clandestine wiretaps, several Las Vegas casino owners and executives. On the strength of the information they had gathered, then-Attorney General Robert F. Kennedy had even proposed that a federal strike force simultaneously raid most of the Strip's major casinos. Only Sawyer's last-minute intercession kept the federal marshals on ice.

Furthermore, wiretapping was illegal under Nevada law, so none of the material collected by the FBI was admissible in court. At the end of the day, the G-men knew something was rotten in the state of Nevada, but they couldn't give prosecutors the evidence they needed to prove it in front of a jury. In 1966, the organized crime section of the Justice Department still maintained an active interest in Las Vegas casinos, and several prosecutors were licking their chops at the possibility of building a federal tax evasion and conspiracy case against casino owners without the benefit of wiretaps.

So Sawyer had good reason to be leery of Caesars, particularly after the revelations from Chicago, though any doubts he privately held did not keep him from congratulating the owners, present and absent, at the riotous opening celebration in the Circus Maximus.

Nate Jacobson, incensed at the slur against his business, demanded that the *Sun-Times* print a retraction. They didn't. Somehow, in the excitement of the opening, he never got around to filing libel charges against the paper, which might have led to a court trial in which he would have to prove beyond a shadow of a doubt that there were no hidden mob investors in the casino.

Less than two weeks after Caesars Palace opened, the Gaming Control Board summoned Jacobson, Sarno, Price, and Zarowitz to a closed-door meeting to discuss the possibility that money was being skimmed and diverted to the underworld. The details of this meeting were never made available to the public.

When questioned by reporters, Jacobson strenuously denied any "hoodlum link," but this did little to halt the allegations. Asked if he was satisfied that Caesars Palace was free of gangsters, Gaming Commission chairman Milton Keefer replied that the body hadn't reached a conclusion either way. Later, the Commission quietly announced that they could find no evidence that organized crime interests were skimming money from Caesars Palace. This hardly had the ring of vindication.

Investigators thought they'd found conclusive proof of a Caesars/mob tie in September 1966, when Chicago police raided a sports betting center on the north side of the Windy City. In addition to $11,000 in cash and numerous sports betting slips, police recovered the phone book of the occupant, Norman Fox. In it, they found phone numbers for several well-known gamblers, including Frank "Lefty" Rosenthal, then of Miami but soon to move to Las Vegas, and Elliot Price. Fox's cause wasn't helped by the two telephones that kept on ringing; police detectives spoke to more than thirty bookmakers calling in their totals for the day. But as far as Las Vegas went, the raid was a dead end. Fox refused to talk, and no direct connection to Caesars Palace was ever proven. Once again, however, the public read about a link between "hoodlums" and Caesars Palace.

It was to get worse. Late in 1966, reports of a "Little Apalachin" meeting in Palm Springs, California, held in October 1965, began to circulate, and Caesars was once again part of the story. The name was a reference to the November 1957 meeting of alleged organized crime associates at Joseph "the Barber" Barbara's Apalachin, New York, home, which was disrupted by a local police roadblock. Dozens of reputed mobsters were arrested as they attempted to flee the scene. Though none ever revealed the true reason for the meeting, the public accepted it as proof of a national criminal conspiracy.

The Palm Springs confab was much smaller, though it led to a sensational trial, with allegations of big-time sports betting, fearsome mobsters, and suicidal showgirls.

Vincent "Jimmy Blue Eyes" Alo and Anthony "Fat Tony" Salerno apparently spent the 1965 Dodgers/Twins World Series at the Palm Springs home of two Las Vegas showgirls, Carolyn Kikimura and Natalie Loughran. Elliot Price and Jerry Zarowitz joined them, as did Miami Beach bookmaker Ruby Lazarus. Nearly a year later, a federal grand jury convened to investigate the meeting, word of which had leaked out. One of the showgirls attempted to commit suicide by diving out of a moving car and into Wilshire Boulevard traffic rather than testify. Two psychiatrists examined her and testified that she was stable enough to withstand the rigors of testimony, though at one point she ran crying from the courtroom.

Prosecutors were trying to establish that Lazarus had made several calls to a Terre Haute, Indiana, restaurant that handled more than $3 million in bets on the World Series, and that Zarowitz had called Las Vegas with odds information. Lazarus served seven months in jail for contempt for refusing to speak to the grand jury, and was ultimately convicted of lying to the panel about whether he used the phones in the Palm Springs house to place bets with several bookmakers.

This was small-scale villainy, though. Thanks to Lazarus stonewalling the grand jury, prosecutors could fashion no more links in a chain to tie Palms Springs, Miami, and Las Vegas to a national criminal conspiracy.

Jerry Zarowitz managed to wriggle out of an indictment in the case, and he continued to reign at Caesars Palace. But Jay Sarno was now feeling the pressure. Caught between Zarowitz on one hand and the Justice Department on the other, no one could blame him for trying to escape the Palace he had built.

Most Las Vegas business leaders saw in Howard Hughes' arrival and subsequent casino-buying spree a new hope for their city. Nevada governor Paul Laxalt, who succeeded Sawyer in early 1967, declared that Hughes had "put the Good Housekeeping stamp of approval" on the state. Through his purchases, the billionaire bestowed virtue by association on the rest of the casino industry. It was said that he brought "college-trained, technically oriented men who based their decisions on business-school criteria" into the gambling business, putting the bookmakers and bootleggers out to pasture. At last, Nevadans had found someone who could wash away the taint of organized crime.

But not everyone was happy with the new order. Those who'd prospered under the old regime began chafing under various new restrictions almost immediately. Partly, this was inevitable: as casinos got bigger, they became less personal. Decision-making devolved to committees, and formal regulations supplanted the autonomy of floor managers. About three months after Hughes had bought the Sands, the clash between old and new exploded into violence, and tilted the balance of power on the Strip even further toward Caesars Palace.

Frank Sinatra had not been having a good day. He had lost $50,000 playing on credit at the dice tables, drinking heavily all the while. He wasn't a happy drunk. When the casino manager refused to extend him any more credit, he threw a tantrum. Within an hour, he had driven a baggage cart through a plate glass window, trashed his hotel room, and pulled out all the telephone jacks in the casino's switchboard room. Somehow the executives on duty coaxed him into their twenty-four hour coffee shop, the Garden Room, where they sequestered him while they sent for reinforcements. Sinatra stewed there with his longtime Sancho Panza Jilly Rizzo standing silently nearby.

The managers called Sands majordomo Carl Cohen, one of the best-respected casino operators in Nevada history. "Carl was the classiest guy in Las Vegas," Steve Wynn remembered. "Everybody loved Carl Cohen." Casino maven Jack Binion said that Cohen was the only casino boss who could handle the nuts and bolts of game operations, including the tough business of security, as well as the finesse work of guest relations. With Sinatra in a blind rage, the suits knew that only Cohen could handle him. They woke him up and, since he didn't want to disturb his wife by dressing in his bedroom, he arrived at the coffee shop with his pajamas poking out of his pants.

"You give me credit or else, goddamn it," Sinatra screamed. "I built this joint, goddamn it. I used to own it. I don't give a shit about Howard fucking Hughes."

"Frank, calm down," Cohen replied. "Let's sit down."

"Fuck this place," Sinatra replied once he had been settled into a seat across from Cohen. "What the hell? I always got a marker. I built this joint. The guy tells me I can't have a marker. Goddamn it, what am I, a bum? I can't get money?"

"Frank, Frank, he gave you fifty grand," Cohen said. "You've got to pay it. If they see that you don't pay the marker, they're not allowing you more. They've got instructions. You have to sign a check."

"Fuck that," Sinatra retorted. "I ain't signing it."

"Everybody's got to sign a marker here," Cohen explained. "It's the new rules, new owners. They got Haskin and Sells, the accountants, checking the books."

"I don't give a fuck about Haskin and Sells."

"Anyway, Frank, I can't do it. Don't you understand, we don't own this joint anymore. The guy from Texas…."

"Fuck the guy from Texas." He became more irate at the mere mention of Hughes. They had been rivals for Ava Gardner's affections years before, and their mutual dislike had soured into hatred. Before Hughes's arrival, Sinatra had been the man people had thought of when they heard the word "Vegas." Now Hughes had bought the whole town and Sinatra couldn't even get credit.

"I'm telling you I want the money. I'm telling you first thing—"

"I'm not going to give you the money," Cohen cut him off. "I can't. And don't go screaming at me. I can't do it." Sinatra's eyes widened at this final refusal.

"Listen, no fucking Jew bastard that I made is telling me what I can do," he screamed, his face purple with rage, as he pushed the table over, spilling a cup of hot coffee on Cohen.

The 275-pound boss jumped to his feet and punched the singer in the mouth. Sinatra crumpled to the floor, two of his teeth shattered, blood streaming down his chin.

Striking Frank Sinatra was tantamount to regicide in Las Vegas. Cohen later said that he hadn't consciously decided to deck the star; the shock of the scalding coffee triggered an instinctive punch. But intent did not matter: the Chairman of the Board was on the floor.

"Jilly, get him, get him," he demanded. Rizzo had handled many a tough guy at Sinatra's request before.

"Not him, Frank, not him," came the reply. Cohen's reputation was such that even Frank Sinatra's best friend couldn't imagine laying a finger on him.

Sinatra was too infuriated to speak. Cohen, embarrassed that he had lost his cool, didn't say a word either. Rizzo helped his friend off the floor and, holding a handkerchief to his mouth, guided him out of the room. The punch hadn't improved Sinatra's disposition. Those who were there say they could see the smoke coming out of his ears, his rage all the greater for his impotence.

"I built this hotel from a sand pile, and before I'm through that's what it will be again," Sinatra vowed when he regained his composure.

By the following year, he'd be taking the stage at the Circus Maximus. Thousands of slick players, wise guys, and wannabes who orbited his star moved down the street with him. The Sands never recovered; the high rollers were few and far between in the years after Frank, and it ended up hosting bus junkets before being imploded in 1996 to make way for the Venetian, an Italian-themed convention resort, shopping mall, and casino. That same year, Caesars Palace announced yet another expansion. Frank Sinatra no doubt smiled.

But Jay Sarno wouldn't long enjoy the glory. He had already decided to leave the casino he'd built.

But the question was, where would he go? A more prudent man would have moved into a lower-profile line of work. Sarno could have easily accepted a loan from Jimmy Hoffa's pension fund and set up a cab company, a laundry business, or a restaurant supply outlet. But he was hooked on the action of the casino and the status that came with being a hotel man. Having tasted paradise at Caesars Palace, he couldn't give it up.

No, Sarno had to build another casino. In more ways than one, he would be jumping out of the frying pan and into the fire.

NINE

You Want It All or You Don't Want Nothing

When Jimmy Hoffa entered Lewisburg Federal Prison in March 1967, he announced that "Allen Dorfman speaks for me," confirming the dapper Dorfman's role as his surrogate.

Dorfman was a complex man who ran with a rough crowd. He had met Hoffa in 1949 and had built an insurance business with the union leader's help. Steven Brill, in his 1978 study *The Teamsters*, depicted Dorfman as a bullying, foul-mouthed hoodlum in a suit paid for by hard-working truckdrivers and dockworkers. But his friends saw a handsome, charming guy with a winning smile. He certainly had qualities that endeared him to Sarno: he was a gambler, loved golf, and enjoyed the company of beautiful women.

At this point, Sarno needed all the friends he could get. Leaving Caesars was proving tougher than he thought. By November 1967, he had a loan commitment from Dorfman and a piece of land about a mile north of Caesars Palace. Zarowitz glared at him every time they crossed paths; it would be good to get as far away from him as possible.

Sarno had been kicking around plans for a "Roman Circus" adjacent to Caesars Palace before things soured there. Las Vegas had no attractions for families, he had noticed; a casino owner who offered something for the kids might clean up. Now he decided to build it as a free-standing attraction. He named it "Circus-Circus," though the hyphen soon disappeared.

"It's the ultimate circus," is how he explained the unusual name.

But he found things more than twice as hard as they'd been a few years earlier. Once a payoff here and a promise there would have gotten him a permit to build the Taj Mahal, but already this wasn't the Las Vegas that he had built Caesars in. At the urging of Governor Paul Laxalt and helped by the behind-the-scenes lobbying of banker Parry Thomas, the legislature passed the first of the laws that would open the casino business to publicly-traded corporations, continuing the legitimization that Hughes had begun when he bought out Moe Dalitz and his former bootlegger partners from the Desert Inn.

Barely a year after his triumph at Caesars Palace Sarno could feel the dice getting cold; where things once came easily, they were now bought only with toil, if it all. Only two years earlier, a commitment from the Teamsters pension fund was all the letter of introduction Sarno would have needed. Now he waited in line like everyone else.

In December, he applied for permission from the Clark County Commission for a 34,000 square-foot casino with an attached lounge and restaurant. This was a major break with precedent.

Since the El Rancho Vegas opened in 1941, hotels had been essential parts of Strip casinos. They let casinos keep players close enough to the tables to assure that, over the weekend, most of them would leave their money in the house's drop boxes. Even if a gambler got lucky over the course of a few hours, the lure of the tables would prove too much for him and he would give the house ample opportunity to win its money back. Over time, the house had to win. Without a hotel, though, players had no reason to stick around. They'd take the money they'd won from you and gamble it back at whatever casino kept their luggage—playing with house money at the wrong house. Nobody planned to build a casino without a hotel unless they were having serious money problems.

So the commissioners wanted to see Sarno's money before signing the permits.

They were right to be leery. In theory, the casino business was a can't-lose proposition, but the real world was messier, and because of poor management, excessive skimming, or just plain bad luck, several Las Vegas casinos had gone belly-up. Earlier that year, the Gaming Control Board had ordered the undercapitalized Bonanza casino closed. The county commission didn't want history to repeat itself. Padlocking a casino and throwing Las Vegans out of work never played well at election time.

"Where's the money coming from?" they demanded to know. Sarno produced loan covenants and lease agreements, and his lawyer argued that everything was in order. Yet Sarno's word was not enough; the committee demanded that he sign a resolution of intent detailing his financial arrangements. Satisfied that, should things fall apart, Sarno would be left holding the bag, on December 23 the commission gave its approval. He could start building.

As Circus Circus moved forward, Sarno was being pulled into a circus of another kind at Caesars Palace. Locked out of the casino by Jerry Zarowitz, blocked from most of the major business decisions by Nate Jacobson, he had busied himself with "promotion," a deliberately nebulous area that took in everything from interviewing prospective new cocktail waitresses to dickering with talent agents.

For a man at the mercy of his own enthusiasms, Sarno was supremely intolerant of cranks. Since he had presided over Merlin's impromptu benediction at Caesars' opening, he had learned to consider the stack of letters and messages from would-be promoters on his desk an annoyance. It was usually the same story: someone with no detectable talent and no track record wanted to use his palace as their catapult to stardom.

That's why he was at first indifferent to a series of messages from a motorcycle rider who wanted to use his parking lot for an exhibition.

He didn't realize it at the time, but Sarno was up against a virtuoso gambler and bullshit artist. Robert Craig Knievel, born in 1938 in Butte, Montana, had by 1967 transformed himself into Evel Knievel, a red, white, and blue leather jumpsuit-wearing daredevil motorcyclist. Knievel wanted to be known as the greatest risk-taker of all time. But fate hadn't smiled on him yet, something he hoped a jump at Caesars Palace would change.

Until the summer of that year, his biggest stunt had been jumping sixteen cars—a difficult task, to be sure, but hardly the stuff of legend.

Still, he was building a reputation, and in December 1967—while Sarno was pleading his case before the county commission, and touching everyone he could for money for Circus Circus—Knievel set a world indoor-jumping record at the Long Beach Sports Arena.

Jumping in an arena, though, was just a stepping-stone to greater glory. Knievel had already announced that on Labor Day 1968 he would jump over the Grand Canyon in a jet-propelled motorcycle. Before he could finance such a stunt, which would make him the undisputed king of the daredevils, he would need money. So he came to Las Vegas.

Casinos, he knew from firsthand experience, had deep pockets (as a gambler, he was Sarno's equal) and did just about anything to promote themselves. While in town to see fellow Montanan Roger Rouse fail in his bid to unseat WBA Light Heavyweight champion Dick Tiger on November 17, 1967, Knievel took a fresh look at the fountains in front of Caesars Palace. Though today they pale in comparison to the Mirage's volcano that sits next-door and the Bellagio fountains across Flamingo Road, at the time they were *the* signature attraction on the Strip. Promoted as the world's largest privately-owned fountains, they were a nearly impossible jump; there just wasn't enough room in the parking lot to accelerate to a speed that could get a cyclist over them. Nearly impossible, though, just meant that it could, with luck, be done. And the setting—in front of a modern-day Roman temple advertising Theodore Bikel in *The Fiddler on the Roof*—would make the rider famous. It would get scads of publicity, which would help him line up more jumps so he could start bankrolling the Grand Canyon shot. The 29 year-old was full of confidence and not ready to take no for an answer.

Knievel was a man of contradictions, a self-described "conservative wildman" who had graduated to motorcycle heroics from safe-cracking and con-artistry yet implored children to live the clean life. He didn't smoke or drink coffee, but had no problem in drinking men twice his size under the table. Though he risked his life on his motorcycle (he had already survived four nearly fatal crashes), he buckled his seatbelt and drove safely under the speed limit on the highway ("I don't want to give anyone a chance to kill me before I kill myself," he explained to a reporter). "I don't smoke dope," he assured audiences in his pre-jump talks. "I get my highs on terror and victory."

Gambling brought another high. He made his first public motorcycle jump in Butte to settle a barroom bet. For Knievel the athletic and technical aspects of jumping were secondary to the gambling aspect. Splitting time between Butte and Hollywood, he spent plenty of time in Las Vegas, at the blackjack and craps tables.

After getting an initial brush off, Knievel appealed directly to Sarno. He had seen the hotel man at the Rouse-Tiger fight, in his element in the front row. Wearing an impeccable suit and tie, he threw his arms up when Tiger TKOed Rouse in the 11th round of a hard-fought match; he had placed a winning bet. Suit or no suit, this was, Knievel thought, a kindred spirit.

"My name is Robert Knievel," he said when he finally got through to Sarno, "and I'd like to talk to you about putting on a motorcycle exhibition. I'm the greatest stunt jumper in the world." This was debatable. "I've been on the Joey Bishop show." This was true. "The way I see it, if we work together, we can put something together on New Year's, a great way to get your fine casino some publicity."

"I don't have time for this bullshit," Sarno said, and hung up. Sarno instructed Evelyn not to put the nut's calls through.

But he didn't say anything about H. Carl Forbes, the president of Evel Knievel Enterprises, and the next day Sarno gave Forbes a phone audience. He sounded honest, maybe a little square, as he explained, in broad generalities, what Knievel would do.

Sarno remained unmoved.

"I don't have time for this. I'm not running a state fair. We don't do stunts here."

When Mike Rosenstein, vice-president of Knievel Enterprises (who happened to share a name with Sarno's Atlanta Cabana manager), called him a few days later, Sarno was just as curt, but his ears pricked up at part of Rosenstein's pitch.

"We can get you national television exposure. We'll have representatives of every major news organization here to cover the jump. You can't lose."

"Yes we can. What if your guy can't make the jump? This is a waste of time."

Then Carl Goldberg called, an older man with a trace of a Russo-Yiddish accent that reminded Sarno of his father. When the *goniff* got down to brass tacks and asked for $10,000 for the right to clog up his parking lot for a week and maybe wreck his fountains, Sarno hung up.

He threw a passel of press clippings that Rosenstein had mailed him in the trash, and told Evelyn that she wasn't to let anyone from Evel Knievel Enterprises through.

But he hadn't said anything about the media, and Evelyn knew that as far as her boss was concerned any publicity was good publicity. Calls trickled in. Was it true that Evel Knievel was going to jump over the fountains? Writers from *Sports Illustrated* and the *New York Times* wanted to know if the stunt was really going to happen. A movie production company was anxious to secure the rights to film the event. ABC was nearly certainly going to broadcast it.

"It's the damnedest thing," Sarno confided in Harry Wald. "Everyone wants to know if this guy's going to do this."

"It might be worth talking about," Wald conceded.

"If we've got this many people calling the hotel before we even announce the jump," Sarno said, "there's no way it doesn't make front-page news across the country."

He had Evelyn put a call in to Carl Forbes, who received him politely. Mr. Knievel, he said, would be in Las Vegas next week, negotiating with another hotel; it would be best to finalize the arrangements before then.

They agreed to a contract for three jumps: one on Sunday, January 1, a second on Wednesday January 4, and a final one that Saturday. Knievel was to get $4,500 plus $500 for expenses. Sarno thought he had gotten the better of the deal. With so much advance interest, he could see the crowds flocking to Caesars to see the cyclist make the jumps.

New Year's 1968 was sunny, with temperatures peaking in the mid-forties; just about as unremarkable a Vegas winter day as possible. Yet there was something special in the air—the possibilities of new beginnings cutting through the previous night's hangover, perhaps, or just the chance to see a man tempt death. By noon, a crowd had begun to gather outside of Caesars Palace.

Despite Knievel's predictions, the media remained mostly indifferent. *Las Vegas Sun* gossip columnist Joe Delaney had given it a one-line mention in his column published that morning, and ABC Sports demurred on sending a crew—though they agreed that, if Knievel filmed it himself, they'd consider airing it. So Knievel contracted with his friend, actor and director John Derek, to film the jump as a work for hire.

The night before the jump, he had lost a big piece of his $4,500 at Caesars, playing alongside Jay Sarno. After they'd both been cleaned out, he confessed the truth to Sarno: there was no H. Carl Forbes, Mike Rosenstein, or Carl Goldberg. Each of them was a figment of Knievel's imagination, given a distinctive vocal timbre and diction by the former conman. Nor had there been a national media frenzy about the jump; again, it had been Knievel seeding the pot.

"I'll be damned," was all Sarno could say. He wasn't angry; he was in awe.

He had made one of his few real friends.

Around 2 o'clock, Knievel left his room, already visualizing the landing ramp. Dressed in his star-spangled leathers, he walked through the casino, one of the few places besides a jump ramp where he didn't look completely out of place. He dropped a bet on red at a roulette table. Black came up. Undeterred, he ordered a shot of Wild Turkey and downed it quickly. This was one of his pre-jump rituals, a way for him to calm his nerves.

At the casino's entrance, he rendezvoused with Sarno, a few other Palace functionaries, and a pair of goddesses that Jay had seen fit to lend him: if anyone was going to risk his life and get Caesars in the news, he had do it in style. With two of the Palace's beauties flanking them they walked outside.

"Well, good luck, Robert," Sarno said, and shook Knievel's hand. Sarno had brought his two sons, Jay and Freddie, to meet the daredevil and see the jump. The three headed to the top of the porte cochere, a prime vantage point for the stunt.

Sarno was amazed by the size of the crowd. By now, more than ten thousand people had gathered, eager to see Knievel make—or miss—the jump. They filled the parking lot that surrounded the fountains, keeping a respectful distance from the takeoff and landing ramps that Knievel and his mechanic, Art Parker, had set up, stood on cars in the Dunes parking lot across Flamingo Road, and lined the low roof of the Flamingo across the Strip.

There was a thrill as Knievel stepped into view, squinting in the sun.

"You're about to see history made," he lectured his audience, though most of them couldn't hear him as he explained the physics behind the jump. They didn't come to see a man talk; they came to see him fly.

The crowd quieted as Knievel mounted his 450-pound, 650cc Triumph motorcycle with "Color Me Lucky" painted across its gas tank. He tooled around the takeoff area, popping a few wheelies and assessing the conditions. The wind was a little stronger than he had planned for. He wasn't sure if he would have enough power to get across the fountains. It didn't feel right. There was no way he should try this jump.

"Nothing gets done if you wait till you feel right," Knievel said to those who could hear him over the engine's roar. It could have been Sarno talking.

Knievel made a practice sortie up the jump ramp. He perched at the top, saw the landing ramp farther away than he thought it should be, and turned around.

Back at the bottom of his approach, the cyclist took one last look at the thousands of onlookers, then accelerated towards the fountains.

Knievel and his cycle raced down the approach and up the ramp, hitting a flawless takeoff. In about a second, he broke through the parabola of the fountains. A man was flying through Jay Sarno's fountains at nearly one hundred miles per hour. With his sons at his side, Sarno felt the dice in the air with his entire bankroll on the line. It was thrilling. It was sick.

Then rider and cycle landed with a thump as the back wheel thwacked the ramp's steel extension, which bounced under the impact and forced the front wheel down hard. Knievel flew forward off his bike, losing his grip on the handlebars. Sarno heard more than saw the crash from the top of the porte cochere. Instinctively tucking his head, Knievel skimmed his outstretched hands over the bottom of the ramp. His body, now moving with only the momentum of the impact, flipped over, heels over head, and Knievel's upper back and neck absorbed most of the landing on bare asphalt. Had he not tucked his head, he probably would have snapped his neck.

Knievel continued to bounce and roll like a ragdoll across the parking lot, slamming his pelvis and crunching bones from his wrists to his ankles. His bike skidded alongside him until both crashed into bales of hay that had been placed at the edge of the parking lot.

For a split second, everyone stood still. As security struggled to hold the surging crowd back, a small clutch of people—including Knievel's wife, Linda—raced to the body that lay next to the smoking cycle.

Incredibly, Knievel was conscious.

"I'm sorry. I didn't make it, did I?" he asked Linda as Dr. Joseph Fink, Caesars' resident physician, struggled to assess his injuries. Knievel was alert when he was loaded into an ambulance and taken to the Southern Nevada Memorial Hospital.

Doctor Armand J. Scully fully examined Knievel in the intensive care ward and revealed to the public that he would be in the hospital for four to six months. His patient was very lucky to be alive, and if he survived he would likely be a cripple.

The next day, Knievel had surgery to reduce several of his fractures and was comfortably resting, conscious and upgraded to fair condition. Doctors mulled fusing his pelvis, which would have ended his cycling career, but ultimately decided not to do the procedure. Still, they warned that his recovery would be slow.

"He's going to be here a very long time," Scully told reporters. His condition, doctors assured the public, was dire. In later years, the Knievel legend would tell of a 30-day coma, but at the time it was merely said that he was in very bad shape.

"Geez, dad, is he going to make it?" a concerned young Jay asked his father as they came out of the hospital.

"Oh yeah, he's fine. I just talked to him," Sarno assured his son. "We're just doing this for the publicity."

The daredevil left Southern Nevada Memorial Hospital on February 12. On crutches, he was already planning his comeback.

The gambit worked: Knievel had botched the landing, but he had succeeded in making himself a superstar thanks to his miraculous survival against impossible odds. The Caesars Palace jump gave him the biggest headlines of his career, and his nauseating crash only made people want to see more. After a series of jumps culminating in a jet-propelled leap over Idaho's Snake River in 1974 (he crashed again), Knievel became a bona fide American icon, a patriotic daredevil whose likeness decorated some of the top-selling toys of the 1970s.

The jump fixed the Caesars Palace fountains in the public consciousness. Since it opened, the property has been expanded, renovated, and remodeled so as to make it unrecognizable. But one feature remained untouched: Jay Sarno's fountains. Had Knievel's jump not rendered them so iconic, they might have gone the way of the Circus Maximus, Bacchanal, or screen block exterior. But the fountains remained.

The Knievel jump also planted the seed of Caesars Palace as the host of main-event sports. Motorcycle daredevilry was hardly the World Series, but it got Caesars Palace into *Sports Illustrated*. In later years, Caesars would pursue a variety of sporting events including Formula One racing, tennis, and, most famously, championship boxing. Knievel and Sarno's unprecedented marriage of a casino and a sports spectacle paved the way for all of this.

For Sarno, the best part of the jump was that he had found a friend, an intimate. Years later, after a round of high-stakes golf at the Las Vegas Country Club, Sarno summed it up.

"Kid, you're no different than I am," he said as they relaxed in Knievel's over-sized motor home. "We're like kissing cousins."

Knievel watched as his friend went on.

"You want it all or you don't want nothing. And you and I know as well as anybody in the world we can't bust these casinos."

"Yeah, and it's even harder to beat the bookies. I've lost more money betting on football this month than I've made playing golf."

They sat for a moment.

"So who do you like on Sunday? New York or Dallas?" Knievel asked.

"Without a doubt, Dallas. I'm putting a dime on them, at least."

Jay Sarno was so appalled by the Flamingo's ordinariness during his first visit to Las Vegas in February, 1963 that he decided to set up shop across the street. *Courtesy UNLV Special Collections.*

Taken in May, 1965, this view of the Caesars Palace construction site shows the new Diamond of the Dunes tower across Flamingo Road. *Courtesy UNLV Special Collections.*

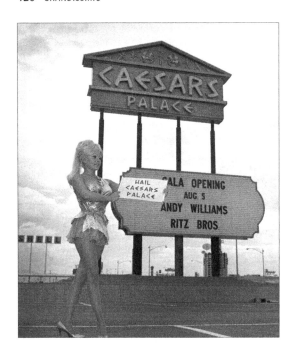

Caesars Palace would give Las Vegas something new: a complete fantasy resort where even the sign was part of the theme. *Courtesy Las Vegas News Bureau.*

The caesar featured on the Palace's opening invitation, its logo, and its promotional artwork bore a strong similarity to Jay Sarno. *Courtesy UNLV Special Collections.*

The fountains that Jay Sarno insisted belonged in front of Caesars Palace became one of the resort's most recognizable fixtures, and certainly its longest lasting. Although virtually everything around them has changed since the opening of Caesars in 1966, the fountains remain a constant. *Courtesy Las Vegas News Bureau.*

Mingling with Vegas royalty: Steve Lawrence, Jay, Eydie Gorme, and Caesars president Nate Jacobson in August, 1966. *Courtesy UNLV Special Collections.*

The Bacchanal was the culinary centerpiece of Caesars Palace. Jay sits here surrounded by the gourmet restaurant's staff, including the wine goddesses and executive chef Nat Hart, standing to Jay's left. *Courtesy Las Vegas News Bureau.*

At the other end of the spectrum, the Noshorium coffee shop offered a more casual but no less carefully themed restaurant that epitomized the fantasy guests could experience at Caesars Palace. *Courtesy Las Vegas News Bureau.*

Jay with his family, shortly after Caesars Palace opened: son Freddie, daughter September, baby Heidi, Joyce, and son Jay. *Courtesy UNLV Special Collections.*

Joyce and Jay ringside for the opening night of Don Rickles and Bobby Vinton, February 3, 1969. *Courtesy UNLV Special Collections.*

Caesars Palace takes its place on the Las Vegas Strip. The Dunes is to the south, and the Flamingo directly across the street. Further on are the Castaways, Frontier, and Stardust hotels (left) and the Sands (note the circular tower), Desert Inn, Riviera, and Sahara (right). Downtown Las Vegas is visible in the distance. The Strip-front fountains are the only element still remaining intact at the "Four Corners" today. *Courtesy UNLV Special Collections.*

Having arrived in Las Vegas with the opening of Caesars Palace, Jay poses for a triumphal portrait at his casino. Note the Greek key motif on the piano, another reminder of the all-pervasive classical theme at Caesars. *Courtesy UNLV Special Collections.*

TEN

Raising the Big Top

The thrill of Evel Knievel's jump didn't last. Before long, Knievel was barnstorming the country trying to build support for his Grand Canyon run and Sarno was back in his office, with Nate Jacobson down the hall and Jerry Zarowitz glowering at him every time he walked past the casino. Jay didn't slow down to make small talk with him.

As winter turned into spring, Sarno started spending more time at the Circus Circus construction site. Between managing what was left to him at Caesars and planning his new casino, Sarno's days were full. At night, of course, there was still plenty of time to gamble.

In the spring of 1968, children were very much on Jay Sarno's mind. He now had four; the oldest two, Jay and September, were in elementary school, with Freddie a bit younger and Heidi, born in 1966, still a toddler. His marriage was reaching the point of no return, but Sarno loved being a father, loved seeing the world through his children's eyes. Now, he was seeing just how few things there were for families with children in tourist Las Vegas.

Since the 1950s, a few Strip hotels had provided small day care facilities, like the Desert Inn's Kachina Doll House, but there wasn't much for kids to do. Most other hotel owners could have told him this was for a very good reason: Las Vegas was built on fast gambling, free-flowing booze, and the promise (realized or not) of easy sex, not exactly wholesome family fare.

Sarno, though, saw an opening.

"If we do something that's never been done, we won't have any competition," he told Stanley Mallin, who he was lobbying to join him. "Imagine something like Disneyland, but with gambling for the adults. It can't miss."

"But it's a crazy idea," Mallin said. "Who's going to bring their kids along while they gamble?"

"Plenty of people," Sarno argued. "It would be great for the city if we could build something for kids. And don't worry, we'll make some money out of it, too. As a matter of fact, we'll be able to get the best circus acts in the world. They'd be happy to take less money so they can live in the same place all year round."

Sarno was right about the last point, and combining adult and children's attractions wasn't, on the face of it, a lousy idea. The casino he designed, however, was thoroughly unwholesome. The giant pink and white big top would have at its core a gambling casino, with all the usual smoking and drinking, and carnival games of chance that kids could play nestled between the slot machines and craps tables. Several restaurants and a theater featuring burlesque shows were to ring the casino, with live circus acts performed above the games.

But Sarno wasn't done. As his marriage to Joyce continued to break down, his preoccupation with sex spilled over into his work. He would do more than shorten the skirts on the cocktail waitresses or even stage a topless revue in the theater, like many other casinos did.

"Here's the show-stopper," he told Mallin. "We're going to have topless shoeshine girls."

"That's crazy!"

"Bullshit. It's brilliant. What red-blooded man won't go nuts with a half-naked broad shining his shoes? And we'll have topless trapeze artists, too, bouncing around above the casino. Whether he looks up or down, he'll get an eyeful."

Even for Las Vegas this was a bit much. Gambling in major casinos is considered a positive social and economic good; topless shows were accepted in the 1950s; casinos and bars never close; and prostitution is commonplace. But Vegas gets nervous when sex and gambling get too close. Prostitution is illegal in Las Vegas and Reno (though it has long flourished *sub rosa*), and even today the Gaming

Commission can fine a casino for tolerating public sex within its confines or just advertising with too much raunch.

It would have taken a miracle for Sarno to get approval for bare-breasted employees to mingle with customers on the casino floor, even if he weren't planning a casino that at least partially catered to children. But Sarno, like many compulsive gamblers, was used to counting on miracles. Psychiatrists call this "magical thinking." It's the kind of leap beyond logic that made Axel Freed, James Caan's character in 1974's *The Gambler*, double down on a hard eighteen while playing blackjack at Caesars Palace. In a scene that Sarno would have understood, Freed gets the three he knows is coming. The impossible can happen.

A more prudent businessmen would have aimed at something less audacious than topless trapeze artists, but a more prudent businessman wouldn't try to solve his financial problems by building a casino.

So Sarno got started. He hadn't retained Melvin Grossman as architect, opting instead for Homer Rissman this time. Rissman was in the midst of a distinguished career for which he would earn a Silver Medal from the Nevada chapter of the American Institute of Architects before his 2001 death. He had begun practicing in Chicago, where he designed several apartment buildings, before moving to Santa Monica in 1954. Rissman built his first Las Vegas Strip casino, the Hacienda, in 1956. He designed all or part of the Frontier, Bonanza, and Silver Slipper casinos before securing the Circus Circus commission.

Rissman executed the unconventional ideas that his client gave him. Patrons entered the casino on the second floor, passing through a foyer lined with funhouse mirrors. From below, air jets activated from inside the ticket booth could strategically lift women's skirts. After purchasing tickets, guests passed through turnstiles and found themselves on a giant oval balcony. Walking to their right, they'd find a Bavarian beer hall, assorted carnival games, and a cocktail lounge, before reaching the entrance to the buffet on the other side of the oval. Crossing this midway point, they'd discover a revolving carousel bar, more midway games, a fur shop, and a hot dog stand before winding up back at the entrance.

Gamblers had several ways to get to the casino itself. They could amble down a curved "Grand Staircase" straight out of the Morris

Lapidus portfolio, slide down a chute, or whiz down a fireman's pole. Once on the ground floor, they were free to shoot dice and pull slot machine handles while watching live bands on two platforms above them or ducking as aerialists swung on ropes directly above them. More midway games lined the sides of the casino, just feet away from the adult games. A go-go bar, shooting gallery, delicatessen, and theater lounge rounded out the entertainment offerings.

As the big top took shape, the Nevada Gaming Commission became increasingly apprehensive about the casino's prospects, both financial and moral. Sarno defended his project with verve at a February 1968 commission meeting. After an hour-long presentation, the commission granted Sarno and his partners a preconstruction license with eleven conditions attached. Most of them had to do with the casino's finances and executives, but the commission reserved the right to review all advertising and publicity releases—an unprecedented intrusion into casino business, but one that was justified by fears that the "elaborate motif" would lure child gamblers.

Sarno made other concessions, denying that he had seriously planned to introduce the bare-chested girls and pledging that all circus acts would be suitably modest for the commission's tastes. In addition, he guaranteed that children would be barred from playing any carnival games that the commission felt were too close to true games of chance.

Though he had a loan from the Teamsters, Sarno's break with Nate Jacobson meant that he couldn't rely on the Baltimore insurance man's Rolodex for his backers. So he brought in Jud McIntosh, a self-made Georgia millionaire who'd stepped into Caesars Palace after its opening. McIntosh had befriended Mallin in Atlanta. He was a placid investor with deep pockets who didn't mind letting Sarno take the lead, and Sarno tapped him as the casino's treasurer. Mallin, too, was back, in an expanded role, as vice president and secretary. Several other investors rounded out the ownership group, including the Rogers brothers, siblings from Texas who'd also invested in Caesars.

With their provisional license in place, construction continued, with Johnson Construction, headed by Rob Johnson, serving as general contractor. This time, with no Nate Jacobson or Jerry Zarowitz, Sarno was the undisputed master.

"My decision to enter Circus Circus stems from our success at Caesars and my complete confidence in the taste of Sarno in what the public wants in this entertainment area," McIntosh declared to the press. Mallin was no less deferential, adding that even though he had been aware of Sarno's "unusual flair for showmanship" since their days at the University of Missouri, "his idea-a-minute pace never ceases to amaze me."

The flood of new concepts meant almost daily changes to the blueprints. Walking through the construction site, Sarno couldn't help but see that things would flow better with the bar ten feet to the left or the stage shifted back a bit. Despite the building's simple design, every day brought new delays and ballooning costs. The opening day was pushed back from August to September to October.

Sarno also found someone new to argue with: executive vice president Burton Cohen. The two had met five years earlier, when Sarno had unsuccessfully pitched Caesars in Cohen's law office.

Cohen had come a long way since that meeting. He loved the intellectual challenge of practicing law and once wanted nothing more than to plod along with law until he became a federal judge. But when he got the chance to become a part-owner of the Frontier hotel in Las Vegas, he reconsidered. He worked out a five-year plan: move to Las Vegas, grow the business, sell his shares high, then retire to Florida to practice law, taking one case a year if he wanted.

"That way," he later explained, "I didn't have to worry about keeping time charts and sending out bills."

Fate, however, in the form of Howard Hughes, intervened. When Hughes bought the Frontier in 1967, shareholders like Cohen got back only their initial investment, which Cohen had borrowed. He couldn't retire to Florida on that. Then Hughes moved Cohen over to the Desert Inn. Unsatisfied with his boss's instructions to "not make waves," Cohen was receptive when approached by an intermediary on behalf of Sarno and Mallin: would he be willing to build, open, and manage their new resort?

Cohen said yes. He soon found that he spent most of his time controlling his boss. It was a challenge because not all of Sarno's ideas were bad ones.

"He had a champagne appetite with a beer income," Cohen later said. "Great visionary, great ideas. And then if you want the child built, you ought to put Jay on a nice long cruise so that when he comes back you can say here's your child that you conceived."

With Circus Circus, though, Cohen did not have the luxury of putting Sarno on a luxury liner. They clashed just about every day.

For example, Sarno came up with an idea for a restaurant that would put the Bacchanal to shame. He had gotten Sid and Marty Krofft, sibling puppeteers who would soon begin their television career with Hanna-Barbera's *The Banana Splits Adventure Hour*, to design an animatronic forest that would be the centerpiece of a tiny new eatery.

"It's the most incredible thing!" he gushed. "The tree trunks and branches really move! While you're eating, the trunks come down and embrace you."

"It's incredible, all right," Cohen admitted when he saw the sketches. "But there's no way we can afford this. It seats maybe fifteen people. We could never charge enough for the food to make this work."

"But it's an attraction," Sarno insisted. "It's absolutely unique. No one else has anything like this. We'll get so much publicity for this, we'll make up the difference in the casino. It's going to be the only thing that anyone's talking about."

"It's a phenomenal concept, I'll grant you that. But there's still no way in the world that we can afford this."

Cohen won this argument, after several days. But it was nothing compared to the knock-down brawl over one of Sarno's sacred cows, the second-story entry to his casino.

"This is the only way that it'll work, Burt," Sarno said. "We're going to have all the carnival games on the second floor. Parents will drop their kids off up there, then come down to gamble."

"But what about people who don't have kids? Nobody is going to walk up a flight of outside stairs to get in. You know how hot it gets."

"We've got to do it that way. The commission would never let kids walk through the casino."

"There's got to be a way around it. This isn't going to work."

"You don't know that. No one's ever tried this."

"Exactly. They've got to come in on the ground floor."

"Why?"

"Because that's the way it's always been done, it's what people are used to."

"Why?"

"Suppose someone's handicapped, in a wheelchair. How are they supposed to get in?"

"Don't let them in."

"You can't do that!"

"You're like everyone else, you're afraid to try something new."

"It's not that it's new, it's that it's a horrible idea."

"Why?"

For almost an hour, Cohen struggled with his boss's "whys." In the end, he had no answer (or at least none that Sarno would accept), and the casino's only entrance remained on the second floor.

As soon as the concrete was poured for the Grand Staircase, Sarno was unhappy. Cohen saw him gesturing broadly to Rob Johnson at the base of the ramp. He hurried over.

"What's going on, Rob?"

Johnson chose his words carefully. "Jay wants the ramp moved over." Sarno nodded.

"Jay?" Cohen asked.

"Yeah, Burt. Look at it. It doesn't have the right flow here."

Cohen let that sink in.

"Rob, take a walk." Johnson decided to check on the crew working in the theater.

"For Christ's sake, Jay, I'm kiting checks to try to get this place open. Do you have any idea how much this change order would cost us?"

"But it's going to work much better if we move it three feet this way," Sarno pointed.

"Jay, you're not moving that ramp."

Sarno threw his keys on the ground, his face red.

"Why the hell do you have to fight me on everything I want to do?"

"If I don't, who will?"

Sarno thought about that.

"You're right," he said, picked up his keys, and walked away.

The ramp stayed where it was.

With Cohen keeping the change orders to a minimum the casino started to take shape. Though the candy-striped big top looked startlingly different from the gentle aqua glow and classical reproductions of Caesars Palace, Sarno actually used many of the same concepts. The giant oval rising out of the desert looked like the famous Caesars ellipses. In the theater annex, he designed a special oval-shaped office for himself. And, of course, there were fountains. Since his shallow footprint at Circus Circus lacked a deep setback, he flipped the fountains so they ran lengthwise down the Strip. They took up more than three hundred feet of street frontage, and their forty-foot jets of water periodically changed color.

Sarno had been planting reproductions of famous statues in his hotels for ten years, but with Circus Circus he commissioned the Great Montyne, an artist who moonlighted as a circus performer, to create twelve original 12-foot tall statues for the fountain areas. Giant clowns, gorillas, and elephants towered over passersby. Montyne also signed on for a year-long run under the big top. Promoting himself as the world's foremost hazard balancer, Montyne built his routine to a thrilling climax: the "Climb of Death," wherein he balanced on one finger over a cluster of gleaming swords, daggers, and spears.

To the side of the fountains, "the world's most unusual sign" announced the casino. This was the golden age of Las Vegas neon: in the years before Circus opened, the Dunes, Stardust, and Frontier dueled for the title of world's tallest sign. Sarno didn't have the budget to reach the stratosphere, so instead he had the Young Electric Sign Company create a working carousel that revolved and played circus music.

He continued to tinker, deleting some attractions, modifying others, and making new additions. One late addition became a signature feature: the "monorail of beauty" that encircled the mezzanine. Every hour, a train decorated with ponies glided around the circuit. The most beautiful women Sarno could find rode the ponies, doffing their hats and swaying as they made their way around the casino. It was another excuse to hire good-looking girls, and another distraction in a casino that was already dizzying. That, however, was becoming the motif of Circus Circus—not a carnival, but chaos.

Meanwhile, Caesars Palace was still his day job. Sarno scored another triumph on March 10, 1968, when Ed Sullivan broadcast live from Circus Maximus. The show featured typical Sullivan fare, with the McGuire Sisters, Jack Carter, Liza Minelli, Allen & Rossi, and the Fifth Dimension performing. In addition, Theodore Bikel presented a scene from *Fiddler on the Roof*, which was currently playing in the Circus Maximus.

His moment on the national stage didn't satisfy Sarno. He threw himself into Circus Circus, sketching constantly. He hadn't felt this good since Caesars Palace had started to take shape.

Sarno found that he was spending almost no time at Caesars Palace. He didn't mind. Now that the place was up and running, there wasn't much for him there. He had the architects plan an expansion tower, with an oversized top floor suite reserved not for high rollers, but for him: the sketches included rooms for each of his children and ample closet space for him and Joyce. But by the middle of 1968, Jay knew he would never live in that suite. And Circus Circus didn't have a hotel yet, but if it threw off enough cash to get him a loan, he knew just what kind of rooms would work best.

Sarno wasn't the only one looking to get out of Caesars Palace: his landlord Kirk Kerkorian wanted to as well. The former boxer was a quick study; he knew how well the casino was doing and suspected that it would do better without the guys from Miami hanging around the cage. So a few months after Caesars opened, he decided to become an owner.

With his successful aviation ventures, he wouldn't need to sell shares to former (or current) bookies to get the place started. Instead, he would form a corporation and, thanks to the changes in the gaming regulations, sell shares to the public. To get the best of the best employees, he wouldn't farm out human relations to cigar-smoking former hoods; he would offer top managers stock options and let them put together their teams as they saw fit. Like Sarno, he wanted to remake the Las Vegas casino, but along much different lines: it would be an efficient resort that would pay solid dividends.

Kerkorian hired Martin Stern, Jr., an architect who had designed expansions at the Sahara, Sands, and Riviera, to build him a 1,500-room colossus of a casino hotel on Paradise Road, on a former racetrack adjacent to the Convention Center. This would be, by his reckoning, the largest hotel in the world, and he intended to wring a profit from it by sheer economies of scale: Las Vegas not as Sin City, but as entertainment factory. The International, as he would call it, would be the tallest building in the state, and like a beacon would stand for the triumph of good business sense over the city's shambolic past.

The flier had seen enough of Sarno and Jacobson's stumbles at Caesars to know that you didn't go into a business like this blind. To train his staff, he bought the Flamingo from Morris Lansburgh (and, indirectly, Meyer Lansky), bringing Nevada's casino industry one step closer to the clean-shaven corporate era. He hired Sahara president Alex Shoofey to run the place, and planned a modernization and expansion campaign that would knock down the neon champagne tower. It was a new day.

Now that he was an owner, Kerkorian didn't see much point in being landlord to a casino that would soon be a rival. It was lose/lose: if Caesars didn't do well, he wouldn't get paid, and if it prospered, he was doing something wrong at the International. Plus, and this was no small consideration, the International wasn't exactly cheap—at $50 million, it would cost more than twice as much as Caesars. So in September 1968 he sold the land under Caesars to Desert Palace, the casino's holding company.

This left Sarno and Jacobson one less complication in the sale of the casino; the new owners could now be presented with a tidy package that included everything from the land to the cocktail napkins—and the guys from Miami.

As opening day for Circus Circus approached, Sarno became even more confident. He was sure that, despite the naysayers, it couldn't lose. After all, casino veterans had been nearly unanimous in predicting quick ruin for Caesars Palace, which had proved so profitable. Sarno made plans for the biggest opening party ever seen in Las Vegas and gave numerous interviews touting what he called "the most unusual casino concept ever devised." It was, according to an early ad, a "green felt Disneyland" with musical slots, flying pink elephants, death defying trapeze acts, and carnival attractions like a "beootiful [sic] naked girl frozen in a solid block of ice."

"We are going to have action—a spirit of fun and gaiety," he assured *Las Vegas Review-Journal* readers on the morning the casino was to open. "The customer will be confronted with jugglers, fortune tellers, trapeze and high-wire acts operating right over the gambling area. We have signed the finest circus acts in the world."

Customers would see dealers and cocktail waitresses coming on shift down a fire pole, with trampolines, unicyclists, a weight guesser, and a dish spinner livening things up. But that wasn't all.

"Then all of the sudden comes a Highland Marching Band. There's a girl selling balloons, over there is a very provocatively-dressed shoeshine girl, here's a fellow leading two pink elephants, you can ride them or pet them. You can play a slot machine with our Money Monkey, who jumps for joy if you win or holds his head in sorrow if you lose.

"There's another monkey who runs a store. If you want something, give him the money and he'll bring you the product.

"Our slot machines outshine the Houston Astrodome scoreboard. You play them and they will play tunes, ring bells, and flash multi-colored lights."

The focus on slots was ahead of its time. At the time, slot machines were drab, low-paying amusements that casino managers derided as "not real gambling." But Sarno saw that the future of the business lay in the mechanical games. Advancing technology was already making more lively games possible—the bells and whistles that Sarno touted. As slots improved, they would draw more players. So he designed Circus Circus to hold an unprecedented number of them: where Caesars had had about two hundred machines, Circus opened with more than seven hundred. In the 1970s, slot machines would continue to improve, offering higher jackpots and more varied game play. Gamblers flocked to them, and by 1983 they would make more money than table games in Nevada.

"There's a baseball toss game. You throw a ball at a target and knock a beautiful girl out of bed, who will dance for you, and then get back in bed to cover up, waiting for the next challenger." Sarno had already inked Los Angeles Dodgers pitching legend Don Drysdale to open the attraction with the ceremonial first pitch.

"Suddenly overhead a man leaps 60 feet into a wet sponge.

"If you are hungry, there are 14 bars and restaurants—more than any other establishment in the world. You can eat from 50 cents to $2.50, and the latter cost is the charge in one of the top gourmet restaurants ever devised.

"But our super gimmick," he went on, "is that in our twenty or so carnival games, the player cannot lose—for every dollar they play they will get $2 in merchandise based on retail prices. At long last, nobody will lose in Las Vegas." Prizes included television sets, fur coats, and golf clubs.

This might have been Sarno's private heaven: girls popping out of their clothes everywhere, cheap food never more than a few steps away, and games of chance that couldn't lose. It was everything he could imagine a man would want in a casino. Giving so much to the customer when other casinos just had cocktails and lounge acts, he didn't think it was possible Circus Circus would fail.

Despite the mounting delays, Sarno insisted the casino would open on schedule, now set for the middle of October. As the second week of the month came, newspaper ads trumpeted that the casino, which was "positively" opening on the 18th, "ain't kids stuff." The cartoon ringmaster made that clear: she was wearing knee-high boots, a jewel-studded g-string, and a flowing tux and tails that just barely failed to cover the crescents of her overflowing breasts and posterior. For those who didn't get it, she held a six-foot long whip.

Sarno, though, wasn't cracking the whip quite as effectively as he wished. He had won some and lost some, and up until the end he stuck to his guns on a final point: the restrooms were to be upstairs.

It was crazy—why make gamblers go farther from the tables than they had to when it came time to answer nature's call—but

Sarno, following his own logic, was insistent. Eventually, Cohen, with Rob Johnson's help, was able to convince Sarno to back down, and as they prepared for the opening, Cohen was particularly proud that players wouldn't have to hike up a flight of stairs—or shimmy up a chute—to use the facilities.

Sarno was all nerves as the date approached. He was able to score another coup: the Ed Sullivan show would be broadcast, live, from the casino shortly after the opening.

Finally, the big top was ready to open its doors; the acrobats were ready to take to the air, and all the slot machines were installed.

It was show time.

ELEVEN

Ringmaster

Even though it drew more than ten thousand guests—a Las Vegas record at the time—Circus Circus's October 18, 1968 opening night bash was a let-down for Jay Sarno.

With no must-see headliner *á la* Andy Williams and Sarno's patron, Jimmy Hoffa, languishing in Lewisburg Federal Penitentiary, this party lacked the star power of the Caesars launch. Only two years earlier, Jay Sarno seemed like the future of Las Vegas, but Las Vegas had already changed.

Howard Hughes had become the state's biggest employer, and Kirk Kerkorian's mammoth International was rising out of the desert. The legislature had already started changing the rules, allowing publicly-traded corporations to own casinos. Within a decade, Hilton, Holiday Inn, and Ramada would join the club. The money to build the future would come from Lower Manhattan, not Miami or Baltimore.

Sarno was on the losing side of history.

Still, he threw a good party. Without Nate Jacobson trying to steal the glory or Jerry Zarowitz glowering at him, he was undeniably in charge. He emceed the twilight ribbon-cutting ceremony, giving credit where it was due, but clearly the center of attention. A 90-foot long yellow streamer, extending from the top of the roof to the ground, billowed in the wind as gamblers, government officials, reporters, and Hollywood stars, many in costume, waited in the parking lot. With some help from Jud McIntosh, Stan Mallin,

United States Senators Alan Bible and Howard Cannon, and Las Vegas Mayor Oran Gragson, Sarno sliced the ribbon with a giant pair of shears, turned on the fountains, and released five thousand balloons into the sky.

A new casino, even one with finances as shaky as Circus Circus's, was still a big enough deal that the state's governor paid tribute to a project that was putting Nevada voters to work. Earlier in the week, he had issued a proclamation lauding Sarno and his associates as "imaginative creators and developers" who were carrying the state into the future, declaring the seven days after the casino's opening "Circus Circus Premiere Week."

More than fifteen hundred VIPs poured through the turnstiles while the hoi polloi continued celebrating in the parking lot. Sarno, dressed as a ringmaster in top hat and tails, was the first to shoot down the slide to the casino level. He wasn't the only one dressed up; this was a costume party. Little Bo Peep drank a martini while countless harem girls filtered through the crowd, and several costumes inspired by shows and attractions at other casinos on the Strip enlivened the festivities.

When the doors opened to the public at last at 10 p.m., the line waiting to get in, four abreast, stretched more than a block. Sarno's triumph seemed certain. He would surely be hailed as the man who brought the "family-style" casino to town.

"Circus Circus is a new type for Las Vegas," he crowed to a reporter. "We have a kiddy room for the little ones, a second floor where teenagers can play games with beautiful prizes, but no money, and a pit on the ground floor with the finest games for adults in town." He scoffed at those who said that the circus acts wheeling above would distract gamblers.

"The old story of the man who made four sevens in a row and when his wife fainted, he stepped over her to make the fifth pass, holds true here," he insisted. "The show will attract others and never faze the real players."

Sarno was speaking for himself; when the dice were in the air, nothing else mattered. But he was an addict. Unfortunately for him, most Vegas visitors weren't so obsessed; even the confirmed gamblers found cartwheeling aerialists distracting. Casual tourists who wandered in on a lark couldn't quite wrap their heads around it. But on that first night, Sarno only saw a world of potential. He gamboled around the floor, shouting orders here, pulling out a handkerchief to polish a slot machine handle there, wishing revelers all the best, barking orders at change girls and janitors.

Casino manager George Devereaux was doing his best to undo whatever damage Sarno did, hurrying behind him and making sure that all the employees did the tasks they were assigned, not what Sarno thought they should be doing.

Wiping the sweat from his brow, Devereaux turned to Burton Cohen. "Only for you would I do this," he said.

"Look at *me*," Cohen answered. "I look like a penguin in this get-up." He did bear a passing resemblance to Burgess Meredith as Batman's television nemesis, top hat and all. "But I'll be damned if I let Jay ruin this opening." He resolved not to rest until his boss was safely in bed.

But Sarno had an unnatural stamina that night. When the invited guests were gone and a curious morning crowd filtered in, he still buzzed around his casino. Finally, around noon, Cohen saw him sitting at a blackjack table, eyes wide open. He motioned for him to come over—there had been a small problem that he had already solved in one of the restaurants but which, he figured, would divert Sarno's attention for a while—and didn't get any response. He walked over and waved his hand in front of Sarno's face. Nothing.

Over the rattle of the slot machines, Cohen could hear him snoring. Cohen arranged for Sarno's driver to see him home, then went to bed himself. Circus Circus was open.

Circus Circus did have something for everyone, as Sarno had planned. The restaurants included the Café Metropole, by day a coffee shop and buffet, by night a gourmet restaurant whose slave girls served a lavish meal, wine included, for $2.50, in "Bachannal splendor." In the Bavarian Beer Fest, diners could draw their own beer in chilled steins and construct sandwiches from a heaping array of twenty different meats for only a dollar as a piano player led a sing-a-long. Throughout the casino, Sarno dared his guests to eat as much as they could: the self-service Donut Parlor was an all you can eat or steal stop for pastries, coffee, and milk, and the appropriately-named Diet Buster let customers gorge themselves on cakes and pies or create their own sundaes topped with hot fudge, crushed pineapple, marshmallows, and cherries for a buck. Downstairs, Jackie's Ess-n-Fress deli was a more traditional eatery, as was the upstairs "Snack Train" food court, where guests noshed on tacos, pizza, egg rolls, and corn on the cob.

Sarno had made sure no one would leave his casino hungry; he also did his best to see that they'd be entertained. No one could avoid the circus acts, of course, but if anyone needed more, Sarno was happy to oblige them. On the mezzanine, peep show booths let gawkers see "the world's most beautiful girls, in the flesh," by inserting a quarter. The small Ooh-La-La Theater featured burlesque and comedy acts, including Breck Wall's perennial sketch revue "Bottoms Up," which ran in Las Vegas more or less continuously from 1964 to 2007.

The *pièce d' résistance*, however, was the Hippodrome Theater. Sarno had commissioned a new musical comedy, "The Piece-Full Palace" for the room. Based on the imaginary history of Las Vegas circa 1868, the drama featured a book by Warren Douglas and music by television pioneer Steve Allen. Producer Jerry Shafer helmed the "madcap Hollywood-Western romp" whose hit breakout number, "Dirty, Rotten, Vicious, Nasty Guys," was punctuated by a shoot-em-up and the cast breaking into the boogaloo. Several characters from the Old West, including Calamity Jane and Billy the Kid, featured in the production, which was livened up by a bullwhip duel, gunfire, fistfights, and acrobatics. "A raucous put-on of a Vegas that never was," concluded reviewer Bill Willard. It was a suitably light frolic for the big top casino.

From the outside, everything seemed to be clicking. *Time* magazine reported in November that the casino was drawing 15,000 guests a day, an incredible number for the time. Some visitors grumped at the diversions, dismissing them as superficial attempts to build a Disneyland casino, but others were enthusiastic. "It's just like when I was a kid," a retired steamfitter told the magazine. Another customer claimed that "for me, it only adds to the excitement of gambling." As if on cue, a nearby slot machine hit a jackpot and promptly struck up a rousing Sousa march.

But beneath the surface, a far more sinister story was unfolding. Sarno beamed as he played ringmaster, but he was actually in the fight of his life. The casino was crowded, but it just wasn't making money. And it needed to make money, quickly. The problems had started before the casino opened. The subcontractors and vendors wanted to be paid, but Sarno was broke. By shuffling bills and making sincere promises, he created a fiscal perpetual motion machine that delivered nothing but promises.

Then Sarno's biggest creditors got together and compared notes. They could throw Circus Circus into bankruptcy if they pressed their demands together. With what looked like a pretty big stick, they requested a sit-down. Sarno, sensing this wasn't an argument he could win, introduced them to Burton Cohen.

"He's got a much better sense of the logistics," Sarno explained before ducking out. After he was gone, Cohen spoke.

"Gentlemen, let's put our cards on the table."

"Damn it, enough's enough," the creditors' spokesman said. "None of us have been paid yet, and the place has been open a week. You're not taking play money from your customers, are you?"

As a lawyer, Cohen knew exactly the size of the barrel they had him over. So first he calmed them down, then laid out a plan that would see Circus Circus pay off its current obligations, and as its cash flow increased begin to pay down the arrearage.

"If this place goes bankrupt, you'll get pennies on the dollar," he said. "This way, it might take some time, but you'll be paid in full."

Of course a bankruptcy judgment was legally binding, and Cohen's plan rested entirely on the goodwill and financial acumen of Jay Sarno. But either his eloquence or a sudden faith in Sarno swayed the creditors, and they decided not to push for bankruptcy. They, too, would gamble that Sarno could turn things around.

Outside that room, Sarno didn't inspire much faith. Considered a tolerable eccentric when Caesars was smashing records, he became less tolerable as Circus failed to live up to expectations. He never passed up a chance to get himself on television. This rubbed traditional Vegas bosses—who stayed well out of the limelight—the wrong way.

No other boss would have consented to be mentioned on the Peter Jennings report broadcast on the November 25, 1968 ABC Evening News; Sarno starred in it. The camera zoomed in on Sarno to start, just as he gulped down a glass of wine and smacked his lips. A lithe Asian woman in a toga dress appeared and began massaging Sarno's temples while another woman approached, offering a bunch of grapes and a kiss on his cheek. It was almost grotesquely indulgent.

"His name is Jay Sarno," Jennings began in voiceover. "He dines alone, as is often his custom, in the Bacchanal Room of his Caesars Palace hotel in Las Vegas. The wine girls were hand-picked by him. They're a necessary part of his life and his image.

"Sarno is a builder of hotels and casinos, perhaps empires. Caesars Palace was designed with the Roman one in mind. Jay Sarno defies tradition. He believes he can accomplish practically anything. His edge, he believes," here the camera zoomed uncomfortably tight on his eyes, "is that he knows what the public wants." And then Sarno spoke.

"I think I'm a queer duck, an unusual duck. I don't think I'm a common man. I kind of have common tastes, a feeling for what they might like, which is a pretty good trick in itself, but I'm a loner, different, a little sad. Most creative people are." Here he paused, staring straight ahead. The camera moved in slightly.

"In this whole company I'm one of the few creative people. I'm not proud of it, I just am. Which is as true as the fact that I'm one of the fattest guys in the company. I'm 5 foot 8, that's a fact, that's not an opinion. I'm creative, that's a fact. I take no special pride in the fact that I am. It's an asset that I am. It's like a guy who can sing. I wish I could sing but I can't. I can close my eyes and see a building, and people, and dealers," now the screen showed aerial shot of Circus Circus, "and performers and all of it going on just now like I'm looking at it in real life. That's my ability. I have a new idea every three minutes. Some people don't have one in three years or three lifetimes."

He went on, telling Jennings about the "humdinger" of a giveaway he was working on (a car an hour, for several days; he didn't come close to having the money to do it) and his plans to bring a new attraction to Circus Circus. He explained that it would be a snake. Jennings wanted to know why.

"Well, I don't know, a snake is a fascinating animal and there aren't that many to choose from, you know. Of course most of the animals are smelly and dirty. Snakes are cleaner and easier to handle. They only eat once a month."

Here he paused, then started again, almost arguing with himself. "Well I don't mind them eating, I'd rather have them eat every day, as a matter of fact three times a day, because we could charge to see 'em feed because he only eats *live* animals." He stopped here, letting Jennings appreciate this. 'Now I *know*, we're gonna be jammed at feeding time. Would you pay to see a snake eat twelve chickens? *Alive?*"

Jennings said nothing.

"Right in front of your eyes, swallow 'em whole?"

Still nothing.

"Yes you would. A lot of people would if you wouldn't."

Wrapping it all up over a montage of Sarno walking through his casinos while acrobats twirled and players pulled slot handles, Jennings gave the final word.

"The people near Sarno figure him *the* paradox. Good yet evil. Kind yet cruel. Common, by his own admission, yet uncommon, perhaps unique. Peter Jennings, Las Vegas, Nevada."

His partners were horrified: their casino's majordomo looked like a complete nut on national television. Sarno couldn't have been happier: this was an homage to a creative genius. Yes, he seemed a bit eccentric. But weren't all geniuses supposed to be out there? He even ran an ad in the *Los Angeles Times* that called his sanity into question.

"His partners are wondering if they should STOP THIS NUT before he gives away all the profits," screamed the type. Jay Sarno peeked over the bottom of the ad, a conical party hat perched on his bald pate. "Jay Sarno is the guy who invented a new kind of fun casino," the small print read. "It jumps 24 hours a day with the kind of fun and games that made Vegas famous. But his partners are worried that Jay has flipped. Almost everyone who comes to CIRCUS CIRCUS walks out with big, expensive prizes that they've won playing his carnival games. And he's practically giving food away. Two bits buys most everything! He serves gourmet dinners with wine for two-fifty. There are peep, cooch, and Broadway shows plus big-top aerialists, trapeze artists, wild animals, and wilder girls. You'll see it and still say, 'It's unbelievable!' Enjoy CIRCUS CIRCUS the way it is…before his partners send the man in the white coat to cart Jay Sarno away."

The ad captured everything that was wrong with Sarno's Circus. The dealers and gamblers couldn't help but be distracted by the acrobats whirling overhead. High rollers didn't want to push aside Tanya the elephant to get to the tables, nor did they want screaming kids running around the place while they played serious money. Like a true three-ring circus, Sarno's new casino had something for everyone, but it also had something everyone hated.

Opening without a hotel further handicapped the casino. Publicly, Sarno had claimed that Circus Circus was such a unique attraction that it didn't need a hotel to make money. Privately, he bemoaned his lack of rooms and never stopped trying to borrow money to build them.

Because he didn't charge to see the circus acts, Sarno felt justified in levying a two-dollar admission fee. This was unprecedented: casinos were supposed to lure people in with a variety of free or cheap attractions, then get them to drop everything in their pockets on the casino games. Making them open up their wallets before they got inside was counter-intuitive. Burton Cohen fought him tooth and nail on this; but Sarno refused to give in.

All this was too much for Cohen. In early 1969, Fred Benninger, an intimate of Kirk Kerkorian called. How would Cohen like to run the Flamingo?

The hotel's president, Alex Shoofey, was taking his team to the soon-to-open International, so there were several openings at the Flamingo, including the top spot. Cohen jumped at the chance to get out of Circus. He had had enough of Norball the Ape Man spooking the blackjack players. Running the Flamingo wouldn't be a cake walk. There was plenty of dead wood to be cleared out, and Kerkorian's plans for expanding the place were ambitious, but he was up to the challenge.

"Once you've worked for Jay Sarno," he told Benninger, "everything in life is easy."

Losing Cohen didn't bother Sarno that much. He was convinced that there was nothing wrong with Circus Circus besides fleeting bad luck. But Cohen's departure left Circus with an insurmountable handicap: runaway skimming. Usually, skimming was part of the devil's bargain that casino owners made: in exchange for funding, help with operations, or running in junkets of big players, they would have to tolerate it. In moderation, almost everybody won: the casino owner got to run his joint and the boys back in Chicago or Kansas City, along with a variety of folks along the way, from dealers to bagmen, got a cut. The citizens of Nevada were the only ones who really suffered; with revenues under-reported, the state didn't get its expected share of taxes. Skimming only moderately depressed reported revenues at most houses, but with Circus Circus already on a thin margin, any amount of pilfering was catastrophic.

Under casino manager George Devereaux, there was no organized skimming. But when Cohen left so did Devereaux, and after him a revolving door of managers either permitted or orchestrated the skimming. If Sarno knew the details, he was powerless to stop it. In public he might have been the ringmaster, but Sarno wasn't about to get into the lion's cage and crack his whip.

Meanwhile, Caesars Palace was still on the auction block. In December 1968, a deal to sell the resort and its property to Denny's in exchange for an undisclosed amount of stock was announced. It seemed like a fine match: Denny's had just acquired two other restaurant chains and was undergoing a phenomenal growth spurt. The company had recently gone public, and Nevada legislators had just approved the change to the state's gaming laws that permitted publicly-held corporations to own casinos.

The marriage between the future purveyors of Grand Slam Breakfasts and Las Vegas's finest casino fell through, though Denny's founder and chairman Harold Butler had been bitten by the casino bug. It was an unfortunate malady. Two years later, he was forced to step down after his attempted purchase of the Parvin-Dohrmann

Company, which owned the Stardust, Fremont, and Hacienda casinos, was thwarted by SEC allegations of insider trading.

Another fast-food chain stepped forward. Lum's, a Florida-based company, was best known for its hot dogs cooked in beer. The brothers who founded the business, Clifford and Stuart Perlman, had started in the dry goods business in their hometown of Philadelphia. In Florida, they expanded a single Lum's location to a 450-restaurant chain, more than one hundred retail clothing stores, and a meatpacking business. The hot dog empire was worlds away from the high-rolling casino at Caesars, but the Perlmans made the best offer for the resort: $58 million for the hotel that had cost $19 million to build three years earlier.

It was the deal of a lifetime—a 300% return on investment for the shareholders and at last an exit from the mobbed-up casino for Sarno. But factoring in the $5 million paid to Kirk Kerkorian for the land and the ongoing expansion project made it less of a bargain, as did the terms: Lum's only paid about $10 million to get the keys to the casino, with an additional $20 million due in January 1970, and the balance over the next five years.

At attorney Mickey Rudin's urging, Sarno took the offer. The Nevada Gaming Control Board had ratcheted up the pressure on Caesars, asking the state to levy a $100,000 fine against each stockholder after the casino was caught "rolling out the red carpet" to twelve notorious members of the Kansas City underworld. The charges came after Clark County Sheriff Ralph Lamb arrested 18 members of a hundred-person May junket from the barbecue capital as they boarded the plane after a week of wining and dining at Caesars. Sarno himself had ordered the group be given free rooms. "Catering to persons of notorious or unsavory reputation," the complaint said, "tends to reflect discredit on the state of Nevada and is a violation of the regulations."

If the Gaming Commission, who made the final decision, seconded the Control Board's recommendation, the casino would have faced a cumulative fine of more than $3 million. Caught between Zarowitz and the gaming police who refused to tolerate the mobbed-up Caesars regime, Sarno felt he had little choice but to take the best offer he could get. He got short-changed.

When it came time to make the $20 million payment in January 1970, the Perlmans pleaded for more time.

"We should take the hotel back," Mallin told Sarno. "They've breached the contract."

But Rudin, claiming to have spoken with a high-ranking official in the Justice Department, urged them to do otherwise.

"They're not going to let you guys do this because Lum's is a public company. They have widows and orphans who'll be wiped out if their stock gets wiped out, which is just what'll happen if this deal falls through. They're not going to let you take it back."

Years later, Mallin said, "I don't know if it was true or not. But we believed him and we were naïve."

The Perlmans had walked into a hornet's nest, regardless. In December 1970, federal agents stormed the casino cage as part of a 26-city, 160-warrant cross-country round-up. They opened lock boxes belonging to Jerry Zarowitz, Elliott Paul Price, and Sanford Waterman, a casino executive vice president, seizing more than $1.5 million in cash. They couldn't figure out exactly what Zarowitz was doing there, since he was no longer officially associated with the casino. The agents guessed he was either skimming cash from the tables or masterminding an interstate sports betting operation. The arrests sparked a sprawling legal action that would not be settled until 1976.

Then the Securities and Exchange Commission began taking a closer look at the conditions of the Caesars sale. Apparently unswayed by concern for widowed and orphaned stockholders, the commission filed a complaint in New York's U.S. District Court in December 1971, charging numerous violations of securities law in the purchase.

According to the complaint, unaudited financial statements failed to explain why the casino had lost $1 million in the five-month period preceding the sale, when it had made $2.2 million in a comparable stretch the previous year, with no discernible drop in business. It's likely that Zarowitz had stepped up his suspected skimming. Lum's, in proxy filings to issue stock to former Caesars shareholders to solicit shareholder approval for the acquisition and to borrow money for the purchase, failed to mention these financial irregularities or that Zarowitz, though he officially held no ownership stake in the casino, was receiving $3.5 million as part of the sale. The lawsuit named Lum's, Caesars Palace, and thirteen people, including Sarno, Mallin, Zarowitz, Nate Jacobson, and the Rogers brothers, as defendants.

Even with the SEC lawsuit hanging over their heads, the Perlmans aggressively expanded, finishing Sarno's tower addition. Clifford Perlman moved into the penthouse suite Sarno had designed for his own family. The brothers sold off their Lum's restaurants and other food service and retail interests, renaming their company Caesars World. In 1972, the company bought the Thunderbird, a casino hotel about a mile north of Caesars Palace, and announced plans to demolish it to construct the Mark Antony, a thousand-room casino hotel. Those plans never came to fruition, but Perlman did lure Burton Cohen to the Thunderbird with promises that he had be given imperium over the majestic Mark Antony.

Ultimately Caesars World agreed to several restrictions to settle the SEC suit. The court, with the presumed acquiescence of Nevada regulators, mandated a series of financial controls, including independent audits, and it barred the company from buying any new casinos unless it received three years' worth of audited financial statements. In addition, the settlement set up an independent department to review all personnel, operations, and security, responsible only to the CEO and shareholders of Caesars World.

With its securities issues in the past, Caesars World continued to expand, adding towers, making Las Vegas a mecca for world championship boxing, and even opening non-gambling resorts in the Poconos. Yet allegations of improprieties would continue to surface. Years later, at unlikely hands, the Perlmans would receive their come-uppance. In the early 1970s, Jay Sarno could only watch as the brothers built his casino into an empire, paying him grudgingly with money that, he felt, should rightfully be his. This would be only one of the injustices he would brave in the coming years.

Around the time that Circus Circus opened, the Cabana empire started to take on water. Sarno had stepped away from any new

Cabanas when he moved to Las Vegas, but since the Cabana chain was still part of his promotional corona, it hurt.

Sarno had gotten attorney Jerry Rosenthal involved with the Cabanas back in 1961, when Rosenthal arranged for Doris Day and husband Marty Melcher to invest. Rosenthal had made his name as a "tax specialist" with a client list that included many Hollywood stars. But he was a deceitful, underhanded confidence man. Day called him "an oppressively evil force" in her life, and even Rosenthal's own nephew admitted he was "a smooth, astute, skilled, crafty crook with a beguiling way about him." Sarno, who wasn't the best judge of character, warned his nephew Jonathan to "stay away from that guy" and described him as "evil incarnate."

Over the years, Rosenthal continued to direct Melcher's investments on Day's behalf. The oil wells, ranches, and hotels, he assured Melcher, were phenomenally profitable. They'd invested a great deal, as Melcher forced his wife to scrimp on household essentials.

"We need all our money for Rosenthal's investment program," he explained. "Without tax shelters we'll be turning over everything to the government."

Rosenthal never provided specifics, and Melcher didn't press him. When his wife questioned the wisdom of those investments, Melcher implored her to trust him, as he trusted Rosenthal.

In 1963, Sarno had ceded management of the Dallas and Palo Alto hotels to Cabana Management, a company that Rosenthal created to run the hotels on behalf of their major investors, the Melchers. According to a later complaint recommending Rosenthal's disbarment, Cabana Management claimed money for services that were "for the most part, contrived, a sham, fraudulent, exaggerated, and, in some instances, duplicative of claims made by Respondent's law firm for the same services."

With Rosenthal both balancing the books and auditing them, the theft might have gone on forever if fate had not intervened. On April 20, 1968, a few months before Circus Circus opened, Melcher died of complications from a heart condition. His death brought the Rosenthal house of cards tumbling down. "The hotels are bankrupt, all the oil wells are dry, and there aren't any cattle," Day's son Terry tearfully informed her after finally forcing Rosenthal to show his hand. Ultimately, Day and Terry sued Rosenthal for malpractice, winning a $22.8 million judgment against him, including $4.6 million dollars for his mismanagement of the hotels. The judge ruled that the hotel investments were so ill-advised that they "would be humorous but for the tragic consequences."

The Cabanas got swept into the legal maelstrom. Rosenthal, more interested in lining his pockets than promoting the hotels, had run them into the ground. A fight between Day and Rosenthal for control over the properties didn't help, and in 1969 a bankruptcy court ordered the Dallas and Palo Alto Cabanas sold to the Hyatt Corporation. Their management of the hotels left something to be desired, and both went into a slow decline.

The Dallas Cabana had an appropriate fate, given Rosenthal's legal history. Hyatt bought it and re-christened it the Dupont Plaza, but just couldn't draw visitors. In 1985, Dallas County bought the hotel for $9.2 million and, two years and $5 million later, reopened it as the Bill Decker Detention Center. Even with a captive audience, though, Sarno's Texas outpost still wasn't a hit; in 2008, officials closed the jail, which was rapped as costly and inefficient. Since then, the jail has re-opened to accept prisoners as the county's correctional needs dictate, but it seems destined to be demolished.

Sarno's first big project, the Atlanta Cabana, has already fallen victim to the wrecking ball. In 2002, the hotel was razed after a plan to reclaim the building from its decline (it had become a Quality Inn, and its intricate tilework covered with plaster) fell through.

The Palo Alto Cabana, on the other hand, was saved in 1996, when Silicon Valley hotelier B. B. Patel bought the hotel, which had been slated for demolition and redevelopment as tract housing. Patel embarked on a $20 million renovation and in 1999 it re-opened as the Crowne Plaza Cabana. Since then, a few local journalists have acknowledged Jay Sarno's foray into Palo Alto and the city's unique contribution to the evolution of Caesars Palace.

S arno was glad to be away from the sinking Cabanas, but he desperately clung to Circus Circus. He had poured his life into the casino, and losing it became a very real possibility. Unlike Caesars, which ran smoothly after a few opening-night jitters, Circus Circus was dogged by problems. There was the skimming, which Sarno couldn't control, but there were also operational problems—many of them caused by the two-dollar admission charge. Tourists would pay it, if only out of curiosity and to see the "free" circus acts. But locals took offense at the idea. Taxi drivers, in particular, loathed it. At this time, casino chips were still accepted as de facto currency across town: people paid for everything from groceries to their electric bills in casino chips. Cab drivers, who'd accepted the chips from customers in good faith, were outraged when they learned they would have to pay two dollars to enter the casino to cash their chips; this simply wasn't done.

Bad press from the cab drivers' complaints (at one point a demonstration of more than a hundred of them nearly turned into a riot) highlighted the issues Circus Circus was facing. It soon became public knowledge that the casino was balancing on a knife edge of financial acrobatics, which made it even harder for Sarno to convince vendors still owed money that things were looking up.

These financial problems couldn't be swept under the rug. The Gaming Commission, still leery of Sarno's seat-of-the-pants financing, refused to grant him a permanent license to run the casino; instead, they extended the casino's license on a month-by-month basis.

By the early spring of 1969 Sarno and the Commission had fallen into a pattern. He would appear at his licensing hearing, assuring the commissioners that everything was under control, making promises—the casino would soon be in the black, contractors would be paid, its investors properly licensed—that even he knew he couldn't keep.

If he could keep them off his back, with some luck, things really would turn around. And, he constantly reminded everyone that there was always the prospect of getting a Teamster loan to pay for a hotel tower. The Teamsters had been loaning him money to stay afloat, and, with or without Jimmy Hoffa's help, they'd see that if they ever wanted their money back, he would have to add rooms to Circus Circus.

But in late March, Sarno was stunned when Gaming Commission chair Jack Diehl announced that his license wouldn't be renewed.

"He made some rather brash statements," Diehl told the press, "that he knowingly or unknowingly couldn't carry out. Now the axe has fallen on him."

The Commission was hesitant to throw eight hundred voters out of work, but it had had enough of Jay Sarno.

Through his lawyer William Morse, Sarno pleaded for just one month more. Diehl said no dice. Sarno hadn't just made bad decisions on the casino floor; he had been accepting loans from just about anyone, promising them the chance to be paid back in stock. The Commission had heard rumors of mob involvement at Circus Circus, and this was a red flag that the mob was setting up shop. It doubly hurt Sarno that he hadn't bothered to ask the Commission's approval before making these deals. Nevada might have promoted itself as the anything-goes last frontier, but the commissioners weren't going to let Jay Sarno write his own rules.

His employees hoped that something would be worked out. So did his creditors. Tension mounted as the deadline approached.

On April 30th, hours before the doors were to be padlocked, the Commission announced that it was rescinding the shut-down order and giving Circus Circus another one-month extension.

The night before, Diehl had called a special meeting of the Commission to respond to an offer Sarno had extended. In a letter carefully worded by Morse, Sarno announced his resignation as president of Circus Circus. He further informed the Commission that he would be placing his 20 percent interest into a trust. To save his casino, he was willing to sacrifice himself.

Treasurer Jud McIntosh stepped into Sarno's shoes as president. And things seemed to settle down at the casino—at least, it stayed out of the headlines.

And that might have been all the Gaming Commission was looking for.

TWELVE

What'll It Take to Make You Happy?

With Sarno just about out of the picture, things settled down at Circus Circus. The casino inched into the black. But Sarno was itching to get back into his office. Through William Morse, he kept a channel to the Commission open: could he come back yet? Could he please come back?

By January 1970, Morse had managed to persuade the Commission's chairman, Jack Diehl, that Sarno had reformed. There would be no more handshake loan/stock purchase agreements, and he was willing to take whatever medicine the Commissioners offered.

That month, the Gaming Commission voted unanimously to welcome Sarno back into the fold. He took up the mantle of Circus Circus president again, with the full faith and credit—more or less—of Nevada gaming regulators behind him.

Sarno threw himself into running Circus as never before. This exacerbated the growing tensions between him and Joyce. He found it difficult to juggle his work, which more often than not took place after hours, and his home life. He loved his children, without qualification. But he wasn't a hands-on parent most of the time. Raising the kids, as far as Sarno was concerned, was Joyce's job. He was happy to keep them entertained, to shower them with bigger and nicer gifts than their classmates got, and to throw them parties that their friends would remember into adulthood. Birthdays on the Caesars Palace yacht, blowing out the candles as the boat cruised the waters of Lake Mead, hanging out at the hotel pool in the summers, Thanksgiving dinners where anyone, including actor Tony Curtis, might show up—growing up as a Sarno meant a charmed life.

But their day-to-day lives—getting them to school, nursing bumps and bruises, studying with them for tests—weren't his job. To be fair, he wasn't the only father of his generation to feel that way.

As Circus Circus prepared to open, the children came to watch the acrobats get used to their new home. The Canestrellis, one of the opening trapeze acts, let the kids join them on the trampoline, teaching them flips, pikes, and hurkeys. After the casino opened, the Sarnos continued to warm up with the Canestrellis before their performances, much to the envy of the other kids in the audience.

The kids also had the run of the midway level. Allowed to play any game she wanted for free, Heidi, the youngest, peeled tickets off the roll and won more stuffed animals than she could fit in her room.

It wasn't all trampolines and teddy bears, though. Sarno's indulgences only went so far. Never physically abusive, he could nonetheless make his children feel the full force of his impatience. The brusque putdowns that left subcontractors cursing under their breath could reduce his kids to tears.

Freddie enjoyed having a dad who was as into sports, particularly golf, as he was. But his brother Jay had no time for games. In the early 1970s, teen rebellion usually meant tuning in and dropping out. Under the influence of his libertine father, Jay became a prematurely responsible adult. Instead of cavorting with the Canestrellis or spending the weekends on the links, he would work: first as a general assistant at Circus Circus, then at other jobs as he got older.

Jay Sarno was a magnanimous—if sometimes distant—host to his extended family. He installed his brother Louis, who was still looking for a break, at the Circus Circus liquor store and even found his mother-in-law a job taking tickets at the bumper car attraction. If anyone needed anything, they knew to call Jay.

When his older brother Sam's daughter Sara got married, Sarno heard the young couple didn't have a television set; he ordered them the latest, biggest color model, not even asking about the price, and had it delivered.

His brothers and sisters, nieces and nephews were welcome to visit any time they liked. They were not exactly encouraged, but it was understood that if they needed a vacation, Jay would see to it. Sarno was proud to be the provider of the family, at last: his brother Herman could never offer anything this swank to them.

Sam, the family doctor, was thrilled to have a little brother who was nearly famous. He had almost become a celebrity himself in Morehouse, Missouri, when he made it known that his brother was partners with Doris Day, back in the Cabana days, and was over-awed when he came to Las Vegas: his kid brother, who he had helped put through college, could walk into a casino and immediately attract a host who bowed and scraped to "Mr. S." Special tables were set up for his family in restaurants, and they had the best seats at all of the shows.

Sam's wife made sure to pick out the right furs and jewelry to wear in Las Vegas; she didn't want to look like a bumpkin. But they were small-town people. They could wade into Jay's world with their pants rolled up to the knees, but they could never dive underwater and breathe. Sam had a regular poker game back in Morehouse, but seeing his brother lose $30,000 in a few minutes at craps was incomprehensible to him. How could you live like that?

For his part, Jay couldn't believe that this was the brother he had grown up idolizing, had even contemplated following into medicine. "Why don't you guys move to the city and raise your children where they can get an education?" he asked, unable to believe that there might be any benefits to small-town life.

Sarno's extended family saw only the good side: the free rooms, comped meals, and star treatment. They loved it. But used to thrift, they broke the only rule of Las Vegas royalty: throw money around as if it were on fire. Sarno had to give them money to tip the maitre d' and waiters as befit the emperor's kin.

"Look, I've got a reputation here," he told his cousin Marion Portman once, giving her a wad of bills. "Don't do cheap things."

Outside of the casino, Jay dabbled in many enterprises, from real estate speculation to a planned nationally-franchised bumper-car operation, and he offered his extended family ground-floor investing opportunities with each of them; usually they offered no return and little in the way of explanation about where the money went. His nephew Jonathan—Herman's son—got roped into the would-be bumper car empire.

"Kid, you want to be a film-maker," Sarno had told Jonathan. "You're not going to make any money, so you have to have some security in your life." He hit all the right buttons—his nephew's admiration for him, his artistic longings, and his fears of an uncertain future.

To a young man who implicitly trusted his uncle, everything made perfect sense. Sarno talked him into signing over his nest egg—about $90,000—to him with no receipt and no solid idea of when or how he would see his money back.

Usually, it ended there: Jay got his money, and his relative had another lesson in risk analysis. But Jonathan's mother Lillian was livid when her son told her what had happened to his inheritance; it had been years, and his uncle hadn't sent him any dividends.

"That's really shameful, what you did," she said after she had gotten her brother-in-law on the phone. Sarno had tussled with Teamster honchos, minor Mafiosi, and federal agents; he quailed before Lillian. Jonathan got a check the next day, with all of his money returned.

So for his relatives, as for Peter Jennings, Jay Sarno was a riddle: generous but conniving, a point of pride, yet often an embarrassment. It was as if, having worked so hard at crafting a persona who could be at home in the suites of Las Vegas, even those closest to him couldn't distinguish what was real and what was for show.

After he resumed control at Circus Circus, Sarno celebrated by moving his family from the pleasant but plain house on Maricopa Way to a 4,800 square-foot showplace on Brown Circle, a neighborhood adjacent to the exclusive Rancho Circle development. A home here meant you were part of the establishment; casino owners, bank presidents, and judges were your neighbors. The house, at 2808 Brown Circle, was a long, rambling rancher with five bedrooms and a master suite, a sunken living room, and a pool surrounded by apricot and plum trees.

It was the kind of house that begged for visitors, and Joyce entertained regularly. She found herself in a small but close-knit group of casino owners' wives who had much in common: they didn't, as a rule, have their own career; they were relatively new to town; they were rich; and they weren't the center of their husbands' attention. So they lunched together and served on the hospital auxiliary and put together programs for the National Conference of Christians and Jews. They dabbled in moderately progressive politics and staged the Miss Teen Nevada contest.

Joyce turned the Brown Circle home into a hub for this kind of work. It made her husband's usual absences a little easier to cope with, but they still hurt.

Meanwhile, on the Strip, Sarno was bothering people by being too present. The state's most powerful man, Howard Hughes, found him particularly infuriating. The billionaire—whose eccentricities made Sarno look like the man in the grey flannel suit—dreaded the very notion of a circus-themed casino mere blocks from the hotels he had bought, fouling the city he wanted to remake in his own image. After reading a newspaper article about the project when it was still on the drawing board, Hughes dashed off a memo to Robert Maheu.

"The aspect of the Circus," he wrote, "that has disturbed me is the popcorn, peanuts, and kids side of it. And also the Carnival Freaks, and animal side of it. In other words, the poor, dirty, shoddy side of Circus life. The dirt floor, sawdust, and elephants. The part of a Circus that is associated with the poor boys in town, the hobo clowns, and, I repeat, the animals. The part of a circus that is synonymous with the common poor man—with the freckled face kids—the roustabouts driving the stakes with three men and three sledge hammers, etc., etc.

"It is the above aspects of a circus that I feel are all out of place on the Las Vegas Strip. After all, the Strip is supposed to be synonymous with a good looking female all dressed up in a very expensive diamond-studded evening gown and driving up to a multi-million dollar hotel in a Rolls Royce. Now, you tell me what, in that picture, is compatible with a circus in its normal raiment, exuding its normal atmosphere and normal smell."

Circus Circus became an itch that Hughes couldn't scratch, maddening the notorious obsessive. He fumed as it opened less than a mile away from his vacuum-sealed suite at the Desert Inn. The circus casino was one more reminder that Las Vegas was far less tidy than Hughes would have liked, and that he was powerless to change it. Originally planned to be the New Rome at the center of the billionaire's growing empire, Las Vegas had lost its charm. In November 1970, Hughes departed Las Vegas under even more mysterious circumstances than he entered it—smuggled down a staircase on a stretcher, his whereabouts a mystery to his ostensible right hand, Robert Maheu.

He didn't leave to get away from Jay Sarno. In fact, he was spirited away from Las Vegas because of machinations within his own inner guard. But Sarno did his part to make Hughes repulsed by his would-be neon sanctuary.

For his part, Sarno thought he was an upstanding public citizen. After all, he had created an attraction at Circus Circus that benefited the entire community; where else could you get into a circus for practically nothing? He saw himself as a spokesman of sorts for the Nevada casino industry, a guy who was happy to step into the limelight for the benefit of his community. He liked the attention, and any publicity was good publicity for the casino. That's why he talked his way into the 1971 James Bond film *Diamonds Are Forever.* Starring Sean Connery, the film has an extended Las Vegas sequence featuring a casino named "The Whyte House" (actually a disguised International Hotel), owned by Willard Whyte, a thinly-veiled Howard Hughes. At one point, the plot carries Bond and others into Circus Circus, where the Flying Palacios spin overhead, blackjack dealers wear ridiculous polka-dotted clown shirts, and Tanya the Elephant shakes her head with glee after hitting a slot jackpot.

After winning a stuffed dog containing the film's macguffin at a booth on the midway, Bond girl Tiffany Case (actress Jill St. John) steps into a sideshow booth that promises to show the incredible Zambora, who may be girl, gorilla, or both. Inside, Jay Sarno, dressed in blue smock with an outrageous red cravat, speaking in a parody of his father's Yiddish accent, introduces the featured attraction.

"Ve must varn you that in every scientific experiment there is always a danger, so keep in mind dese curtains is an exit. God forbid something should go wrong in here, get out of here." A motionless Zambora, suspended in a "transcendental state," is revealed in a cage. After Sarno fusses with a control panel, the girl is replaced by a rather obvious-looking man in a gorilla suit, who breaks the bars of his cage, sending a screaming mob of children out through the curtains and clearing the booth for the next paying crowd. Case exits stage right, and the adventure moves on.

It was a tiny role, a bit of horse-trading that let EON Productions film inside Sarno's casino. But Sarno saw it as his big cinematic break. He ordered dozens of publicity stills of himself in costume and sent them out with a press release announcing his star turn.

Sarno even tried to improve his looks. He didn't seriously stick to a diet, but he did take to wearing, on formal occasions or when he especially wanted to impress someone, a toupee. It did make him look younger when he wore it, but he wasn't fooling anyone. It didn't help that he wore it haphazardly, so his employees and acquaintances didn't have time to buy the fiction that, after a quarter century, his scalp had decided to sprout hair again. But it didn't matter to Jay; when he was in the mood to have hair, he now had a full head of hair.

The line between reality and fantasy was becoming increasingly blurred.

For Sarno, one element of reality couldn't be ignored: his casino needed a hotel. Since it was losing money, he couldn't pay for it out of cash flow. No bank would lend him the money. And the Teamsters pension fund was no longer a sure thing. A few years earlier, he just had to call Hoffa or Dorfman and everything would be taken care of. Now there were new rings to kiss. Sarno had approached Nick Civella, reputed boss of the Kansas City mob, to ask for help in getting the loan.

Civella, whose influence within the Teamsters union was ill-defined but substantial nonetheless, terrified Sarno. "I think I'm going to be killed when I go meet with him," he told Stan Mallin. "You need to come along with me."

"For protection?" Mallin asked cautiously. He had heard the rumors of things Civella had done.

"No, it'll give me legitimacy. He wouldn't dare do anything in front of a witness."

Against his better judgment, Mallin accompanied him to the meeting. They both returned.

As a result of meetings like that one, in March of 1971 the Teamsters gave him a $7.6 million loan and work started. Designed by architect Lee Linton, the fifteen-story, 414-room tower rose directly behind the big top casino. The expansion included a Japanese style spa, a clown-shaped Olympic-sized swimming pool, a new coffee shop, and an expanded showroom.

Building the hotel was triply important to Sarno. It would revitalize Circus Circus. It would make him a bona-fide hotel man again. It would also give him a home. As his relations with Joyce deteriorated, he was spending most of his time in a suite at Caesars Palace. With a suite in his own casino, Sarno would be living in a beautiful bubble: he would rise when it suited him, make some phone calls from his office downstairs, then head over to the Las Vegas Country Club. After that it would be dinner, some gambling, and back to Circus with whatever conquest he had picked up along the way. Having the tower finished wouldn't just improve his balance sheet. It would make his life just about perfect.

In getting the Teamster loans that kept Circus open and then paid for the tower, Sarno had become intimate with an entirely new circle. Although Hoffa might have contended with mobsters in his rise to Teamster power, Sarno had no direct dealing with that wing of the underworld. Sure, he frequented the bookies and sportsmen of Atlanta and Miami Beach, but they were just, like him, businessmen who weren't too choosy about their partners and financing.

With Civella—and others—getting their muzzles into the henhouse, Circus Circus became one of the most notorious mob haunts on the Strip, with suitcases of cash dispatched back to Kansas City and Chicago under the watchful eye of Carl Thomas, a Civella associate. Sarno found himself trapped in a vicious cycle: he would borrow Teamster money, which would give guys like Civella more power to skim from the casino; the casino would lose more money, which would lead to an even bigger loan; which led to more skimming.

One sign of gambling addiction is chasing losses. A man bets $25 on a college football game on Saturday and loses; so he bets $50 on Sunday, hoping to break even; after he loses that bet, he goes in for $100 on the Monday night game. Before long, he's placing bets not to win, but just to get back above ground. Needless to say, those who chase their losses just dig themselves further and further into debt.

Sarno was repeating precisely this pattern of behavior with the mob guys who he now had to beg for loans.

It was about this time that Tony Spilotro first walked into Circus Circus. Thanks to his fictionalization as Nicky Santoro, played with hyperactive menace by Joe Pesci in Martin Scorsese's *Casino*, Spilotro is a household name. Having established himself as an enthusiastic law-breaker by the time he dropped out of high school, Spilotro quickly became a force to be reckoned with in the Chicago underworld. By the time Sarno had opened Caesars Palace, Spilotro already had to his credit a string of gruesome murders, some of which involved brutal torture.

About the time that Sarno got the loan for the Circus tower, Spilotro moved to Las Vegas to oversee the Chicago mob's substantial cut of the skim in that town.

Spilotro chose Sarno's casino for his base. On paper, he was granted the concession to operate a gift shop. In reality, he didn't spend his time ordering snow globes: he was watching the flow of money and, increasingly, establishing himself as the most feared man in Las Vegas. Like others, he came out for a fresh start, but his reputation preceded him. Those who knew what was good for them gave Spilotro a wide berth.

Sarno had no illusions. "Mr. Spiltro's such a nice man," his youngest daughter Heidi once remarked after running into the always-gracious Spilotro at Circus.

"No, he isn't," was all Sarno could say. If even a tenth of what he had heard about Spilotro was true, it made him sick to think that a man like that was even in the same city as his children.

Thanks to his connections Sarno was more powerful, but his life had an extra sliver of danger. For a gambler like Sarno, that wasn't necessarily a negative; every day brought the added chance that someone might take a shot at him. And though the thought of being murdered filled him with terror, there was a certain pleasure in the uncertainty that fear conjured up.

In the end, Sarno convinced himself the compromises might have been worth it. When the hotel finally opened in July 1972,

Sarno was ecstatic. He had done the impossible: held on to Circus Circus and added a hotel. So he allowed himself a little present. In the plans for the expansion, Sarno built himself the ultimate middle-aged semi-bachelor pad in suite 1410, taking up the center slice of Circus' top two stories.

His eldest son Jay later joked that the suite looked like it was designed by a hooker on acid. A masterpiece of red, gold, and magenta, the main room was dominated by a giant curving staircase—lifted from the Fontainebleau lobby—and oversized bookcases with hundreds of serious-looking leather-bound volumes. A sliding ladder was needed to get to them. They made Sarno appear a man of letters.

If anyone had bothered to actually climb the ladder, they'd have seen a full run of United States Department of Agriculture reports from the 1930s, Wisconsin highway planning tomes, and not much else. Sarno had bought them by the yard from a supply house and had never cracked a cover.

So much for Sarno the scholar. But he wasn't applying for a MacArthur foundation grant; he was trying to impress the Vegas gentry. He largely succeeded.

"That Sarno—bright guy, very studious" some of his visitors said; any man who'd surround himself with such learning had depths they could only guess at.

One night, Sarno threw a party. As usual, he was running late. His son Jay, now in high school, found himself roped into serving drinks.

Then his father made his grand entrance in a three-piece suit, toupee firmly in place (this was an occasion, after all). He made a production out of removing a pocket watch from his vest, flashing it for all to see, and checking the time.

One of the bottle blondes in attendance turned to young Jay and said, "Your father is just so elegant." She was completely sincere. To the teen, who'd been living with his father's "elegance" all his life, this was the most garish, phony, gaudy, absurd thing in the world.

So, emulating his father, he half-closed his eyes and turned his head up in a pose of royal indifference and said, "Yes, ma'am, we come from a long line of distinguished Polish peasants."

Later that night, Jay told his dad the story. His father was furious. Though he constantly bragged that he was a self-made man, Sarno hated the idea that anyone would find out just how humble his origins were. He wanted nothing of the stench of the St. Joseph packinghouse district ruining his luxury suite, let alone the ghosts of Szczuczyn.

Sarno had come to Las Vegas to reinvent himself. With the right clothes, the right apartment, and the right guests, he could pretend to be the man he wanted to be. Any intrusion on that fantasy was unwelcome.

A few months later, feeling a little low, Jay Sarno decided to call a friend he hadn't heard from in a while. Allen "Ace" Greenberg had been one of his ZBT brothers back in college who had gone on to a successful career on Wall Street.

"I'm having some problems," Sarno started. Greenberg settled in: this could be anything from money troubles to a mob hitman. "Joyce and I are fussing."

"Hmm." Thank God I don't have to listen to him kvetching about his problems getting a loan for the hotel, Greenberg thought. "What's the problem?"

"She doesn't like me screwing young girls."

There really wasn't too much Greenberg could say, but Sarno wanted to talk, not listen, anyway.

Sarno's marital problems started with his own infidelities. He had long stopped sneaking his dalliances like fudge brownies hidden in his desk drawer; having gotten away with so much over the past fifteen years, he now dropped any pretense of taking his marriage vows seriously. But he was still a doting father and still wanted Joyce for those occasions when a wife was required.

"Why are you getting mad?" Sarno would ask when she protested, "I buy you a Rolls Royce. I only buy them convertibles." He meant it, too. Intimacy was something you paid for; one or two nights was worth a necklace or a few bills peeled from the wad he always kept in his pocket; a week or two merited a fur coat; anything longer term meant Sarno calling the Ford dealership.

While Sarno spent his days presiding over Circus and his nights chasing skirts. Joyce spent her days running the house and her nights crying in the living room after the kids had gone to sleep, usually chasing her sorrows with a drink or two.

In the early years of her marriage, Joyce's only sounding board was her mother, who answered all talk of unhappiness with three themes: *doesn't he provide for you?*, *where will you go?*, and *but think of the children.* Without much resolve of her own, Joyce grew to accept her lot as the best of a bad situation which, when you really thought about it, wasn't that bad at all, really.

But as Joyce gained a broader circle of friends in Las Vegas, she began to see a different picture. Some of them were content to be part of the beautiful wife/beautiful kids/beautiful mistress circle. Others weren't. Stan Mallin's wife, Virginia, finally convinced her that she didn't have to tolerate Jay. It wasn't the Fifties anymore, and she wasn't a 23-year-old in fear of spinsterhood. She had options.

For a man who spent nearly every night in the arms of other women, and whose soul-mate and real confidant was his long-time mistress, not his wife, Sarno didn't take Joyce's "That's it. I'm getting a divorce" very well. He flew into a rage, then decided that the best way to punish her was to subject her to the most soul-crushing thing that *he* had been subjected to: a rigorous investigation.

Just like the IRS, the FBI, and the Get Hoffa task force had done to him, Sarno had his wife followed, photographed, and wiretapped. Surely he would catch her doing something wrong, something he could use as leverage in divorce court.

Thousands of dollars and a few private investigators later, Sarno had nothing. They hadn't even caught Joyce running a yellow light, much less anything that would tilt scales weighted down with the considerable heft of Sarno's infidelities.

After making the proceedings as painful as possible, Sarno found himself a free man in 1973. Joyce kept the house on Brown Circle, while Sarno moved permanently into his Circus Circus suite. The kids, who stayed in the hotel with Sarno on the weekends, actually found the arrangement acceptable; in addition to enjoying full run of Circus on the weekends, their mother was happier during the week.

Finally liberated, Sarno hoped to tie the knot with Carol

Freeman, but she rebuffed him. If he would have divorced Joyce back when he moved to Las Vegas, she would have jumped at the chance to be with the man she loved. Now she was married to Jimmy Hassell, a singer with Kenny Rogers and the First Edition, and had a child of her own. She also knew enough of Sarno's extracurricular conquests to appreciate that Jay could never be faithful. Still, they played cards together most nights, and she remained his soulmate. Jay kept hoping that they'd make it official someday.

With Joyce now his ex-wife and Carol not making any demands, any restraint Sarno might have known fell away. Every woman he found marginally attractive got the full Sarno charm.

"What'll it take to make you happy?" he would ask. "A coat? A car? Make *me* happy and you'll never want for anything."

He got a few offended stares, a few polite demurrals, but he learned that, in Las Vegas, he could buy plenty of happiness—for the moment, at least.

THIRTEEN

Friends, Hustlers, and G-Men

With the hotel complete, Sarno emerged as a Las Vegas power broker. He became known among the city's strivers and second-tier hustlers as a man who could get things done, a man who could put you in touch with the people who really mattered in Las Vegas.

Now that he had a place to properly entertain them, Sarno enjoyed having real friends over, too. For him, that meant, mostly, two men: Evel Knievel and Allen Dorfman—at least after Dorfman served a one-year prison term for wire fraud and conspiracy. Sarno had gotten closer to Knievel as life dealt them both a few bum hands. Sarno had temporarily lost his casino, and Knievel's dream of jumping the Grand Canyon kept slipping out of reach. When Knievel was in town, Sarno put him up in a huge upstairs wing of his suite. Sarno or Mel Larson, vice president of marketing for Circus Circus, got Knievel anything he wanted, including show tickets for his kids.

But the perks meant nothing to Knievel; he would have stayed with Jay no matter what. It was having someone he could look in the eye as an equal that brought him back to Jay and Las Vegas. Surrounded by genuine admirers, sycophants, and users, Knievel, like Sarno, had few straightforward relationships in his life. As life got increasingly turbulent for both men they found some refuge in each other's company.

Sarno's friendship with Dorfman grew in the early 1970s. He owed Dorfman everything: without Dorfman's intercession, he never would have gotten his foot in the door to get the Teamster loans that had helped him keep Circus open. But it was also nice to spend time with a guy who liked the good life and didn't mind swimming with the sharks.

For about ten years Sarno and Dorfman—with their families—spent their winter vacations together at the Jack O'Lantern Lodge, an Eagle River, Wisconsin, resort that Dorfman had bought as a fantastic winter home in which he could entertain his closest four dozen friends over the holidays.

As with everything, Sarno didn't vacation in a small way. Christmas with the Dorfmans meant moving Joyce, Jay, four kids, Joyce's mom, a babysitter, a few essential assistants, and any hangers-on from the casino who wanted a free trip to Wisconsin. Bellmen from Circus Circus hustled trunks of winter gear and suitcases into station wagons; Sarno's driver ferried the immediate family to the airport in the middle of a baggage convoy.

The kids especially looked forward to the resort's fleet of snowmobiles. Through an arrangement with Dorfman, the Arctic Cat company based its snowmobiling team at the lodge. His guests were free to take the team's massively souped-up racing models out to a frozen lake for speed tests or go screaming through the trees and down hills.

Sarno staged a "Dorfman Winter Olympics," with families organized into teams, competing at snowmobiling, skee ball, table tennis, gin rummy, and a host of other indoor and outdoor games. He organized the fun, seeding the teams and presenting trophies; as in the casino and in life, there were winners and losers—and you could get action picking the former. He even had a craps table flown in so the guys could shoot dice at night.

Vacationing from his Las Vegas casino, Sarno brought a casino with him, including Evelyn, who continued to balance him.

On one trip to Eagle River, though, Evelyn finally reached her breaking point.

"You're so lucky, to get to go on a paid vacation like that," one of the other secretaries told her. "I've seen the pictures. Everyone has so much fun."

"Oh, Mr. Sarno makes sure we all have a good time," she said, "but I'm a southern girl. I can't stand it being so cold. And anytime you go outside you have to get all dressed up in those clothes. What's the point? You ride on the snowmobile for about three minutes and that's about all you can take before you have to go back inside to warm up."

"But you can just relax, sit by the fire."

"No, I've got to be up before everyone else to make sure everything is ready. I'm still working when I'm up there. I'm on call 24 hours a day, like a nurse. It's no vacation."

After that trip, Evelyn thanked her boss profusely, then informed him that she wouldn't be going back the next year. He offered her any snowmobile she wanted, and was mystified when she still refused.

The next year, she pulled young Jay aside before the family left for the airport.

"I'm going to give you the tickets," she said, "because if I give them to your father, he'll lose them." She handed him the thick stack and waved goodbye as the caravan departed.

"Who's got the tickets?" his dad yelled, long after they'd arrived at the airport.

"I do," Jay replied.

"Good, check in," Sarno told his pre-teen son, "We're going to the coffee shop." He handed Jay a twenty-dollar bill to tip the red cap and drifted off for a quick nosh. With some amusement, the ground crew checked the mounds of luggage under the supervision of a lone child. At the gate, he got to pick his families' seats, and he took the opportunity to puckishly give September a seat far away from everyone else. Young Jay then strolled back to the coffee shop and told his father everything was taken care of.

"Where do we go?" he asked.

"Gate 22," Jay answered.

"Where's that?" asked his father.

"That way."

"Follow Jay, everyone," Sarno shouted, and the whole entourage trudged after their pint-sized guide. In his own way, he was teaching his son responsibility.

S arno remained close to Jimmy Hoffa as well. After Hoffa's release from prison in 1971, Sarno visited him regularly, although he often had to use discretion. As Sarno's own problems with the federal government mounted, he couldn't be seen publicly with his old friend. Under the pretext of taking his son on a fishing vacation, he headed to Hoffa's Michigan home.

Once, when Hoffa visited Sarno in Las Vegas, he saw young Jay outside experimenting with his model rockets.

"What are you doing there?" he asked. "Are you sure that stuff is legal?" Hoffa, of course, was no stranger to incendiaries; on his say-so, more than a few had been detonated in a recalcitrant trucker's lot.

"Yes," Jay answered, matter-of-factly explaining the permissible payloads and thrust allowed under U.S. rocketry codes.

"Good, kid," Hoffa responded. "You don't want to go to jail."

Hoffa knew what he was talking about. But he should have been warning Jay's father, who made the most of his new connections with the city's underworld. He started each day in mid-morning with a lavish breakfast prepared by his private chef; those who had favors to ask or scuttlebutt to share were free to visit him as he dined; they could ask for anything they liked, from Eggs Benedict to Belgian waffles. And, if they needed help getting a business proposal into a casino—say, a concession to sell movie tickets or rent cars—he could put them in touch with the right guys—guys who could make sure no one else tried to muscle in on their territory.

Sarno chose some of the best of them as partners; instead of just making introductions, he would actually help finance their start-up. With Circus still not showing a profit and Joyce scooping up most of his official income in alimony, he tried to diversify as much as he could. Ten grand a week here from one partnership, twenty grand there…it got him a few more minutes at the crap table, at least.

Despite his financial reverses, Sarno was gambling more than ever. Benny Binion's Horseshoe, which had just hosted the first World Series of Poker, was his favorite place to play because Binion, whose motto was "the sky's the limit," would take any bet, no matter how large. Sarno lost most of them. One night, he reportedly brought half-a-million dollars in a shopping bag and blew it all.

S arno didn't just gamble at the craps tables. Despite serious health problems, he remained a devout golfer, one who remained so true to the sport because of the incredible opportunities it afforded for gambling. It was his passion.

"I hear you're a good golfer," a new acquaintance once volunteered.

"I'm not a golfer, I'm a fucking nut," Sarno responded. "Last week I lost forty fucking thousand to Puggy Pearson in Pebble Beach." Pearson, best known today as the winner of the 1973 World Series of Poker, was one of the clique of hustlers who agreed on one thing: as long as Jay Sarno was around, none of them had to get a real job.

Sarno needed his golf fix nearly every day. Usually, it was a foursome at the Las Vegas Country Club, which is still one of the favored hangouts of the Las Vegas establishment. Betting thirty thousand dollars a game (the equivalent of more than $160,000 today) was middle-stakes action. Losing forty thousand dollars to Puggy Pearson was memorable, but mostly because of the setting, not the money.

They bet on everything: the entire game; each hole; who scored the longest drive on each hole; who got closest to the pin. Often, they took along a hanger-on—who the winner would generously tip—to keep track of the action. Once they were done playing, more money changed hands over gin rummy in the clubhouse.

It was the thrill of the contest, not knowing whether he would win or lose, that drove Sarno, not a love for the game itself, even though he was a fine player. His partners, however, saw to it that whether he won or lost wasn't usually left to chance.

With his eyesight failing thanks to unchecked diabetes exacerbated by his diet, Sarno rarely knew exactly where his ball or those of his partners landed. Jimmy Chagra, one of the most notorious characters in Las Vegas in those years, reportedly only won when he played Sarno. He wasn't the only one to take advantage. Whichever "friend" had volunteered to caddy for him might kick his ball into a pond. Another supposed best friend, an always-smiling, instantly likable guy, usually played on his side. More often than not, his friend would have an off day and Sarno's heroics couldn't give them the victory. While Sarno was at the snack bar having a post-game nosh, money quietly changed hands.

Sarno knew what was going on but was so desperate for the companionship and the action that he let it continue. He also internalized his losing: it wasn't him, it wasn't his friends—it was the clubs. In a typical week, he might get three new sets of clubs, and, finding that they didn't help things much, give two away. He would have been better off trading out his friends, but where else would he get that kind of action? No honest man would bet tens of thousands of dollars against him.

But the friends stayed and the clubs went. "I've given away more golf clubs than anybody in the country," he bragged.

In fact, at times it was the clubs: his friends sometimes found ways to alter their loft or the lie, completely changing the shot. It might seem like overkill for guys who could also spot the ball at will, but beating Jay Sarno at golf was their livelihood.

Despite this turnover, he still accumulated enough golf gear to fill a specially-designed oversized closet (dubbed "the pro shop," it was about half the size of his office). And, just like he couldn't quite decide between his wife, his mistress, or the latest girl of the week, he found it impossible to select the USGA-sanctioned fourteen clubs for a game. So, it was decided that, for his game, the limit would be waived. He saw a bag the size of a trash can at Las Vegas Golf that displayed the latest set of drivers that had been marked down and appropriated it as his own bag. For such a good customer, the manager was only too happy to oblige. Stuffed with dozens of clubs, it was unmistakably Sarno.

One hot summer day, Dorfman and Sarno took their sons boating down the Colorado River, ending up in Page, Arizona, where Dorfman's Gulfstream awaited. Then they ran into some trouble: the pilot informed Dorfman that they would have to wait until nightfall to take off—at such high temperatures, it was unsafe to fly. They'd either have to reduce weight by a few hundred pounds or sit and wait.

"That's completely unacceptable," Dorfman responded after conferring with Sarno. "We've got a tee time in Las Vegas this afternoon."

The pilot refused to budge, and Sarno volunteered to leave the kids at the double-wide trailer airport in Page. Once he and Dorfman were playing golf, the pilot could return for them. It sounded like a fine way to get the weight down.

"Don't leave us here! Are you crazy? You can't leave us!" the kids clamored. But Sarno wouldn't give up his golf game. He finally wheedled the pilot into admitting that, with permission from the tower, they could execute a special performance takeoff that would probably get them into the air.

To young Jay, this sounded like fun; he and the Dorfman boys, their mothers nowhere to disapprove, agreed, without any regard for or real understanding of the danger. Sarno and Dorfman just wanted to make their tee time. The pilot had been slipped a few hundred dollars. It was worth risking all their lives not to miss a golf game.

"It's going to be a little wild," the pilot warned before taxiing past the end of the runway into a graded overrun area. Five hundred feet into the desert, with the plane bumping along in the dirt, he did a 180-degree turn. Facing the runway, the pilot locked the brakes and ran the engines up to full power.

The plane shook like crazy. Dorfman smiled and slightly tightened his grip on his arm-rest. Sarno was thinking about the par three fifth hole. The boys were squealing with delight; this was like an Apollo moon rocket. Suddenly the pilot popped the brakes and everyone was thrown back in their seats.

The plane screamed through the sagebrush and onto the tarmac. The runway got shorter and shorter, with Lake Powell looming closer and closer. Just as the wheels lifted off, they were over the lake and gaining altitude.

The adults made their tee time and young Jay got a fun story to tell.

"Mom, it was great," he gushed. "We got to do a special performance takeoff in the Gulfstream." He didn't omit a single rattle or vibration as he described the wild ride.

"What has your father gotten you into now?" was his mother's response. "I can't believe that man would do that. How ridiculously irresponsible."

Even when Sarno tried to show responsibility, he did so recklessly, taking on risks that other casino owners shunned. They preferred a sure thing; he loved playing with fire.

On June 5, 1973, Circus Circus and nineteen other Las Vegas casinos received letters demanding $100,000 in cash. The anonymous extortionists had a simple demand: if each casino did not contribute their share to a $2 million payoff, they would destroy seven unspecified casinos by electrically-timed bombs that had already been programmed to explode.

Extortion by bomb had been an occupational hazard of running a casino since the days of Monte Carlo. Nearly all threats were made by cranks looking for easy money, but you could never be sure: there was always the chance that they were deadly serious. In fact, seven years later, a bomb planted by a former gambler angry over his losses exploded in Harvey's Wagon Wheel casino in Lake Tahoe, taking a huge chunk out of the hotel tower.

The letter worried Sarno, who dealt with a lot of cranks and usually didn't get flustered.

"This seems to be better organized than anything we've seen before," Sarno told the papers. Yet he wanted to get involved. Most of the other owners were content to forward the letters to the FBI, quietly search for any suspicious packages, and increase their security patrols. But Sarno agreed to serve as liaison between all the casinos and the FBI. Following the instructions in the letters he began negotiating with the extortionists. It was a quick negotiation: he asked them where they wanted to pick up the money, and they told him.

Sarno first "sent" two FBI agents disguised as Circus Circus security guards to Hoover Dam to deliver the ransom money. The extortionists became suspicious of other vehicles in the vicinity and refused the pickup. They then set a rendezvous at Davis Dam, about forty-five miles south of Hoover Dam, but got skittish again. Fearing that Jay might be asked to deliver the money personally, the FBI insisted that he undergo a crash course in firearms training.

Then the plotters called with a third drop, asking that his security guards go to a Los Angeles motel and await further instructions. After waiting a day and a half, the "guards" received a phone call telling them to charter a helicopter and fly to a spot in the San Gabriel Mountains, where they were to leave the money in a waiting car and leave. Instead of leaving, though, the agents hid themselves in the vehicle. At the appointed time the extortionists drove up, rammed the parked car, and tried to grab the money inside. The agents emerged, guns drawn, and took the would-be bombers into custody.

The masterminds turned out to be Ray and Kristina Sterrett, a married couple in their forties with one child, who ran a trailer court in Sidney, Nebraska. Their Las Vegas adventure earned them an indictment on extortion charges that carried a twenty-year prison sentence. They hadn't planted a single bomb.

When the FBI announced the arrests Sarno enjoyed a hero's welcome in Las Vegas. "Sarno Helps Bust Casino Bomb Plot," the *Review-Journal* trumpeted. Sarno even lavished praise on the FBI, noting their meticulous attention to detail: "They even went so far as to pick out agents that looked like our own security guards." In light of his past brushes with the Justice Department, this was gracious indeed.

Sarno thought he had friends in the FBI, but he had powerful enemies in an organization that was even more important to Las Vegas in the early 1970s: the Teamsters Union. Since coming out as a Jimmy Hoffa loyalist, Sarno had earned the hatred of Frank Fitzsimmons, Hoffa's putative seat holder. Hoffa had hand-picked Fitzsimmons to run the union during his "holiday" at Allenwood Federal Correction Facility on the basis of his loyalty: since their days together in the Detroit local, Fitzsimmons had been a gofer for the ferocious Hoffa, always happy to grab the coffee or run an errand. He was lightly regarded by the rest of the union leadership, who Hoffa did not trust to mind the house while he was away. But once ensconced in the president's office at the Teamsters' palatial Washington headquarters, Fitzsimmons came into his own. All those who wished to remain in the new president's good graces had to pay fealty to him and disown the jailed Hoffa.

Allen Dorfman retained his control of the Central States Pension Fund and was sufficiently respected (or feared) to be grudgingly accepted by the new order. Jay Sarno was not so lucky. Fitzsimmons let it slip, while golfing at La Costa with a party that included Dorfman, that he thought Sarno was a "thief" who had tremendous chutzpah to ask the union for another loan to build a second hotel tower. Personally, he despised Sarno and wanted nothing more than to see him run out of Circus Circus, which was already eating up $17 million in Teamster funds.

Dorfman immediately reported Fitzsimmons' remarks at La Costa to Sarno. Sarno knew that he rubbed people the wrong way, but this was much more serious than another casino owner not wanting him at his table at a charity gala. So Fitzsimmons was on his mind early in the afternoon of October 16, 1973, when he got a phone call from William H. Miller, owner of the Thoroughbred Lounge, a Strip sports book, and promoter of the Wednesday night fights at Circus Circus. Miller told Jay he had gotten a call from his son, Tim Miller, who told him to immediately call a telephone number in Phoenix. The elder Miller did so, and a man identifying himself as Larry May answered. After introducing himself, he said that he wanted to "do Jay Sarno a favor." A man known to him as Joe Moretti, May said, had offered him a contract to kill Jay Sarno. May said that he declined the offer, but learned that another man, "Big Ben" Harrison, had accepted $5,000 for the contract. He had come to town and was to murder Sarno as the hotel man left Circus Circus.

Sarno didn't know anyone named Joe Moretti, and though he was sure that plenty of people would like to see him dead, Frank Fitzsimmons was the only one, he thought, who was worth mentioning. His chief of security Harry McBride assigned a security guard to remain with him around the clock and notified the Las Vegas Metropolitan Police Department. Having established what he thought was a rapport with the Las Vegas field office of the FBI during the bomb plot saga, Sarno contacted his "friends" in the Bureau as well. He advised the agents of the alleged threat to his life, and they duly opened a file on the matter.

At their first meeting in his offices, Sarno told agents that he had never heard of anyone connected with the contract. But the next day, he changed his story. He now remembered that May had been a guest at Circus Circus about a month earlier, introducing himself to Sarno as a just-released ex-convict who was "down on his luck." Sarno said he had felt sorry for May and gave him $50, as well as one night's room and board at Circus Circus. But May needed more than free lodging to brighten his mood: he ran up a forty-two dollar bar tab that, Sarno said, "was not part of the deal." The hotel sent a bill to the Missouri address May had given on his registration sheet which was returned as undeliverable. Sarno produced copies of the paperwork in question. He now told agents that he wasn't sure whether the threat on his life was legitimate or not, but he was positive that if anyone wanted him dead, it was Fitzsimmons.

Undecided as to whether the case was now a potential contract murder or an attempt by May to extort money from Sarno, agents continued to investigate, now with a closer eye on May himself. They learned that Harrison was, indeed, known to the Phoenix police, but could not find him in Las Vegas. Two weeks later, they discussed the facts of the case with Assistant United States Attorney Lawrence Semenza, who advised them that there was no clear-cut violation of the extortion statute there. The case was closed.

Sarno never figured out whether the threat was legitimate. He was used to creating fantasies; now, he couldn't tell what was real and what was fiction.

A few months after the reported contract on his life, Jay Sarno's FBI jacket boasted five files. One was devoted to the Larry May affair. Another detailed an attempted kidnapping. Sarno himself was the subject of three additional investigations, each of which stemmed from his association with Hoffa. A memo filed in January 1974 also noted ominously that Sarno was "currently under investigation by the IRS."

This was not a new development: in 1971, the Internal Revenue Service had opened a virtual branch office in the bowels of Circus Circus so that they could audit the hotel without having to schlep papers to their Downtown offices. Once settled in, they showed no signs of leaving. The FBI had been dogging Sarno since he moved to Las Vegas, their accommodating treatment in the bomb plot notwithstanding. But when Sarno proved too slippery for any criminal indictments, the IRS took point on the government's investigations. Tax agents and investigators became as familiar to Sarno as his barber or favorite waiter.

"I don't know quite when I became under audit," Sarno said after a few years, "but it seems like a way of life."

The IRS had been running a more or less continuous audit of Circus Circus since its opening in 1968. This was one of the penalties, Sarno learned, of borrowing money from a man that Robert F. Kennedy had pledged to put in jail. It didn't matter that Kennedy was no longer Attorney General or, indeed, that he had been assassinated before Circus has opened. Once engaged, the gears of government continued to grind.

The agents didn't have much to work with—their ongoing audit turned up nothing felonious after years of investigation—but their bosses were convinced that Sarno was undoubtedly a front for hoodlum interests. So the inquiry continued to swell: at one point, the IRS insisted on copies of all paperwork to verify the status of the casino's assets, from $9.00 items to $100,000 ones.

The investigation of Jay Sarno became a continent-spanning cottage industry for federal attorneys, investigators, and agents. In the early 1970s Sarno's nephew Larry Corash, who'd offered his opinion on Caesars' tackiness to his uncle nearly a decade before, was married and living in Washington D.C. He had finished his training as a doctor and his wife Michelle, an attorney, had been hired as general counsel in the Department of Energy. One night, Michelle and Larry attended a party where everyone chatted about where they worked and what they were doing. A gentleman from the Justice Department stole the show.

"I'm working on this fascinating investigation of this guy in Las Vegas, Jay Sarno," he declared, then gave as detailed a summary of the case as prudence would allow. Since it involved Las Vegas, the Teamsters, and intricate intelligence work, he had the floor for a few minutes.

"Oh, that's very interesting," Larry replied when he finished. The next day, he called his father, who had been investing in Sarno projects at his wife Sara's insistence since the Cabana days.

"What do you know about this?" he asked after he told the story.

"Actually, I know quite a lot about that," his father replied. He had gotten a few friendly inquiries from the Justice Department about his investments with Sarno and had decided to unwind his involvement with his brother-in-law. "I just think there are too many issues there," he concluded.

Sarno felt he could talk his way out of almost anything, but he didn't want to play games with the IRS. When his nephew called him with news of the party conversation, he already had a plan.

"This is serious business," he told Corash. "You need old guard people—white shoe, waspy people—to handle this."

So he hired Harris Kerr Forster, a venerable New York-based accounting firm, to oversee the books, and White and Case, a well-established law firm, to deal with any possible legal issues relating to his personal and business tax liabilities.

The first real skirmish came in June 1972, when a Mr. Arnold, a Las Vegas IRS agent, presented Sarno with a demand for $1 million in withholding taxes, payable immediately. Circus Circus had enjoyed a gentleman's agreement with the previous agent in charge of collections under which the casino paid its withholding taxes after "a little lag." Now, Arnold threatened to close the casino if Sarno didn't come up with the money immediately. Sarno frantically tracked down Teamster officials who were vacationing in Las Vegas and, with their signatures, got Arnold to give him 45 days to come up with the money. Jud McIntosh was able to lend him $300,000. Another $700,000 from Parry Thomas's Valley Bank helped him stave off disaster. While he was assembling the loans, Arnold's superiors over-ruled his decision to close the casino, but Sarno was more convinced than ever that he was the target of a vendetta.

In January of 1973, the audit entered a more intense stage with the arrival of criminal tax investigators. While the agents apparently had carte blanche to investigate anything they felt didn't look right, several issues presented themselves as likely red flags. Sarno's biggest problem was $600,000 in business partnership losses that he and Mallin had claimed on their personal federal income tax returns over several years. Though the IRS had, at the time, allowed the claims and therefore given him back more than a half-million dollars, it was now investigating the possibility of fraud. At the very least, the tax officials were mulling the possibility of another civil adjustment, in effect forcing Sarno to pay back every allowance he had claimed over the past few years.

Additionally, Sarno had claimed $1.8 million in gambling losses on his 1970 return. Though that's actually a conservative figure for the amount Sarno might have lost that year (it pencils out to less than $5,000 a day), the Audit Division was challenging the deduction; again, this would force, at the least, a civil adjustment. Since Sarno didn't have nearly enough money to satisfy these debts, he dreaded such a judgment.

Complicating Sarno's trouble was a nearly $500,000 refund he was requesting for his personal 1969 tax return; he was told that, if he correctly filed a series of carryback forms, he could get the money returned to him. Stanley Mallin had applied, separately, for a $100,000 refund. While both were sure these were legitimate claims, the IRS wasn't going to take their word for it, and verifying them took time. But the pair needed the money as quickly as possible: should the IRS disallow their business losses for 1968 to 1971, they'd use the proceeds to pay these off. If not, they'd be able to at last satisfy some of their creditors.

Conditions were dire at the casino. It seemed incapable of operating in the black. IRS agents expected a skim, but could not turn up any solid evidence to confirm it, so officially it remained a case of a small business struggling through tough times. It wasn't through lack of trying. Many department heads voluntarily took pay cuts; Sarno and Mallin worked without salary for a few months, and even the union leaders agreed to pay reductions, though things never came to that. All the while, the envelopes going back to Chicago and Kansas City only got fatter.

As it became increasingly obvious that Sarno couldn't turn things around on his own, he contemplated selling Circus Circus, but he owed far more on it than it was worth. The gas crisis had wreaked havoc with the casino business, and the bump in business he had been expecting from the hotel just didn't happen.

Unable to sell, he considered leasing to a pair of entrepreneurs, Bill Bennett and Bill Pennington, both of whom had come to the casino industry relatively late. Bennett, born in 1924, had built up a chain of Arizona furniture stores before selling them in 1962. He invested his millions in a financial services company that went bankrupt, leaving him penniless. The natural-born salesman and manager found himself looking for a new career. He was in luck. In 1965, the Del Webb company was expanding its casino operations. The sunbelt developer already owned the Sahara and Mint casinos in Las Vegas, and was in the forefront of the transition in casino ownership. Under the old system, dozens of owners had free rein in the count room, skimming off casino income for their underworld sponsors or personal gain. In his casinos, Webb bought out all the other owners and instituted strict cash control procedures. This new corporate order meant a stronger bottom line.

In accord with its new management philosophy, the company's president L. C. Jacobsen looked to hire men who had not previously worked in gambling to run the Del Webb casinos. This seems counter-intuitive, but Jacobsen believed that good businessmen could learn the specifics of the casino trade, while those who now ran the hotels and had risen through the ranks as dealers had no idea of how to properly run a major business. Jacobsen hired Bennett as a night-shift casino host at the Sahara Tahoe, a newly-opened Webb casino on the South Shore of Lake Tahoe. In his new position, the former millionaire was charged with catering to the needs of casino customers: making dinner reservations, arranging transportation, and whatever else a guest might request in between hands of blackjack. Bennett concentrated on learning how the other departments worked, and he was soon made night general manager before being transferred to the Mint, where he took over as sole general manager. The casino, which had lost $4.5 million the year before, soon became a money-maker, and after Bennett had raised the Mint's annual profit to $19 million, Webb tabbed him to supervise both the Mint and the Sahara Tahoe.

Cashing out $5 million in stock options in 1971, Bennett teamed up with Bill Pennington, a former oil wildcatter who'd gone into the gambling machine business. His Raven Electronics company used an early random-number generator to simulate the game of keno on an electronic slot machine. After splitting with his partners in Raven, Pennington's new firm, Western Equities, offered electronic blackjack; in his sales rounds of Las Vegas, he met Bill Bennett, who assured him the real money was in owning a casino, not providing the machines.

After trying to purchase the Landmark and Four Queens casinos with no success, Bennett and Pennington formed a company, Circus Circus Enterprises, to lease that casino from Sarno and Mallin. Negotiations began in earnest in the fall of 1973 but stalled. Sarno just wasn't a motivated enough seller yet.

Within a few months, however, he would become more motivated than he could have imagined.

FOURTEEN

A Brutal Thing

Jay Sarno thought that he had the market cornered on problems. He and Stan Mallin had the weight of the world on their backs: a failing casino, run-ins with the IRS, and the workaday headaches of every casino boss.

But they weren't the only ones who dreaded getting up in the morning. A man they both knew better than they'd like, Leo Crutchfield, was also struggling. And through sheer pluck and determination, he managed to make his problems their problems.

Crutchfield had first met Stan Mallin in 1968, when he sold Mallin his house on Mohican Drive. Mallin had mentioned that he was partners in a casino that was about to open. Seeing his chance at the big time, he asked Mallin for a favor.

He was a salesman for his brother's Arrowhead Linen Services, a company that serviced several small motels on the Strip. They didn't have the connections to get in with the big boys, but they were eager to get ahead. Even though it didn't have rooms, the restaurants of Circus Circus would use their share of linen. Could Arrowhead bid on the contract?

Stan talked it over with Jay. They allowed Arrowhead to submit a bid. For Crutchfield, the chance to work with a guy like Sarno meant a foot in the door. Who knew what it could lead to? Arrowhead submitted the lowest bid and won the contract.

In addition to working for his brother, Crutchfield had his own operation, the Sudden Service rental car agency, which had its chief office at the tiny La Concha motel. Crutchfield nursed the tiny concern like a hatchling, just begging for it to grow and prosper. When Circus Circus opened its hotel tower in July 1972, Crutchfield secured the right to open a satellite office at the property.

He had visions of renting cars to high rollers, of finally getting ahead. In Las Vegas, a guy whose formal education hadn't gone past the eighth grade could, with a little hustle, make himself a big shot: it was a dream Crutchfield shared with many small-time operators. But he soon found reality was different. The casino's bell captains kept sending customers to his rivals, just to spite him. Mallin said there was nothing he could do. This wasn't the big time. It was frustrating to work so hard and still be so broke.

Sarno often deigned to receive him as a breakfast visitor; over bacon and eggs, he dressed him down for missing his rent payments. Occasionally he was nice enough, sharing a laugh with Crutchfield at someone else's expense, but Crutchfield knew he didn't amount to much in Sarno's eyes. One night, Sarno was walking through the casino with Allen Dorfman. Crutchfield approached, giddy at the thought of an introduction to the Pension Fund wizard. But Sarno brushed him off like he didn't know him, even though they'd had breakfast together that very morning.

It was a terrible thing, being a small-time guy in a big-time town.

But Crutchfield had more in common with the big boys than he suspected. Since June 1972, he had been under investigation by the Internal Revenue Service. In September, Crutchfield encountered Joe Turner, an Audit division agent. Turner announced that he had been charged with auditing Sudden Service's parent company, the Nevada Car Corporation. Crutchfield met the problem head-on. Instead of hiring a lawyer and accountant to iron out any difficulties, Crutchfield tried to buy Turner off. In a town like Vegas, everyone had a price. That's how the game was played.

And so the courtship began. First, Crutchfield offered Turner a $2,000 bribe to make the audit go away. Turner refused. At their next meeting Turner let it slip about how lonely he and his wife were, and how difficult the stigma of working for the IRS made meeting people in a new town; he also mentioned how pretty the girls were in Las Vegas. Crutchfield thought he understood perfectly what it would take to get Turner off his back.

They next met on March 1, 1973, in the coffee shop of the El Morocco, a small Strip motel. After breakfast, they went to Crutchfield's office at the La Concha to go through the books.

"Say, have you got a couple of minutes?" Crutchfield asked when they got to the office. "I've got someone I believe can help you straighten out this audit and clear up a few things."

Turner agreed. They drove to another motel and headed upstairs. Odd, thought Turner; he was expecting to be taken to an accountant's office.

They entered a motel room without knocking. Turner didn't see any financial records, though his eyes popped out at the young woman languishing on the bed wearing only lingerie.

"This is my friend Harry," Crutchfield told her. "He's got a really bad cold. Can you take care of it in about thirty minutes?"

He moved for the door, but Turner blocked his path. For a few minutes they all made small talk. When Crutchfield again tried to leave, Turner left with him.

"Gee, you sure know how to hurt a girl's feelings," Crutchfield complained as they walked down the stairs. "Look, do you want that in the room there? I want out of this audit."

Turner shook his head. Crutchfield upped the ante, tossing him the keys to the car they'd driven over in, a 1973 Lincoln Continental Mark IV.

"Don't worry about bringing it back," he said.

"I don't want it," Turner insisted. Crutchfield then added a boat to the offer; Turner had once talked about his love of fishing. But the IRS agent stood firm.

Crutchfield knew that you didn't get ahead in life by taking no for an answer. A guy like Jay Sarno, he had probably been turned down the first hundred times he had asked for a loan; it didn't stop *him*. The courtship of Agent Turner continued.

Two weeks later, when they met again, Turner broke down and intimated that he would be happy to take cash to help out his new friend. After some back and forth, they reached an agreement: in return for $1,500, Turner would dummy up documents that would reduce Crutchfield's corporate and personal tax liabilities for 1970 and 1971. Crutchfield knew he was right: success came to those who kept trying.

Turner also told Crutchfield about an IRS agent named Smith who headed the Circus Circus investigation. Agent Smith was drinking heavily, in the process of separating from his wife, running around with women, and desperate for cash. Maybe some of Crutchfield's friends, other powerful Vegas businessmen, needed help with their tax troubles, too?

Crutchfield quickly offered himself up as an intermediary between Turner, Smith, and several "hotel owners" who, he said, could use a friend at the IRS. He and Turner hashed out a deal in May 1973: if he could get Sarno and Mallin to pay a bribe of $35,000, he and Turner would each keep $5,000 and the rest would go to Smith.

This might be, Crutchfield suggested, the start of a beautiful friendship.

"All those guys fuck up their taxes," he told Turner. There should be plenty of opportunity for the two of them to solicit bribes. Today Circus Circus, tomorrow, the world.

But Sarno and Mallin wouldn't bite. Over the next few months, Crutchfield pestered them with increasing intensity, to no avail. Mallin and Sarno might have been opposed to bribing an agent of the United States government on principle; they might have mistrusted Crutchfield; or they might have smelled a rat.

Their instincts were correct. Robert Ray Smith was, in fact, a longtime employee of the Intelligence Division of the Internal Revenue Service. This division, which was administratively independent of local agency offices, was empowered to investigate special cases of fraud. In March, just as Turner and Crutchfield struck their deal, Smith had been assigned to investigate Circus Circus for both civil and criminal violations of the tax code.

So Sarno and Mallin were right to say no to Crutchfield. This only made him even more insistent. One day, he called Mallin and said again that his IRS friends could put all of their tax problems behind them with a flick of the pen. Mallin immediately called Sarno.

"What did you tell him?" Sarno asked.

"I told him to get lost, and don't butt into our business," Mallin replied. "I gave him a warning: You'd better stay away. You're going to get in trouble."

"I'm glad you told him that," Sarno responded. "This can get anybody in trouble if you're not careful."

Meanwhile, Agent Smith was getting frustrated. He spent his days only fifty feet away from Sarno and Mallin in the IRS's Circus Circus field office, but they had not approached him.

"I work around them all the time," he complained to Crutchfield, "and they act like they don't even know I'm there." Crutchfield, he demanded, had to produce.

So he continued to call, still getting nowhere. Finally, he confronted Sarno directly, begging him to meet with Smith.

"Get lost," Sarno responded. "I don't like that talk."

By September, Crutchfield was desperate. So were Sarno and Mallin. They were still waiting for Sarno's refund; indeed, the survival of their business had come to depend on that half-a-million dollar bonanza. Their accountants had been through everything and assured them that there was no evidence of any criminal wrong-doing in their books. "You're one hundred percent OK," they told Sarno. But then Clarke Bingham, a partner at Harris Kerr Forster, changed his tune.

"You guys aren't going to get any refund," he told Sarno early in September. "They've got you flagged, whatever that means."

"Don't they have to?" Sarno asked, convinced he deserved the rebate.

"Just forget it," was Bingham's considered professional opinion.

So when Crutchfield made another call to Sarno on the night of the 26th, the hotel man was finally willing to listen; he had exhausted every other possibility.

"Please don't hang up," Crutchfield begged. Sarno stayed on the line. "I'm calling as a friend.

"Smith came to see me today, and I'm telling you, he's going to bury your ass. He's a criminal investigator, and you're in plenty of trouble. Jay, I'm your friend, I'm telling you, meet with this guy. You'd better meet with him. Do me a favor, just meet with him, just listen to what he's got to say, that's all. You don't have to do anything."

"All right, Leo, I'll check with Stan, and I'll let you know," Sarno responded, a bit more courteously than usual.

Sarno called Mallin.

"I've never heard him so hysterical before," he told Mallin. They agreed that perhaps they should agree to meet with this Agent Smith. It couldn't hurt.

Crutchfield suggested that they meet with Smith in the Circus Circus steam room. That way, no one could wear a recording device. He had dimly remembered movies where, when police agents met with suspects, they wore wires, so he knew what to look for. He thought. He had already conducted grossly inept pat-downs of Turner and Smith in his early meetings with them to assure himself that they weren't wearing wires. They were, and those conversations were later used as evidence against Crutchfield in court.

It was "a fantasy" of his, he later admitted, to get the two sides together at last: that was the only way, he thought, to get the IRS off his back, and he would make $5,000 to boot. But it was more than that: it was his chance to be part of something big, his chance to be the star. That's how the Circus Circus steam room on September 27, 1973, became the setting for the most momentous conversation between three naked men in Nevada history.

As Sarno remembered it, he arrived late, stripped down and stepped inside. Agent Smith and Stan Mallin were already there.

Sarno had told Crutchfield that he didn't want to initiate any conversation with Smith. "I'm not saying anything to him. If he says there's something wrong, I'd like to hear what he's got to say."

So he and Mallin sat and stared at Agent Smith. Smith, equally guarded, stared back.

"It was like a Mexican standoff," Sarno recalled later. Sarno and Mallin and Smith sat silently staring at each other, waiting for something to happen. Dripping with sweat, his heart racing, Sarno finally broke the tension in the most noncommittal way he could imagine.

"Well, Bob, what can we do for you?" he asked. "What's this meeting all about?"

It was like a button had been pressed; Smith began speaking mechanically.

"You fellows know that I'm the criminal investigator of Circus Circus, and also the two of you personally," Smith began. "It's now time for me to make my report. And whatever report I make will probably be accepted, because I've been around here a long time." He paused to let this sink in. The sweat rolled down their bodies. Neither Sarno nor Mallin dared interrupt.

"Not only that, but although I'm not in the Audit Division, I've known those fellows for years, eighteen years in the service, and we're friends, and any recommendation I might give would carry a lot of weight. And I know they're considering a lot of civil readjustments. They may disallow some of those large depreciation losses you fellows have claimed." He paused again.

"I know very well if they do, it will break you guys. You'll have to close your doors. There's no way to meet the amount of money that demand will represent. I also know you've applied for a refund. If you think you'll get that refund without my blessing, you're whistling Dixie. I can hold it up. I can get it rejected. I can hold it up so long that they'll take it away in payment of future taxes.

"You'd better believe the IRS, if they want, can make a criminal indictment stick in any casino the size of Circus Circus. You handle so much money that it's easy for them to get a case together."

Sarno fought the urge to smash Smith's face in. He had them by the balls, and they knew it.

"You know that I'm in there eighteen years?" Smith asked, almost to himself. "And I got nothing to show for it? And now is my time to make a buck, make a score. And I'm going to get it while the getting is good."

He folded his hands and looked at Sarno.

"Bob, you know damn well we haven't made any money around this place in years, and there's no need for us to cheat on our taxes," Sarno started. "But if you think you scared me by mentioning criminal indictments and going to jail, you guessed right. You did scare me. I don't like that kind of talk. I think of a criminal indictment and going to jail the same way I think of death."

He had seen his friends Jimmy Hoffa and Allen Dorfman go to jail. They'd survived it. But he knew he wasn't as tough as either of them. Between his diabetes and his heart, prison would kill him.

"What's your suggestion?" Sarno asked. "What could be done about the situation?"

"Well, I could inside of ninety days put in a report with the Criminal Division out of Circus Circus," Smith said helpfully. "Two or three or four weeks after that, I can put in a report that we're off of you and Mallin personally. I can make some recommendations to the Audit Division, because those are highly technical things that are just a matter of opinion very often. It's really kind of an art, not an exact science. I know you should get the tax refund, but without my help you ain't gonna get it. In a few months after that I'll get the IRS off your back and out of your hotel altogether, and you can go back to running your business."

"Well, that would be nice," Sarno said sarcastically. "What would such a unique effort cost us?"

"Seventy-five thousand dollars," Smith blurted, almost before the question had left Sarno's lips.

The two partners looked at each other. Sarno's instinct was to stall for time. Maybe he could talk to someone, find an angel, as he had in the Arnold case. He had gotten Arnold to go away. Surely with a few phone calls he could find a way to outsmart Smith.

"Bob, we have to talk this over," he said. "Can we get back to you tomorrow? Give us a day to think about it?"

"No, it's now. I'm not going to piss around with this, Sarno, you've got to decide now. If you don't make the decision now, forget it. It's over." Smith wasn't going to let the mouse out of the trap so easily.

"Stan, let's go out in the hall," Sarno said, indicating that Smith should wait while they spoke in private.

"You know we can't get hold of that kind of money," Mallin said once they were out of earshot. "That's not $75,000. That's $150,000 before taxes. We've done nothing wrong. We don't owe this money. This is insane."

"Remember, we already had a brush with the IRS," Sarno countered. "You know how vicious and capricious they can be.

Reason is not what counts. You know, this guy is very powerful. He's a drunk and chasing women. If we know it, they know it. Yet they don't fire him. He must be very highly placed, powerful, and well in position there, well-entrenched," he deduced. "You can see he's a red-faced drunk, a vicious guy. We got plenty of trouble. If we get indicted, we'll have to pay legal fees."

"We don't have the money, we don't owe it, nothing's wrong," Mallin protested.

"That's true, but this guy is talking about getting us in jail. It's murder."

"We don't have the money," Mallin said, throwing his hands up. Even if they wanted to pay the bribe, they couldn't.

"Stanley, there's one way we might have the money. If I gave him twenty-five hundred a month, and then when he comes through with the refund check, I could give him the other fifty grand out of that."

Mallin didn't precisely agree to go along with the scheme, but acquiesced, as usual, to Sarno's elephantine will. Now they had to convince Smith to take the deal.

As they moved toward the steam room door, an anonymous hotel guest, bent only on having a good *schpritz*, sauntered through and plopped himself down with a nod of the head to Smith, who sat impassively. Sarno motioned for Smith to join them. The three ended up in the empty whirlpool spa.

"Bob, you know that we're practically busted. We can't pay our withholding taxes. We can't make the mortgage payment. We're trying desperately to borrow some money to keep this place going. It's a brutal thing you're doing."

"So?' Smith replied. There was no way, Sarno now knew, that he could back this guy down. He outlined the offer: twenty-five hundred a month, then a fifty-thousand dollar payment after the refund came through.

"Oh, you want terms?" Smith asked mockingly. "That's going to cost you ten percent of Mallin's refund, too."

Sarno looked at Stan. *If there were any other way,* his eyes seemed to say. He had gotten them out of the Arnold mess. Now it was Mallin's turn to do this one little thing.

"Okay, I'll do that," Mallin agreed. It was done. Sarno left him and Smith to discuss the specifics of their next meeting. By noon, they'd finished their discussion and gone their separate ways.

The following day, Mallin gave Smith $2,500 in hundred dollar bills. A month later, he gave him another $2,500. In a second steam room rendezvous, Smith gave a progress report: he announced that within thirty days he would get the Civil Division out of Circus Circus. The audit would be over. For the next three months, Sarno or Mallin—usually Mallin—gave Smith $2,500 in quick, surreptitious meetings.

Sarno began to believe that he had finally found a way out of the trap. In January 1974, he received approval for another Teamster loan, $7.6 million that would let him add 400 rooms to the hotel. If the tax refund came through, he would have some breathing room at last. Then he got his refund check: nearly $500,000 with interest. Feeling like a free man again, on February 21 he gave Smith $50,000. Life seemed to be looking up.

On the afternoon of Thursday, March 7, a phalanx of police officers and federal agents stormed through the doors of Circus Circus. Some players kept putting money in the slots; others looked up at what they at first thought was another circus act. The employees cursed themselves for not having found other jobs already; they'd known this day was coming. Now the casino would surely be closed, and they'd be among hundreds looking for work.

The troop marched back to the executive officers where they arrested Sarno and Mallin, dragging them out of their casino in handcuffs.

The two ended up in front of U.S. Magistrate Joseph Ward, where they learned that, along with Leo Crutchfield, they had been indicted by a federal grand jury on 17 separate counts, the most important of which were bribery of a public official, conspiracy, and interference with the administration of Internal Revenue laws. As a bonus, Sarno was charged with threatening the life of Special Agent Smith. For this Caesar, the Ides of March had come early.

Turner and Smith had been secretly recording their conversations with Crutchfield, Mallin, and Sarno. A man as unrestrained as Sarno was liable to say outrageous things to a lawn chair; goaded on by an undercover agent wearing a wire, he had spoken even less circumspectly. One of his more extravagant bouts of bragging had triggered the charge that he had threatened Smith's life, on top of his many references to the bribery scheme. With the recordings, prosecutors believed they had him dead to rights.

Sarno was now accused, United States Attorney DeVoe Heaton reported with some satisfaction, of offering the largest bribe in the 112 year history of the Internal Revenue Service.

Sarno and Mallin's bail was set at $100,000 each. Sarno didn't have that kind of cash on reserve, even though he had received a half-million dollar tax refund barely two months earlier. Since he lived at the hotel, he didn't have any property to pledge as collateral. Joyce absolutely refused to put up the Brown Circle house, so Mallin posted the bond for both of them with his own house.

Once again, Jay Sarno proved himself incapable of doing anything in a small way.

FIFTEEN

The United States v. Jay Sarno

In early 1974, Jay Sarno was breaking precedents at an alarming pace. Not only was he accused of offering the largest bribe in IRS history, he and Stanley Mallin became the first proprietors of a major Las Vegas Strip casino to find themselves under indictment for a crime of this magnitude. Nevada regulators, who'd already stripped control of Circus Circus from Sarno once, were in a difficult position. In the court of law, all men were assumed innocent until proven guilty. But those who ran Nevada casinos had to be, like Caesar's wife, above suspicion, at least when things started getting into the papers.

The Nevada Gaming Commission wanted them out of the casino business. But where to find a buyer? Nobody would take a chance on a casino as leaky as Circus Circus. Even if they found a buyer, before escrow closed the trial would probably be over, and two standing casino owners could be headed to prison. This would be an unparalleled embarrassment for the state's gaming industry, and it might bring even more federal scrutiny to Las Vegas. But everyone involved—regulators, other owners, public officials—wanted Circus out of Sarno's hands before the trial. The commissioners knew about Bill Bennett and Bill Pennington's ongoing negotiations to lease the property, and they accepted this as a compromise. Sarno and Mallin must be reduced to landlords with no active involvement in the running of the casino.

Already seriously negotiating, Bennett and Pennington brought in Angel Naves, a Mint casino manager, to handle the daily operations in exchange for a 10% share of the company. But they still didn't have enough cash to pull the deal. So they brought in Mickey Briggs, scion of the Detroit family behind the Briggs and Stratton engine and lawnmower company, who took another 10% of the company. With Briggs' name and the assets of Western Equity as collateral, they finally inked a five-year loan of Circus Circus. Bennett and Pennington took over on May 2.

The Gaming Commissioners breathed a sigh of relief: Jay Sarno was no longer a casino owner. There were small, spontaneous celebrations in many offices up and down the Strip. But Las Vegas wasn't about to get rid of Sarno that easily.

On trial, he believed, for his life, Sarno realized that he needed a tougher hired gun than he could find in any white shoe law firm. Stan Mallin stole a march on him and retained Oscar Goodman, a rising Las Vegas attorney. Goodman had grown up in West Philadelphia, son of a prosecutor with the district attorney's office, and shared many traits with Jay Sarno. Both were bright but not focused on their studies, and both loved to gamble. Though his family was certainly more well-off than Sarno's, Goodman had faced the same type of antisemitism Sarno had in his youth. After flirting with art and writing as possible careers, he went into law. Graduating from the University of Pennsylvania's law school in 1964, he made his way to Las Vegas and took a job with the district attorney's office. Arriving with $87 and boundless ambition, he was ready, like Sarno, to reinvent himself in the desert city.

While Sarno was willing Caesars Palace out of the ground, Goodman became disenchanted with his prosecutor's job. He struck out on his own, making a name for himself as a smart, tough lawyer who, thanks to his rounds of the casinos, had more than his share of civil work from dealers, bellman, and other Strip workers. Goodman vaulted into national prominence in 1972, when he began representing Meyer Lansky and several others as Nevada counsel in the Flamingo skimming case that sent Morris Lansburgh to jail. Ultimately, Goodman succeeded in having the charges against the wily Lansky thrown out, but in March 1974 the proceedings were still ongoing. This case fixed him forever in the eyes of prosecutors as a "mob lawyer," and in the coming years he would represent many other alleged organized crime figures.

Not coincidentally, Goodman also represented a number of bookmakers, including Jerry Zarowitz and Elliot Price, in a massive 26-city bookmaking case. This case, which began with the series of raids and arrests in December 1970 that turned up the $1.5 million in Zarowitz's safe deposit boxes at Caesars Palace, was ultimately tossed out on a technicality. Zarowitz and Price had been raving about Goodman, and Sarno shared their endorsements with Mallin, who promptly hired him.

But Sarno wanted Goodman for himself. He demanded that Mallin give up the attorney. Mallin did, retaining Harry Claiborne as his new counsel. Claiborne, an Arkansas native, had been practicing law in Las Vegas for nearly thirty years, gaining a reputation as a theatrical, charming defense attorney. He had taken the younger Goodman under his wing after his arrival in Las Vegas, and the careers of both were intertwined for years.

With a flurry of pretrial motions, the trial took shape. The recorded conversations made by Smith and Turner were allowed in, and, since the defendants alleged that Leo Crutchfield was really a government agent and not a co-defendant, his trial was separated from Mallin and Sarno's. Crutchfield would be tried, on his own, at a later date.

With Judge Roger D. Foley presiding, the trial in the case of *United States v. Jay Sarno and Stanley Mallin* began on Tuesday, February 14, 1975, with the examination of 57 prospective jurors. At one point, government attorney James Duff asked the jury pool if they had any strong negative feelings about the IRS. After the laughter died down, three jurors indicated that they were angered by the agency's recent decision to begin taxing "tokes," or tips earned by dealers—another way the federal government was "out to get" Las Vegas. They were thanked and excused by the court at the prosecution's request. Another was excused because she "hated to see even animals caged."

After about five hours of *voir dire* examination, Judge Foley impaneled a jury. With a standard admonishment not to discuss the case with each other or outsiders, to maintain an open mind, and to avoid news accounts of the case, he dismissed the panel for the evening.

The next morning, the jury began to hear testimony. The prosecutors, James Duff and Richard Wright, outlined their case: that Sarno and Mallin asked Crutchfield to introduce them to Agent Smith, who they bribed $50,000 for help getting Sarno's $500,000 refund, $10,000 for Mallin's refund, and $2,500 a month for ten months to close the criminal tax investigation of Circus Circus, violating the laws against corrupting public officials and, in Sarno's case, threatening the life a of federal agent.

Duff and Wright called a series of IRS agents who testified about the wiretapping process and the timeframe of the investigation. Under cross examination, Claiborne began to raise some questions about the government's case. In May 1973, Crutchfield had, the IRS witnesses agreed, told Sarno and Mallin that the agency was ready to move on their case and that time was of the essence; yet the two worked down the hall from Smith at Circus Circus for five months without approaching him or any other agent with a bribe. Why was this? If Crutchfield had truly approached Turner and Smith on behalf of the Circus Circus owners, why were agents on record as having told Crutchfield to "go and see" Sarno and Mallin?

Turner then took the stand for two days; during his testimony, the jury heard tapes of his conversations with Crutchfield. Much of it seemed to prove that the car rental mogul had pestered Turner into taking a bribe. But as Oscar Goodman pointed out in his cross examination, the tapes left open the possibility that Turner had manipulated Crutchfield to get at Sarno and Mallin. Turner insisted that Crutchfield, Sarno, and Mallin had initiated the bribe talk, and that in fact he had feared for his life at one point, since they were dangerous men.

Then Smith testified, walking the jury through his investigation of Circus Circus, Sarno, and Mallin. He said it was likely that their partnership losses and Sarno's gambling losses would be disallowed, resulting in, as he put it, "large civil tax deficiencies" for the pair, which they would be personally liable for paying.

Smith offered a radically different version of the steam room conversation than the one Sarno remembered. After they had gotten comfortable in the steam room, Sarno began chattering about how he had done nothing wrong, didn't want to cheat, and didn't like criminal investigators like Smith, but that he "equated going to jail with dying." He asked Smith what he "could do for him," and the agent allowed that he was in a position to make recommendations that "carried a lot of weight." He admitted that he had said that Sarno's adjustments were "highly technical in nature" and debatable, and that he had agreed to accept a bribe.

According to Smith, after discussing the specifics of how he would pick up the money, Sarno impressed upon him the fact that, should anything go wrong and he find himself facing criminal charges, that Smith would be sorry. "You should know that I know the right people," he reportedly said, "and it will never be settled in court."

Smith testified that he feared for his personal safety. At one point he noticed a car following him around town, and he suspected Sarno was having him watched. Still, he continued in his duties.

The day after the steam room summit, Smith accepted the first money from Mallin and inventoried the bills. Claiborne and Goodman agreed that their clients had, in fact, given the money to Smith, and stipulated that the prosecution could introduce into evidence the entire $62,500 collected from Sarno and Mallin without challenge.

For the next several hours, Smith recounted talking taxes with Sarno and Mallin and accepting $2,500 wads of cash from them, each of which was inventoried and stored as evidence. Initially, he did not record several key conversations because he thought Sarno was skittish and was afraid that the hotel man would search him for a wire, but by January 1974, they had gotten comfortable with each other and Smith began recording their conversations. On the 24th of that month, Sarno asked him about Swiss bank accounts. Smith admitted that he couldn't just deposit Sarno's $50,000 in his local bank, so instead he let on that he was "sending the money to Switzerland."

But Sarno didn't completely let his guard down. In front of Smith, he told Mallin, "I'll level with Smith because if he double-crosses me he's a dead man." Sarno then began giving advice.

"Bob, let me tell you about being rich, old boy. Cash is good… show money is what counts. You got to buy something. Everybody that's rich is an owner." He launched into an explanation of how Smith could successfully launder his money.

At their next meeting, Sarno reported having received his refund check—just a shade over $490,000. Smith reminded him not to forget to pay taxes on the $30,000 in interest included in the settlement. They then talked about Sarno depositing the money in a Swiss bank, with Smith sharing research he had ostensibly done on the matter. After testifying that he had received $50,000 in hundred dollar bills from Sarno in the foyer of his office, Smith had answered all of Duff's questions. Judge Foley dismissed the jury for the night.

The next morning Harry Claiborne began his cross examination. He pushed Smith to admit that Sarno and Mallin had known of his presence at Circus Circus for months without approaching him. He then poked holes in Smith's earlier assertion that he had been fearful of his life because he thought he was being followed. Even if there was someone tailing Smith, Claiborne argued, it could have been anyone.

"You're really not the most popular people around?" he asked, and got a negative response. "And you're not really trying to be, are you?" he pushed, to which Smith had to answer, "No, we're not." It was absurd for an experienced investigator to suggest that he feared for his life because of a tail, and Smith admitted that he had given up the investigation into the alleged surveillance after he found no connection to Sarno or Mallin.

After they refused to approach him and when no solid criminal evidence could be found against them, Claiborne advanced in his questioning, Smith had "started a campaign of fear" against the targets and brought up the idea of him paying $75,000 to make their tax problems go away.

Finally, Claiborne tried to explode the myth that Sarno had threatened Smith: didn't people always use the phrase "you're a dead man" and mean nothing by it? Was it possible that the highly-strung Smith had read too much into an innocuous remark? When Sarno said that, if he was indicted, the case would never reach trial, couldn't he have meant that he would fix the judge, not that he would kill Smith, a potential witness?

After Smith's testimony, Joe Turner retook the stand to clarify his earlier indications that a threat had been made on his life in April 1973, during his courtship by Crutchfield. Here things degenerated into slapstick. Under Goodman's prodding, he revealed that he had heard about the possible threat from another agent with the IRS, that he had never actually been threatened. After further questioning, he admitted that the agent in question had been told of the threat by his wife, who felt sorry for Turner's pregnant wife and thought she would best be served by getting her husband off a stressful investigation.

Turner squirmed as Goodman got him to admit that, yes, the agent's wife had concocted the whole thing. The gallery found this development quite amusing, but Goodman was after more than laughs. It did not help the government's case that one of its agents had testified that he had been in fear for his life over a threat he had known for months to be false. The government's airtight case was sprouting leaks.

After Goodman wrapped up his cross examination the prosecution rested and, on the morning of February 27, 1975, the defense took the stand.

In his opening statement, Harry Claiborne laid out the case for the defense: that Leo Crutchfield, because of his own greed and fear of the IRS, had been used by the government to entrap Sarno and Mallin, who would never have contemplated bribing an agent had they not been threatened. It was a case of the government beating up on the little guy (who also had given hundreds of Las Vegans jobs), plain and simple.

First up was Irving "Ash" Resnick, a Caesars Palace stalwart who'd been arrested in a parallel tax investigation the previous March. Resnick had been convicted of income tax evasion and sentenced to a year and a day in prison. Under Claiborne's questioning, he testified that Crutchfield had approached him, anxiously insisting on a private meeting, saying the matter was urgent and that Resnick was at risk. When they met, Crutchfield told Resnick he was about to be indicted and that a friend of his at the IRS could help him out of his tax jam. When he found out that "only" a federal indictment was in the cards, Resnick was relieved. (One can only guess at the rough characters Resnick associated with, when a federal indictment let him sigh with relief.) This furthered the defense case that Crutchfield was trawling the Strip for casino executives that he, Turner, and Smith could entrap on bribery charges.

Goodman then took over, calling James Faso, comptroller of Circus Circus. His job was to review the daily financial situation of the casino, prepare all financial statements, and monitor the construction costs. He talked of his efforts to aid the auditors and of the strain that the audit placed on the regular running of the business. The casino actually hired a man named Alexander Chupa, whose sole job was to act as a "buffer zone" between the casino and the army of internal revenue agents that had camped out in the conference room. Sarno's only conversation with Smith, he said, was to ask how the investigation was coming along, and when it would be finished. On cross examination, Mr. Duff tried to elicit Faso's testimony on cash controls on the casino floor in order to prove the possibility of income tax evasion, but after Goodman's objection Judge Foley admonished him to confine himself to "the scope of the direct." This substantively ended the government's questioning of Faso.

Leo Crutchfield then took the stand, questioned by Goodman. He did not come out of it looking well. Under cross examination, he explained that Joe Turner was a "corrupt agent" because he had "ripped me off" for $1,500. James Duff, for the prosecution, then asked if turnabout was really fair play. "And then you turn around and try to rip off your friends, Sarno and Mallin, for some money, is that correct?"

"Right," Crutchfield admitted. "The way they [the agents] were talking, they were going to get a lot of money from them [Sarno and Mallin], and they had to pay it anyway, so I might as well get a part of it."

Crutchfield insisted throughout Duff's questioning that he wasn't working for Sarno or Mallin. "Nothing proves I was working for them, nothing," he testified. "I was working for Joe Turner."

After Crutchfield stepped down, Goodman called Jay Jackson Sarno to take the stand in his own defense. The jury watched as

Sarno, the armpits of his immaculate suit already darkened with circles of sweat, walked to the front of the court.

Sarno began by explaining how he came to Las Vegas to build Caesars Palace and how he decided to open Circus Circus, conveniently skipping over the reasons he had sold Caesars.

He confessed that the big top casino was "one of my not-so-good ideas, incidentally. It sounded good." With the benefit of hard-earned experience, he added a qualifier: "There are no bad ideas; they're just bad after you try them."

Sarno testified that he had insisted that Faso and the accountants from Harris Kerr Forster cooperate fully with the audit. "We had nothing to hide," he maintained. He then discussed the chain of events that had gotten him into the steam room with a naked IRS agent. Crutchfield, a "persistent fellow," had hounded him for months; Smith, he had been told, was a drunk, a woman-chaser, and "on the take." Finally, after the anguished September 26 phone call, he had agree to meet with Smith just to shut Crutchfield up.

After Sarno gave his account of the meeting, Goodman asked him why he didn't report Smith if the agent had tried to shake him down.

"We wanted to," Sarno insisted, but "just like a guy with a gun at his head, you don't quite know what to do rationally." They had not discussed it with their lawyer at the time, Morton Galane, or their accountants. "Perhaps we were stupid, but we were shaken. Who wouldn't be? We were afraid to report him. Stanley said, and I agreed, 'Hey, this guy can get us buried with his friends. They're not going to take our word over an IRS guy.' He had a big ranking from 18 years there. We didn't think we could possibly win against this man except by giving him the money. He was a symbol of the IRS, of these things we had heard about. We had heard many stories of how viciously they are framing people and bringing in lying witnesses. We heard them so often that we couldn't put them out of our minds."

Next, Goodman asked Sarno about a recorded conversation in which he had let it slip that if his accountant, Clark Bingham, "goofed up" his tax refund request, "I'll want to kill him and I think I've got every legal right."

Sarno told the court, "If I killed every guy I threatened to kill, there wouldn't be so many people on the relief rolls. But I haven't killed anybody. Of course, I didn't mean I'm going to kill him. I'd like to kill my son, but I haven't killed him yet."

The threats he had reportedly made against Smith were just jokes, he insisted, jokes that Smith had been too dense to appreciate.

"I put him on a few times, Mr. Smith, he didn't even know he was being put on."

What about when he said that if Smith double-crossed him, he would be a dead man? That, too, Sarno assured the court, was just a misunderstanding. "That's an unfortunate figure of speech," he allowed. Actually, when he and Mallin learned that one of their credit gamblers wouldn't be paying his debts, they'd joke to each other "we're a dead man," meaning they had as good a chance of collecting the money as a dead man. By telling Smith he would be a "dead man" if he informed on them, Sarno only meant that he wouldn't be able to collect the bribe.

Goodman also prompted Sarno to claim that he was having trouble paying the bribe because he was too honest a casino owner. Sarno explained to the jury, as the tapes revealed he had to Smith, that if they had had "some real skimming" going on at Circus Circus, he would easily be able to pay him in cash. But they didn't, not because Sarno wouldn't countenance criminal behavior, but because they weren't making enough money.

"I'm not saying I'm the holiest man alive," he told the court, "but I want to suggest that no owner living could skim if the place isn't making any money, because if he skims, the place will close, so where is he going to skim out of, a closed casino?"

Further, he explained that he had talked to Smith about setting up a Swiss bank out of necessity, not greed. "In a town this size, if your name is Sarno, you can't deposit sums that great," he claimed. The word would get out, and his creditors would converge on him "like vultures and take it all away."

"The trick," he rationalized, "is to pay your debts systematically, slowly, so that everybody gets some, and you have a little left over, that's what I'm talking about." Hiding the money in a Swiss bank account was just a way of ensuring everyone got paid.

Finally, Sarno took the initiative and offered the jury three reasons why they should not find him guilty, even though he freely admitted to paying the bribe. The first was his family: his son Jay, then sixteen, worked like a dog at school, always buckled his seat belt, and was so honest he wouldn't even think of littering. "He's a son like you dream of having." Then there was his daughter, September, who was "fifteen going on twenty-seven," a beautiful girl who also got great grades. But raising an adolescent daughter was not without its problems. "We're in that stage that's both confusing and confounding," he said, as if asking the jury for advice. "She wants the pill. Do we give it to her or not? That's the fatherly situation I'm involved in."

His son Freddie was a gifted athlete, and it was "the pleasure of my life" to watch him play basketball. Finally, his eight-year-old daughter Heidi, was the apple of his eye. For him to go to jail and not share in their lives was unthinkable cruelty.

The second reason, was his health. "I have gout, I have diabetes, I'm overweight," he said. His eyesight was so bad that he was "totally blind." Even out of jail, he was living under a death sentence.

"But the most terrible reason," Sarno continued gravely, "is the third reason." What, the jurors wondered, could be so horrible?

Sarno started calmly: "I have to be honest and admit, I have a very raucous personality. I'm not like Mallin, who's a quiet gentleman, and everybody likes him, and rightfully so. I have known him since college. I irk a lot of people." If he had an operation on his eyes that his doctor had said was necessary, a simple touch in the wrong spot would render him blind for life. "And I could easily provoke a guy to do that, I realize that," he admitted.

If he didn't have the operation and wore glasses to prison instead, his humiliation would be all the more certain.

"They'll rip them off and crush them underfoot, and I'll crawl around, a laughingstock," he pleaded. "And I'll try to defend myself and I'm going to get a knife stuck in me. Those are my feelings. Maybe I'm a coward. Maybe I'm a coward and that's why it's just the worst thought on earth for me. I would rather go out and get shot or get hit by a car than go to jail."

This nightmare had compelled him to go along with Smith, as sure as if the agent had been holding a gun to his head. "He was obviously so powerful, he looked like a vicious man," he impressed on the jury. "He's a red-faced drunk with that grin of his."

With that to ponder, Judge Foley sent the jury to lunch.

When they returned, James Duff began his cross examination, trying to establish that Sarno had competent attorneys and accountants whom he could have gotten help from if he had really been extorted by a mere IRS agent, a red-faced drunk no less. Sarno had friends in the FBI who'd worked with him on the bomb extortion plot who would gladly have listened to any allegations he made.

Sarno admitted it sounded preposterous. "I didn't say it was sensible, but that's how it was." Having good lawyers meant nothing, he had learned from Jimmy Hoffa and Allen Dorfman. "You know how many guys are in jail that's got bigger lawyers than we got? I was afraid of this man, I certainly was."

He couldn't turn to anyone because Smith would frame him regardless of what he did. "Mallin, you don't need to be proper and right," he recalled telling Stan as they talked outside the steam room, "The IRS buries you anyhow." Goodman noticed a few jurors nodding.

Duff and Sarno went back and forth for the rest of the afternoon. Sarno insisted what he had done was stupid, but not criminal; it couldn't be wrong to protect your life. He hadn't paid a bribe, he had been shaken down.

With Duff trying to get him to admit otherwise, things became contentious. Sarno did not help his cause with his rambling, or by frequently raising his voice to respond to Duff's pointed questions. When he remarked that he'd never "scheme up on" anyone the way Smith had on him, Duff asked incredulously, "You don't scheme up on anybody? How about when you don't pay your creditors? Put your money in a Swiss bank so that your creditors don't get paid?"

"If you choose that interpretation, be my guest," Sarno replied, staring at the floor.

Sarno admitted that he was intimidated by the prosecutor and, indeed, frightened by everybody in the government, "because I know what's in their minds." When Duff asked Sarno if he had yelled at Smith, who also intimidated him, the same way he was yelling in court, Sarno apologized. "I'm excited, I'm frightened, I'm afraid.

You've been more than polite, and I'm very sorry if I've been yelling. I'll try not to."

Duff had no more questions, and the judge thanked and excused Sarno from the stand. Glaring at Goodman, Sarno walked back to his seat at the defendant's table, gathered his things, and left the courtroom.

It had been a disaster.

The phone woke Oscar Goodman sometime after two. With the kind of client list he was building, he was ready for anything. Was a client in jail? Was a client dead? He put the receiver to his ear and tentatively said hello.

"You're fired."

Goodman exhaled.

"Christ, Jay, what's this all about? Can't it wait until we get to court tomorrow?"

"No, goddamn it. Don't bother going to court. I'm getting another goddamn lawyer. Stanley's going to get off and you're going to send me to jail. He looks like a million bucks sitting there, and I look like a schmuck."

"Listen, Jay, we've been through this a million times…"

"No, you listen to me, Goodman. I talked to Stanley and I know that he's going to have a bunch of character witnesses tomorrow, and they're going to testify about what a goddamn saint he is. I want some character witnesses for me. I've taken care of enough people around town, we should have plenty of them."

"Jay, you know that's a bad idea. If we open up the issue of your character, Duff is going to have a field day. Just let it lie. We're building a good case. I think we've got a good jury."

"I don't want to leave it up to the jury! I want character witnesses, someone to say something nice about me. Goddamn it, if Stanley gets off and I don't…"

"Don't worry about that. We're building doubt in the jury's minds. It's going to be…"

"No, I'm worried about it, and that's it. You're fired. I'm not going to go to court with you because you're not putting on a defense for me. I'm going to get a real lawyer who knows what he's doing."

"Fine, Jay, I'm fired." Goodman hung up, rolled over, and went back to sleep.

The next morning, Oscar Goodman dressed and went to court. He sat down at the defense table next to Harry Claiborne and Stan Mallin and made small talk. Sarno chugged into the courtroom barely two minutes before the trial was scheduled to resume. With a nod, he sat down next to Goodman.

"Character witnesses, Goodman, I want character witnesses."

Before Goodman could reply, the bailiff announced that proceedings were continuing, and Judge Foley entered the court.

It was Mallin's turn to face the jury. Harry Claiborne elicited testimony about how he had come to Las Vegas, joined Sarno at Circus Circus, met Leo Crutchfield, and finally delivered a cash bribe to an IRS agent. He offered substantially the same version of the steam room meeting as had Sarno. He was just as frightened as his friend had been by the vicious Smith, but for different reasons.

"My own life was of secondary consideration," he said. His biggest fear was that the government would padlock the doors of Circus Circus. Love for his fellows Las Vegans had driven him to bribe Smith.

"This may sound altruistic, but I didn't want the disgrace of a bankruptcy personally, and I didn't want these thirteen hundred employees with roughly five thousand people dependent on them out of work."

With no asides or embellishments, Mallin finished with his direct examination in a matter of minutes, though it seemed much longer to him. Sarno was quietly furious.

"He's going to walk free!" he whispered to Goodman. "Do something!" Yes, he was in mortal dread of prison; but seeing his best friend found innocent while he went to jail was his real worst nightmare.

Richard Wright immediately began the cross examination, walking Mallin through his version of the Turner-Crutchfield-Smith courtship. Again, his testimony jibed with Sarno's.

"Turning in Smith would have been fruitless and we panicked," he admitted. They were guilty perhaps of bad judgment. "I'm not proud of it. We panicked, and we did bribe the man."

Mallin confessed that when the panic wore off he had considered blowing the whistle on Smith, but remembered what had happened to Daniel Ellsberg after publishing the Pentagon Papers: he had been hounded. The Nixon administration, Mallin told the jury, "had used the IRS as a tool to get back at people." He believed this would happen to him if he told the truth, so he had quietly gone along with the bribery.

The jury looked receptive, Claiborne thought. Would they accept fear of President Nixon as a defense for bribery?

Without knowing it, Mallin almost stepped onto a landmine when answering questions about the Circus Circus gift shop. He explained that the hotel had two gift shops, and that they'd been initially unable to lease out the downstairs one. "Nobody wanted it except this one gentleman. His name was Spilotro." Mallin had to spell the name for the court reporter, and Wright asked him to confirm that Spilotro did not have to bid on the gift shop lease.

Immediately Oscar Goodman, who had already represented Spilotro in a few of his scrapes with the law, leapt to his feet.

"Your honor, I would object, on the grounds that it isn't relevant to any issues thus far."

Wright agreed to move on to another area of questioning without realizing that, with a little prodding, he might have gotten Mallin to confirm in open court a connection between Circus Circus and the Chicago mob.

There was little else of drama in the rest of the questioning: Wright and Mallin dickered over the amount of influence Mallin had over Crutchfield, his and Sarno's state of mind when they offered the bribe, and whether they had tried to intimidate Smith with talk of dead men. Mallin agreed that his partner was a jerk, but a harmless one.

"He's the type of individual that could provoke fights by his very personality, but I have never known him to strike anybody."

Back at the defendants' table, Sarno simmered.

Following Mallin's testimony, Claiborne announced his intention to call a brief parade of character witnesses on his client's behalf. Sarno glowered at Goodman. The government attorney, unprepared for this, protested that he had not lined up "witnesses to testify to their bad character," but Judge Foley allowed the character witnesses nonetheless.

Seeing some agitation at the defense table, Foley asked if Sarno's lawyer would be calling anyone to talk about his client's good reputation.

"I can't get any character witnesses," was all Goodman could offer. Sarno was apoplectic. The trial went on.

First, Dr. Donald Henry Baepler, the president of the University of Nevada, Las Vegas, revealed that Mallin's reputation for truth and veracity was "very good."

Sarno jabbed Goodman in his ribs. "He's going to win. He's going to win."

Next, Robert E. Foster, principal of the School for Retarded Children at Allen J. Stewart School agreed that he had no reason to believe that Mallin's character was not good.

Sarno prodded Goodman again, hard enough to make him flinch. "I know that guy," he whispered, not quite *sotto voce*. "Just ask him about me. Ask him!" Sarno's face was getting red, and his toupee was beginning to slip. "Go on, ask him about me!" The jury turned their heads.

"Mr. Goodman, anything?" Judge Foley asked.

"Nothing at this time, your honor."[503] Foster left the stand.

Claiborne then called John R. Young, with the Young Electric Sign Company, the premier neon marquee installer in Las Vegas. After he testified that Mallin's character was "excellent," Sarno could take no more.

"You bastard," he hissed at Goodman. The jury turned again. This was much more interesting than listening to businessmen talk about Mallin's reputation. Sarno's toupee had slid completely to the side of his head. There was no way the jury would forget this. His hand forced, Goodman rose.

"Judge Foley, I'd like ask a few questions if I may." The judge allowed this while at the prosecution table Richard Wright began flipping through a thick folder that had previously lain untouched.

"Sir, can you share with the court your impressions of Mr. Sarno's character? What is his reputation in the community?"

"He's been very fair with me and very honest with me," Young said diplomatically.

"What about his reputation in the community at large?"

"I…I would say that it's fine." Not unimpeachable, not excellent, but fine. Sarno was even angrier, but worse was to come.

With the genie out of the bottle, Wright rose, smiling like a child on Christmas morning.

"Have you heard that he's allegedly a front man—"

Goodman was back on his feet before he could get the words out, loudly objecting to this "pure innuendo and speculation, dime-store novel-type question."

At side bar, Wright revealed that he planned to go through "a whole list of articles" that established Sarno as a mob front. Judge Foley refused to allow him to pursue this line of questioning. He couldn't ask any questions about the mob in this case; it wasn't relevant. Testimony resumed. After Young declined to volunteer anything derogatory he had heard about Sarno, Wright let him go.

"Damn it, Goodman, that was a disaster. You've got to get someone to say something better about me. There's got to be someone around here who'll testify."

Feeling a bit better now that he knew Wright wouldn't be able to bring up the mob, Goodman agreed. After local builder Stanley Ebner swore to Mallin's good character, Goodman called Chic Hecht, a prominent local merchant, steadfast Republican, and state senator, who swore that Sarno's reputation was, in fact, "very good." Foley refused to allow Wright to ask Hecht any questions at all.

With that, Claiborne and Goodman rested their cases. The prosecution then called IRS agent Francis Ballentine, former Assistant U.S. Attorney Paul Goldman, and Smith as rebuttal witnesses, trying to shoot down the defendants' claims of entrapment. And then, at 5:29 p.m. on the afternoon of March 4, both sides were finished.

The next morning, Goodman and Claiborne argued for an immediate acquittal pursuant to Rule 29 (b) of the Federal Rules of Criminal Procedure. The government's conduct was so outrageous, they argued, as to completely violate their clients' right to due process. This alone should make a conviction impossible.[508]

Foley let the trial continue, though he agreed that the threat charges would be tossed out. After further wrangling over the jury instructions, and with the jury re-seated at last, on March 10 the attorneys prepared to make their final pleas.

In a fiery closing argument, Oscar Goodman impressed upon the jury the seriousness of what they'd heard over the previous two weeks: his clients had paid the $62,500 because they'd been "coerced, extorted, and intimidated" by Agent Smith. In its zeal to "get" the prominent Las Vegas hotel owners, the government had overstepped the rule of law and had engaged in entrapment. He walked the jury through a clearly-labeled chronological chart that showed exactly how Turner had "pushed" Crutchfield into delivering Sarno and Mallin to Smith, who then set the trap.

Titled "GOVERNMENT EFFORTS TO ENTRAP SARNO AND MALLIN," this visual aid had been Sarno's idea.

"We've got a great case, but the jury won't listen to words," he had told Goodman. You need to do something visual, that they can look at while everyone's talking to them, so they can figure this out."

Goodman agreed. Throughout the trial he had referred to the chart, though he was a little surprised when the government attorneys did not object to having a chart that declared unambiguously that the government had engaged in entrapment introduced as evidence. But now they were in closing arguments. He would soon see if the chart had made a difference.

"The jury should be as incensed and enraged as I am about what the government did to these two pillars of the community," he concluded.

In his final statement, prosecutor James Duff claimed that the defendants were grasping at straws. "Sarno and Mallin couldn't claim insanity, so they had to plead entrapment," he thundered. Because the wiretap evidence was incontrovertible, they'd invented the "phony entrapment charge." Then he claimed that the government didn't force Sarno and Mallin to offer the bribe, it had only created a "favorable opportunity" for it, and that Crutchfield was under the control of the defendants, not the IRS.

With the presentations finished, Judge Foley issued the jury its instructions. In addition to the stock admonitions to weigh the evidence carefully, follow the law as stated by the court, and remain unswayed by sympathy, prejudice, or public opinion, Foley told that jury the government had to prove, beyond a reasonable doubt, that there was no entrapment. With the bar for conviction set rather high, he sent the jury off to deliberate at 11:41 AM on Wednesday, March 12.

When they had not reached a verdict by five that afternoon, they were sent home with instructions to return at nine the next morning.

The jury came back with several questions about Crutchfield's testimony and their instructions; these queries kept Foley occupied until after the lunch break, when he finally declared that it would take two or three hours to read back the portions of testimony the jury wanted to hear, and he would not permit it.

"You'll just have to rely on your own recollection," he admonished them.[515]

But they returned with even more questions. Reading one note, Foley became frustrated. He put it down and turned to the jury.

"There comes a time to bite the bullet. You've got to decide this case. And I think it's just a waste of time to keep sending notes like this last one to me: 'Please locate and clarify facts that indicate if Robert Smith in fact does or does not have a heavy drinking problem.' You've heard the evidence. You decide."

With that, he sent them back to the jury room.

Outside, Duff fumed that Foley's remarks had probably tilted the jury toward an acquittal. But less than an hour later they returned and announced they were hopelessly deadlocked. Foley told them that they'd only spent seven hours deliberating; the trial had been an expensive one in time and money, and a decision was needed. If they couldn't agree, the trial would have to be mounted again for the benefit of a jury no more competent than them. "You must take your time," he admonished. "You may be as leisurely in your deliberations as the occasion requires."

But the jury came no further in the next two hours, and was excused for the day and instructed to return the next morning. They remained in the jury room all the next day. Nothing. Foley ordered them to return on the following day, a Saturday.

Sarno needed some action to break up the monotony; he offered Goodman a bet: even money that Oscar couldn't beat him on any of the 18 holes of the Las Vegas Country Club's putting course. Goodman figured that he'd have to beat Sarno at least once; he took the bet. But Jay, personifying grace under pressure, ended up collecting from his attorney.

The jury met at nine and deliberated until after four, when Foley called them into the court. They had now spent over twenty hours arguing and still could not agree on the guilt or innocence of either Sarno or Mallin on any of the thirteen counts before them. Since Thursday afternoon, no one had budged.

The panel was unanimous, however, in swearing that even if testimony was read back and the judge's instructions issued again, it could not agree on a verdict.

With that, Judge Foley declared a mistrial. He thanked the jury for their conscientious service, then moved to rule on the defense's motion under Rule 29 (b), over Duff's objection. Before the jury had retired to deliberate, Foley revealed, he had concluded that if Crutchfield was in fact an agent of the government, the IRS had ipso facto entrapped Sarno and Mallin. He had charged the jury with deciding whether the prosecution had proven beyond a reasonable doubt that Crutchfield was not an IRS agent, and they had proven that they were unable to decide that question of fact.

"There necessarily being a reasonable doubt about entrapment and agency," he concluded, "this court finds that there *is* entrapment as a matter of law, and the reserved motion is granted. The defendants are discharged and their bonds are exonerated. The jury is excused."

Jay Sarno and Stanley Mallin were free.

Sarno was hailed as a conquering hero. "SARNO BEATS IRS TRAP" screamed the headline in the *Las Vegas Sun*, in World War III-size type over the masthead. Walking away from a bribery charge despite reels of wiretaps and bundles of money introduced as evidence embroidered Sarno's reputation as a solid Nevadan. It was almost a point of community pride.

Nationally, however, those with an interest in the case were less jubilant. Some believed Judge Foley had been bought. On the surface, it was not a baseless allegation: Claiborne and Goodman both had several successful trials in Foley's courtroom. In fact, Foley had quashed both the Lansky skimming case and the Price/

Zarowitz bookmaking charge, two major Goodman victories. He was personally friendly with Claiborne, and was among the first to congratulate the lawyer when he was named a federal district judge in 1978. During the trial, he tended to sustain Claiborne and Goodman's objections. At one point the judge even told Agent Smith that he "didn't see any threat at all" in Sarno's admonition that, should the agent cross him, the "case would never reach court."

Suspicions of a Goodman/Claiborne fix followed Foley for the rest of his career, but nothing was ever proven. It's possible that Foley had a predisposition for the home team; Sarno and Mallin had both been prominent citizens, and they had certainly done more good for the community than Duff, Wright, Turner, or Smith. Foley's son was a classmate of young Jay at Bishop Gorman High School; years later Goodman told Jay that this had swayed the judge, who decided that no man who could raise a son as conscientious and hard-working as Jay could possibly be so dissolute as to initiate the bribery scheme. This might have been a case of bias, but not a fix.

Regardless of whether Claiborne and Goodman enjoyed a home court advantage, the jurors who believed Goodman and Claiborne's tale of a government conspiracy were essentially correct. There really was a high-level federal effort to get Jay Sarno.

It later came out that Teamster President Frank Fitzsimmons and several of his cronies had informed on Jimmy Hoffa, Hoffa union ally Harold Gibbons, and Jay Sarno to the IRS between 1972 and 1974. And the connection to the White House was more immediate than anyone could have suspected: Fitzsimmons met with President Richard Nixon in 1972 and secured a promise that ongoing government investigations of the Teamsters would not harm Fitzsimmons or his allies. In return for his political support of Nixon, the government's resources would be marshaled against Fitzsimmons' rivals and enemies. Sarno was high on that list.

Only a few months after Sarno's acquittal, Jimmy Hoffa vanished. Though his body was never recovered and the case remains officially unsolved, it's widely believed that entrenched organized crime elements in the union murdered him because they feared that he might be successful in retaking the presidency of the union and cleaning house. With Hoffa's death, Sarno lost a good friend and ally and was also reminded of the unwise bargains he had made to get Circus Circus built. With the feds muscling Allen Dorfman out of the pension fund, Sarno knew he had little chance of getting any loans for future expansions of Circus Circus, should he resume operating it after Bennett and Pennington's lease contract expired.

The feds weren't about to give up on the bribery case, either. In October 1975, a week after Leo Crutchfield was convicted in his separate trial, a federal grand jury indicted Sarno for perjury. Prosecutors charged that he had knowingly lied on the stand when he testified that Smith had asked him for $75,000 in the steam room meeting. The government also appealed the acquittal in the original case. Sarno was out of jail, but under the constant strain of a running battle with the federal government.

Slowly, however, he gained the upper hand. In January 1976, Judge Foley dismissed the federal perjury charges, ruling that a jury had already failed to convict Sarno on the material charges at issue. The government appealed this ruling, and Sarno remained under a cloud until May 1979, when the Ninth Circuit Court of Appeals finally affirmed the dismissal. The panel upheld the original acquittal appeal as well. Sarno was finally free.

Meanwhile, Sarno and Mallin went on the offensive. With Oscar Goodman representing them, in May 1976 they filed suit against the IRS, seeking a refund of the $65,000 they'd paid in bribe money to Smith. The money was sitting in a Reno evidence locker, where it had been an exhibit in the Crutchfield trial. Goodman argued that his clients had been separated from the money under "duress and intimidation" and that it rightfully should be returned to them. This case made its way through the system for two years, when Sarno and Mallin agreed to drop the suit if the IRS agreed to apply the bribe money, and other funds at issue, to tax bills the pair had rung up since 1970.

The five years lost to the trial and its aftermath took their toll. Even after Sarno had been acquitted, the threat of a guilty verdict on the appeal had made him a pariah with lenders and the Gaming Commission. In 1979 his missed his chance to take back Circus Circus, but he still wanted to be a hotel man again. It was the only thing that made life worth living.

Work on Circus Circus in early 1968: the theater building and main casino are well-underway, and the diggings for the Strip-front fountains are visible. *Courtesy UNLV Special Collections.*

Making his older brother proud: Stan Mallin, Herman Sarno, and Jay at the opening of Circus Circus, October 1968. *Courtesy UNLV Special Collections.*

Taking a break from Caesar, Jay mimics Hannibal, mounting Tanya the Elephant for a gambol around the Circus parking lot. *Courtesy UNLV Special Collections.*

When it opened, Circus Circus had fountains that rivaled those at Caesars Palace. But they never became as iconic, and were removed in a later renovation. *Courtesy UNLV Special Collections.*

Jay gambled everything on Circus Circus's new hotel tower turning things around in 1972. *Courtesy UNLV Special Collections.*

Jay unwinds with Oscar Goodman, who represented him in his 1975 IRS bribery trial. *Courtesy Heidi Sarno Straus.*

Jay in his element, on the golf course with David Janssen, star of *The Fugitive. Courtesy UNLV Special Collections.*

Jay gets ready for a round at the Las Vegas Country Club, oversized bag in tow. *Courtesy UNLV Special Collections.*

The growing estrangement between Jay and Joyce is visible in this view of a family birthday celebration at the Bacchanal in 1969. *Courtesy UNLV Special Collections.*

Jay, in his special occasion toupee and tux, with his lifelong confidante, Carol Freeman. *Courtesy UNLV Special Collections.*

An exiled caesar? The land Sarno managed to lease for Grandissimo was literally on the wrong side of the tracks, a world away from the Las Vegas Strip that he'd redefined. *Courtesy UNLV Special Collections.*

As the Wall Street Journal put it, the Grandissimo would have been "only the largest hotel in the world." It was a combination of superlatives that skeptics dismissed as the latest crazy idea from Sarno, but the Grandissimo was actually a precursor of the megaresorts that began rising in Las Vegas in 1989. *Courtesy UNLV Special Collections.*

A caesar until the end: the strain of the previous years is apparent in this photo of Jay at a Caesars Palace toga party in August, 1983, about a year before his death. *Courtesy UNLV Special Collections.*

SIXTEEN

Grandissimo Dreaming

While Jay Sarno was preoccupied with his trial and appeals, Circus Circus Enterprises had transformed his former three-ring circus of a casino into a carefully-managed business. Sarno had a front-row seat: as part of the lease deal, he retained the right to live in his 14th floor executive suite, gratis. When the second hotel tower finally opened, he moved into an even gaudier suite on its top floor and stayed for years, much to Bill Bennett's consternation.

Angel Naves tended to the daily management of the casino floor and Bennett served as on-site CEO, constantly in communication with Bill Pennington, who remained in Reno. They had bought out Mickey Briggs, who was more interested in the Las Vegas high life than the daily drudgery of running a hotel.

Sarno exasperated Bennett. Only a small circle of top executives were permitted to call him anything but "Mr. Bennett," even when they were socializing together after hours. It was rumored that it had taken his wife several months to bring herself to call her husband by his first name. But Sarno would saunter into the executive offices, often wearing a bathrobe and slippers, with bonhomie for all. "Hello, Mel," he would shout to Mel Larson, vice president of marketing, his voice echoing down the corridors. "How are you? Is Billy in?"

Bennett would cringe, but there wasn't much he could do. Sarno was his landlord, a man whose goodwill he still needed. Sarno treated his lessee like his personal bank: though he made a steady $100,000 a month—about $410,000 in today's dollars—from the Circus lease, he invariably needed an advance.

Bennett could afford to give Sarno the money because he had figured out how to run Circus Circus at a profit. When the new tower was finished in 1975 the room count was close to 800—a respectable figure that let the casino begin the mass marketing that Sarno had earlier envisioned. In later years, Bennett received full credit for opening up Las Vegas to the bargain customers. Yet he acknowledged Sarno as "the greatest idea man to ever hit Las Vegas." Bennett's real genius was properly executing Sarno's concept.

Bennett focused on Sarno's one good idea—opening up the casino business to families and budget travelers—and cut out the distractions, like high roller suites. He remodeled Sarno's casino, building a ceiling over the main floor so that slot players could no longer see the acrobats swinging in the air above them. He sent Tanya the elephant packing, closed down the salacious girlie shows, and brought the carnival attractions under firmer control; no customer of his would be cheated by a carnie huckster. Where Sarno had presented a true three-ring circus with something for everyone, Bennett zeroed in on his target market and dispensed with all the frills.

Like Sarno, he believed that the future of the business lay in slot machines. He introduced innovations like progressive slots, which link together several machines to deliver an extra-large jackpot, to the Strip. He also agreed with Naves that the hotel should offer the lowest rates in town, and tasked Larson with filling those rooms. By guaranteeing an $18 a night room—well below the prevailing industry standard—and offering to book overflow guests in other hotels for the same rate, Circus Circus found itself awash in walk-ins. The shorts-and-sneakers crowd, in large enough numbers, more than made up for the loss of premium customers.

Bennett also cut down on employee theft, sanctioned and otherwise, by firing or buying out those who'd been in on the skim. Somehow, he was even able to convince Tony Spilotro to leave. Spilotro ultimately ended up at Frank "Lefty" Rosenthal's side at the Stardust, a partnership fictionalized and celebrated in the movie *Casino*.

Off the bat, cutting out the skim added at least $100,000 to the casino's monthly balance sheet. Bennett could pay Sarno's lease three times over out of that. By offering managers large bonuses to increase their reported results, Bennett gave them an incentive to track the money moving through the casino accurately. Within months of Bennett's takeover, Circus Circus was at last operating in the black. In 1978, the company opened a Reno branch in a converted department store, which Pennington personally managed. Circus Circus was a success.

Although Mel Larson was devoted to Bennett and became a board member of Circus Circus Enterprises, he also struck up a friendship with Sarno. Larson was new to town, and both he and Jay were unmarried. With Sarno living in the hotel and constantly dropping in to offer his advice (wanted or not) to Bennett, they saw quite a bit of each other.

Larson had not started out in gambling. He had always loved racing cars and in the 1950s had both competed on the NASCAR circuit and directed public relations for the organization. He met Bennett while racing in the Mint 400, and in 1974 agreed to move to Las Vegas to work for him full-time as public relations director of Circus Circus. During the day, he did his chores for Bennett, and at night he did the town with Jay.

"Mel, I just got a new Rolls Royce," Sarno announced one evening. "You've got to come for a ride." Larson agreed, and Sarno eased them out of the Circus Circus driveway and onto the streets of Las Vegas.

"You want to drive?" he asked when they stopped at a light.

"Not really," Larson answered. But Sarno insisted, so Larson got behind the wheel. Even though he was an experienced driver, he took extra caution with his friend's brand new Rolls. But after a mile or so, Sarno got impatient.

"Pull over," he demanded.

Larson put the car in park and got out. "What'd I do? Did I do something wrong?"

"Let me show you how to drive a Rolls Royce," Sarno said contemptuously as he settled behind the wheel. *What the hell*, Larson thought. *I've been driving race cars for thirty years. What the hell does he want?*

"Now watch this," he commanded. The car glided to a stop at a traffic signal. "Here's the way you drive a Rolls Royce. You look over your shoulder at the people on your right, and you look over your shoulder at the people on your left, and you feel good, because you are in a Rolls Royce and they're in just a plain old car."

Sarno hadn't been lying about one thing he had told Bob Smith on those tapes. Cash was good, and if you didn't know how to spend it, you might as well not even have it. Not even five years of hell could stymie his love for life.

Even while fighting the appeals, Sarno had been thinking about his next project. Now that he was free to build again, he was ready to start planning in earnest. He knew he wasn't going to get many more chances, and he was going to make this one count.

Even when he was trying to coax enough money out of the Teamsters to build hotel rooms at Circus Circus, Jay Sarno was dreaming bigger. Early in the 1970s, he contemplated something that would have been called The Centurion, a thousand-room Roman-themed luxury hotel. In mid-1973, he announced that he was about five months away from starting work in earnest. But with Circus Circus' struggles and then his legal fight consuming him, he gave up the idea.

As he was collecting his rent checks from Bill Bennett and fighting off the government's seemingly-endless appeals of his acquittal, Sarno hit upon the idea that, he thought, would bring him back to the big time. In retrospect, Circus Circus might have been a mistake—it was daring, yes, but too mundane to be luxurious the way Caesars had been. And starting small, with just a casino, had been wrong. Jay now knew that big was the only way to go.

So he started thinking and doodling and didn't stop until he came up with the Grandissimo.

Sarno announced the project in December 1976. It was to be a 3,000-room hotel spread out over ten buildings connected to a central casino by moving walkways. In late December, he got the county commission to authorize a zoning variance that would let him build the resort on a 110-acre plot on Industrial Road, an unglamorous access road that runs to the west of Interstate 15. It was literally on the wrong side of the railroad tracks and the freeway but, as Sarno reminded potential investors, with great access to the north-south artery.

Then there was silence as Sarno slowly put the pieces together. It wasn't until the spring of 1979 that he officially organized Grandissimo, Inc., a Nevada corporation that would build his dream casino. He now had definite plans for an epic resort that he could deliver with less-than-epic financing.

The Grandissimo was going to have two phases. The first would see the construction of two buildings: a 15-story, main tower with waterfalls cascading down its concave wings, and 2,500 rooms, an 80,000 square-foot casino, ten restaurants and lounges, and a small shopping mall. Sarno planned two theaters: a 2,500-seat venue dedicated to elaborate stage productions, and a more intimate one showcasing celebrity headliners. Maybe, he thought, he could lure Sinatra to sing for him there.

In addition, an 11-story building linked to the casino by an enclosed two-way elevated walkway would house 700 rooms, giving the resort 3,200 rooms and making it, by Sarno's reckoning, the biggest in the world—certainly bigger than anything in Las Vegas. The resort would have something for the whole family, on a far grander scale than the bumper cars at Circus Circus: three pools, including one on the roof, a gigantic flume ride that would splash guests across the property, and a roller coaster that would roar right through the casino. Sarno also penciled in space for a pinball arcade, but he knew that it was the flume and the coaster that would appeal the most to kids—and give their parents someplace to stash them while they gambled.

Phase two would add four more 700-room satellite buildings to the original structures, connected by people movers. At the end, the Grandissimo would have 6,000 rooms—more than double the size of anything else in town.

"It'll be a miniature Disneyland," Sarno said repeatedly, and he meant it. This was going to put Circus Circus and Caesars Palace to shame.

But it wouldn't be on the Strip; Sarno just couldn't get land there. Instead, he secured an option on the land he had gotten the zoning variance for three years earlier. Sarno paid owner William Peccole, a well-connected Nevada real estate developer, $50,000 for a six-month lease option, and was due to pay an additional $200,000 over the next year, at least until he got his financing in order and could sign a 99-year lease, when payments would start at $600,000 a year.

According to the terms of the lease, he was prohibited from funding construction by borrowing money, so he hired M.S. Wien and Company, a small Jersey City trading house, to underwrite an initial public offering of stock. In December 1979, Grandissimo filed a registration statement with the Securities and Exchange Commission, outlining its plans to issue 50,000,000 shares of Class A stock, to be sold over the counter. With a maximum price of $5 a share, this could net the company $250 million, enough to get construction started.

Sarno put together a pragmatic Board of Directors. He was the chairman, naturally, with Tom Bell of Jones, Jones, Bell, Close, and Brown as a director and executive vice president. That was the same firm that, back in 1964, he had been driven to by his FBI agent chauffeur, and it was still an important connection. He brought Howard Kamm, a former manager of the Aladdin casino, as vice president of gaming operations. Kamm learned the casino business in Havana and worked for Howard Hughes at the Frontier. Peccole placed Donald Ward Ozenbaugh, Jr., a Merced, California, CPA, on the board, while Sarno had Sol and Nathan Rogers, who'd invested with him at both Caesars Palace and Circus Circus, and his longtime assistant Evelyn Spinks. She got a place as a reward for her nearly two decades of service and also to give Sarno another friendly vote if push ever came to shove.

Rounding out the board were Michael H. Singer, a partner in Oscar Goodman's law firm, and Roy Tussey, a former FBI agent, who had investigated skimming at Circus Circus during his service at the Las Vegas branch office from 1971 to 1977. He was tasked with supervising corporate security. Jack Biegger, a prominent local car dealer, Jerome J. Vallen, the dean of the University of Nevada, Las Vegas's College of Hotel Administration, and Oran Gragson, a former Las Vegas mayor, gave the company some cachet with Las Vegas's business elite.

Having prominent locals on the board of directors was just one way Sarno tried to get the community behind the Grandissimo. He also offered select power-brokers a chance to buy blocks of stock at 3 cents per share. Harry Claiborne, who just put on the robes of a U.S. district judge, for example, paid $1,000 for 333,333 shares of stock, which would be worth almost $1.7 million if the IPO went off as planned. Many of Sarno's personal friends and long-time backers got similar deals. He even cut Joyce in for 100,000 shares for $300, a potential half-million windfall. Oscar Goodman (and a few of his partners), former sheriff Ralph Lamb, and *Las Vegas Review-Journal* editor Don Digilio all stood to do very well if the SEC signed off on the Grandissimo stock sale.

Sarno was sure he had all of his ducks in a row. He had taken care of the Vegas end of the operation. Now he had to trust the professionals on Wall Street—technically, Jersey City—to do the same.

J uly 23, 1980, was a slow news day, but the front page of the *Wall Street Journal* still had a few items of note. Billy Carter was being investigated for an unlikely foray into international diplomacy: the president's brother, registered as a Libyan agent, got caught trying to arrange that country's intervention in the ongoing Iran hostage crisis. The national recession continued.

 Squeezed under a chart about plummeting durable goods orders, but still above the fold, was a story about Jay Sarno.

In Gaudy Las Vegas, Grandissimo Casino Is to Be Gaudissimo, the headline read.

This was how the investing world learned of the pending Grandissimo IPO and about the man behind the dream.

It wasn't a sympathetic portrait. The second paragraph let the investing public know that, by his own admission, the casino magnate lost nearly $4 million in Las Vegas casinos between 1969 and 1974. "I'm a lousy bettor," is all Sarno offered in his defense. An unnamed rival casino owner said, "I cringe when I run into Jay at a party." Sarno responded that his success had evidently bred envy.

After recounting Sarno's short-lived triumph with Caesars Palace and high-flying antics at Circus Circus (helpfully dropping a reminder about their Teamster financing), the article announced Sarno's latest campaign against decorum.

"It will just be the world's largest hotel and casino, that's all," wrote the reporter, adding that the project was modestly called the Grandissimo.

The reporter outlined the project's "typical Sarno touches:" the roller coaster, the flume ride, the waterfalls, a 35-store mall, two theaters; sixteen tennis courts, and the swimming pools. Six thousand rooms, more than twice the size of the Las Vegas Hilton (which had opened as Kirk Kerkorian's International). The only thing it was missing was a golf course.

The article noted Sarno was still trying to wrangle the SEC's approval of his $250 million stock plan. "I don't see how it could work," one analyst said, noting the on-going economic slowdown. "The last thing anyone needs right now is a 6,000 room hotel-casino in Las Vegas."

The reporter also uncovered the preferential stock deals. The *Journal* ominously noted that one investor anticipating a $6.6 million windfall, Nicholas Tweel, was a longtime business partner of Allen Dorfman. Along with Dorfman, Tweel had managed to win an acquittal on the same 1964 jury-tampering charges that sent Hoffa to federal prison.

"I wouldn't answer that question even if it would save Nick's life," his attorney replied to a reporter's query about precisely what business Tweel's Triad Trust company, indicated in the SEC filings as the potential beneficiary of the stock sale, was in.

Sarno's family was devastated. His sisters couldn't believe that a respectable paper would print such libelous dreck about their brother, who had been one of the country's most successful hotel men for more than twenty years.

His son Jay called long distance from San Diego. "Sorry about the article," he said.

"What do you mean? It's great!" his father enthused, and young Jay could tell that this was no gallows cheer. He really was as excited as a little boy.

"The phone's been ringing off the hook all day! Everybody's interested in putting some money into this now. I can't talk. I'll call you later."

Jay Sarno liked to say that he only ate one meal a day. It was true, but that meal lasted about fifteen hours. Living at Circus Circus, he was never far from a nosh. He just had to pick up the phone and whatever he craved would materialize—a thrill that never got old. When, in 1981, he bought a rambling two-story home that had previously belonged to Sammy Davis, Jr., at 221 Dalmatian Lane in the Rancho Bel Air development, he hired a full-time chef. Sarno still used the Circus suite, but he liked having the house, particularly on the weekends when he had the kids, who were in their teens and early twenties.

It was a stately five bedroom mock Tudor with separate maid quarters and a master suite with a sauna. The crystal chandeliers that hung in the entrance foyer—actually an atrium framed by a massive wood-paneled staircase—gave the place class, as did the stained glass windows throughout. There was a swimming pool out back that didn't get much use.

Sarno's usual weekend morning began around ten-thirty. He'd wake up, press the in-house intercom, and announce, "Breakfast!"

His three youngest children would rush downstairs, where they were greeted by the kind of spread most families only see on Thanksgiving.

After about an hour of noshing and talking with his kids, pausing frequently to take a call or welcome a breakfast visitor, Sarno would shout to his live-in housekeeper, "Dixie, clear out the breakfast dishes and bring out the lunch."

Out came sizzling plates with enough food to feed a neighborhood. Sarno had gone to bed hungry often enough in St. Joseph. No one would ever feel a hunger pang in his house.

Around two, he had be driven to the Las Vegas Country Club in his limousine, his kids taking separate cars, and would grab a sandwich at the snack shop just before he teed off. His kids would cycle in and out, playing tennis and catching up with friends, while

Sarno played with the usual group of big bettors. On the fourth hole he would stop at another snack shop.

"Temmy," he had call to his daughter September, who had come out on the course to see him, "see what you can find in there." He did the same thing at the ninth hole.

Wrapping up his golf around 5:00, he would enjoy the hot hors d'oeuvres waiting inside the clubhouse. For the next hour or two, he would throw back canapés and deviled eggs while playing rummy, all the while thinking about dinner.

Around seven, he would migrate his family caravan over to Caesars Palace, where a nine-course wine-pairing feast at the Bacchanal awaited. After some time at the dice tables, he would head home. But not straight away: before they went home, he would have his driver pull the limo through a Wendy's drive-through. They made his favorite hamburgers, after all, and what better way to wash down one of the priciest meals in town?

When his driver pulled up to the house, he would head straight for the refrigerator to stock up before turning in for the night.

From the time he raised his head from the pillow to the time he returned it there, Jay Sarno was constantly eating.

This did not improve his health. It would be untrue to say that Sarno had struggled with his weight since a young age; he was fat, and there wasn't much he cared to do about it. But in the late 1970s he started putting on even more weight. He had a series of heart problems, and in 1977 underwent open heart surgery. Long ago he had developed adult-onset diabetes. His eyesight kept getting worse and he was having more and more trouble getting around, but Sarno refused to seriously manage his diet. That's not to say he never tried to lose weight. Around the time he moved into the Rancho Bel Air house, a book called *The Beverly Hills Diet* was burning up the best-seller list. Judy Mazel, the author, had no formal medical or nutritional expertise. Her reinvention as a diet guru unfolded, she explained, after a disembodied voice told the former secretary to leave the freeway and buy cashews, leading her into a health food store, where she began reading diet books. The essence of *The Beverly Hills Diet* (named for the modest town where Mazel located her weight-loss clinic) was to allow dieters to eat only one type of food at a time, never mixing carbohydrates and proteins in the same meal. For the first ten days of the diet, adherents ate only fruit.

Credentialed experts attacked the diet as grossly misstating the science of nutrition, and Mazel herself was slammed as the "showbizziest" of the Carter-era crop of diet faddists. But Sally Kellerman and Engelbert Humperdinck offered blurbs on her book's back cover. What more endorsement did you need than that?

Sarno got wind of the diet but wasn't going to waste his time reading the book. Instead, he got in touch with Judy Mazel.

"You're going to help me lose weight," he demanded. He wanted to hire the famous author as his live-in diet coach. When she protested that her services were needed in her own clinic, which at the time boasted more than two hundred patients, he made it clear he was serious.

"I want to lose thirty pounds in a month. I'll pay you a thousand dollars a pound. So that's thirty thousand dollars. You want it? I'll have the jet fly you up here."

"Can I start on Monday?" It wouldn't be hard, she thought, for Sarno to lose that much weight, since he had an inordinate amount to lose. So she moved into a spare room, watching every bite that Sarno put in his mouth. By Thursday, he had dropped eight pounds. Mazel had to return to Beverly Hills on Friday and with five thousand dollars as partial payment for her services.

When she returned to Las Vegas on Sunday, she put her patient on the scale and saw that he had gained three pounds back.

Mazel was astonished. This flew in the face of everything she knew about nutrition; still eating only fruit at this point, he should have continued losing weight. When she learned that he had not, in fact, stuck with the diet, she became furious. His appetite had just cost her three thousand dollars.

"What do you mean?" he responded when she told him that her plan required at least a modicum of self-control. "I'm not paying you five grand to leave me. If I could do it on my own without supervision, I wouldn't need you."

That was the end of Jay Sarno and the Beverly Hills Diet. Mazel kept the five thousand dollars, Sarno lost five pounds (though he quickly found them again), and it was further proof for Sarno that doctors and experts didn't know what they were talking about.

That's not to say that Jay gave up dieting. When a doctor finally referred him to a nutritionist who wasn't bad looking, Sarno offered her the same deal he had offered Mazel. So she moved into the house and spent all day making Sarno low-fat, nutritionally balanced meals, which Jay dutifully ate. Of course, once she was asleep he had his driver steer the limo over to Wendy's for a hamburger or two. Why did he keep her on payroll when he had no intention of really losing weight? It helped that she was pretty and that he was regularly intimate with her, as well as a friend of hers who liked to stop by.

Carol Freeman was still the closest thing Sarno had to a friend. Jimmy Hoffa was gone; Evel Knievel rarely came by, and Allen Dorfman was facing problems of his own. He had been forced out of the union's Central States Pension Fund in 1974. Even so, he remained a power, feared by tough men because of his connections.

But he was still under a cloud. In 1978, he was the subject of yet another federal investigation. He became the target of the FBI's Operation Pendorf (a portmanteau of "Pension" and "Dorfman" or "Penetration" and "Dorfman," depending on the source), a comprehensive wiretapping investigation that sought to uncover links between Dorfman, organized crime, and politicians.

In 1979, agents uncovered a series of potentially incriminating conversations between Dorfman and United States Senator Howard Cannon, a Nevada Democrat who'd served in the body since 1959. Ultimately, Dorfman faced trial—along with Teamster president Roy Lee Williams and alleged Chicago mob figure Joey Lombardo—for conspiring to bribe Cannon to use his influence on trucking deregulation legislation favorable to the union. Though Dorfman had long been a loyal friend to the dangerous men who'd helped him become rich and powerful, those men now feared what he could tell prosecutors should he choose to turn state's evidence in exchange for leniency.

One day, Freddie asked his father why they hadn't seen as much of Allen lately.

"He's involved with some pretty rough people," Jay answered his son, "He's got to be careful."

"Why doesn't he just get away from them?"

"Well, it's not that easy." Sarno himself had seen just how hard it was to outrun his past.

Sarno had also drifted away from Stan Mallin since the trial. In cross examination, Sarno had vigorously denied that he had Mallin deliver the first several bribes so that if anything went wrong, his friend would be left holding the bag and he would get away scot free. "We're a team, we're partners," he insisted. "Do you think I'd hurt that man?"

But only an idiot couldn't see that Sarno had set Mallin up, and Stan was no idiot. Even as Mallin stood in the docket beside Sarno, he couldn't resist taking a few shots at his friend. "I very often turn a deaf ear to Mr. Sarno," he told the prosecutor during his cross examination, "because he talks a lot, as you saw in this courtroom yesterday. We've had many fights about that. I very, very often turn a deaf ear to Mr. Sarno's statements, particularly when they're not relevant to me."

Not everyone was dismissive. Steve Wynn, who had been at Caesars opening night, had made good on his promise to move to Las Vegas. Owning a piece of the Frontier, he cashed out when Howard Hughes purchased the casino in 1967. Then, through a series of business dealings, including the flip of a piece of land adjacent to Caesars Palace, Wynn took control of Downtown's Golden Nugget. Suddenly, the "kid from the Frontier" became a friend of Sarno's, though at first it was a master-student relationship.

"I'm coming down to your joint," Sarno would say. "Make sure you've got my money waiting for me at the cage." Sarno's credit was always good at the Golden Nugget.

Then things changed. Wynn opened a casino in New Jersey. He had been able to build it thanks to his friendship with Michael Milken, the man who'd unlocked the power of junk bonds—high risk, potentially high-yield instruments that fueled much of the merger and acquisition fervor of the 1980s—for the casino industry. Sarno's pupil had arrived; Wynn was palling around with Frank Sinatra himself in commercials for the Nugget. Sarno still blustered ("Give me the Chairman's suite tonight," he would demand when Frank was out of town), but there was some respect as well.

Looking at the plans for a renovation and expansion of the Golden Nugget, Sarno gave him a look—not shock, but recognition.

"I'm proud of you, Stevie," was all he needed to say for Wynn to light up.

The torch was being passed.

Neither the Grandissimo's dim prospects nor its potentially unethical financing hurt Sarno's standing in the community. If anything, it made him even more of a hometown hero. Here was a man who wasn't just doing good for himself—he was trying to do good for Las Vegas. A few months after the *Wall Street Journal* article appeared, the Anti-Defamation League of B'nai B'rith awarded him its Torch of Liberty at a luncheon organized by casino kingpin Carl Cohen—the man who'd decked Sinatra back in 1967—and attended by some of the biggest names in Vegas. They hailed him for his extensive charitable work for several organizations, including the American Cancer Society, the Boys Club of Clark County, the Boosters' at Bishop Gorman High School and the Variety Club Heart Fund.

"A multi-talented man whose endeavors have enriched our lives for many years," the proclamation read, "Jay Sarno has distinguished himself as a giant in the recreation industry."

Yet despite the *Wall Street Journal's* intimations, raising money for the Grandissimo wasn't easy for Sarno, even though Wall Street was starting to cozy up to the casino business. In 1976, Aetna Life Insurance loaned Caesars World $60 million for a host of improvements, including the tower whose suites Sarno loved. It was the first loan from a mainstream lender to a Las Vegas casino company, and it hadn't been put together by Caesars World president Clifford Perlman or any of the casino's old hands; rather it was a young business school graduate, Terry Lanni, who brokered the loan; he would later helm both Caesars World and MGM Mirage, showing that finance could be a path to the top. But for now, he was just helping serious lenders dip their toes into the casino market.

Steve Wynn had built his Atlantic City casino with Wall Street money, showing everyone that the gambling business could be profitable. But the Wall Street guys could talk to Steve Wynn and walk away impressed; they couldn't do that with Jay Sarno.

The planned IPO never came off, and Sarno was left trying to wring money from potential investors through an endless series of face-to-face meetings that went nowhere.

Sarno had picked perhaps the worst moment in the history of Las Vegas—until 2008, at least—to build the Grandissimo. The city was in the midst of a recessionary slump that saw many casinos ditch glitzy amenities in favor of budget accommodations. Bill Bennett even opened an R.V. park at Circus Circus. With competition from Atlantic City ramping up, international high rollers grounded by a global financial meltdown, and a public image battered by the MGM Grand and Las Vegas Hilton hotel fires, Las Vegas was the last city anyone wanted to bet big on.

Yet partially the fault was Sarno's. He always put more effort than thought into the things he cared most about. When he looked to raise money for the casino he wanted more than life itself, he did it his way. Casino operators who were raising capital in the early 1980s knew there was a right way to do it: you hired someone fresh out of Wharton or Marshall who could speak the finance guys' language as your ambassador. It opened doors and allowed major investors to feel at ease.

Sarno had…Jay Sarno.

He thought that maybe if people could see what he could imagine, they'd open their wallets, so he hired architect Wayne Simonds to execute a few renderings of the Grandissimo, which he framed and set up on gold easels, sparing no expense to make a good first impression with potential investors, in his Circus Circus penthouse. Right before a group of big Wall Street guys arrived to hear his pitch, he called Mel Larson downstairs.

"You've got to come up here and see the drawings. They're beautiful."

So Larson took the elevator up and knocked on the door. Sarno answered it himself, wearing only his boxer shorts, his toupee sitting on the coffee table behind him. Evelyn Spinks sat dutifully at a table, smiling while Sarno showed off the drawings.

There was a knock at the door. Larson, expecting Sarno to excuse himself to put some clothes on, prepared for a few minutes of small talk with the investors. But Sarno opened the front door, introduced himself to the Wall Street contingent, all business in their suits and ties even in the Vegas heat, and started his presentation in all earnestness. Not surprisingly, they declined the investment opportunity.

Another time Sarno had Larson take him and another potential investor up in a helicopter to scout the Grandissimo's site, the same way he would have Larson fly his foursome out to the golf course in Pahrump (about an hour's drive; too long to sit in the limo) when a tournament was clogging the greens at the Las Vegas Country Club, landing right off the first tee.

"That was Jay," Larson reminisced years later. "He did everything in a Grandissimo way."

Anyone with a dollar in the bank and time to kill came out to see the Jay Sarno show, just to have something to talk about over cocktails the next week. More than once he got a firm commitment. Talking on the phone, furiously sketching with his right hand while he ran through the details for the hundredth time, he could almost see the casino. And more than once he got an investor to agree.

"Looks like we got the financing," Sarno would enthuse to his kids over one of their meals together. "Let's celebrate!"

But there was always a comedown. The guy who'd given him a $400 million handshake was actually six steps removed from the actual source of funds; the money had been lost in a speculative foreign exchange trade; the would-be broker had been counting on being able to hustle some cash that stubbornly wouldn't be hustled, or Sarno simply found out, after weeks of faith, that he was an out-and-out fraud.

After a while, the Grandissimo was all that was left of Jay Sarno. His gambling was completely out of control. He no longer bet to win or lose. He was feeding the beast.

Then things got worse. Allen Dorfman was convicted of conspiring to bribe Senator Howard Cannon on December 15, 1982. He faced decades in prison and two more trials for other charges related to the Pendorf investigation. The only way for him to avoid dying in jail was for him to cooperate with prosecutors and inform on those above him in the organized crime hierarchy.

In January 1983, after posting a $1 million bond to gain his freedom during his appeal, Dorfman was walking with business associate Irwin Weiner, towards the Lincolnwood, Illinois, Hyatt Hotel, when two masked gunmen approached them from behind, announced, "This is a stickup," and fired eight .22 bullets. Five of them struck Dorfman in the head, killing him instantly. No one believed for a minute that this was a random mugging gone wrong. His former friends weren't taking any chances.

If something like that could happen to Dorfman, handsome and confident and tough, Sarno wondered what was in store for him.

Like Dorfman, he was also facing a difficult decision about what to say in court. Lee Linton, the architect who designed the Circus Circus tower for Sarno, had been indicted for extortion and tax evasion arising out of a construction kickback scheme at the Aladdin, where he was building an addition. Sarno had been called as one of the first witnesses to testify against Linton in October 1982.

Sarno was going to have to testify about financial transactions between himself and Linton that had a bearing on the tax evasion charges. From any angle, it was a lose/lose decision. He might be forced to say something that would get the IRS on his back again. The hint of unsavory dealings could ruin his chances of getting a gaming license. It's also possible that Sarno didn't want to say anything that could get the real powers behind the Aladdin wondering about how much he knew, and what he might be willing to say to stay out of jail.

Sarno failed to appear, explaining that he had to travel to New York to meet with an anonymous banker who was ready to lend him the money he needed to get the Grandissimo started.

When the trial started, however, Linton entered a guilty plea. Sarno would not have had to testify if he had simply shown up. But because he had ignored a subpoena, the Strike Force attorneys who had assembled the case against Linton insisted Sarno be tried for criminal contempt—a charge that could land him a six-month prison sentence.

Sarno hired yet another lawyer and put up a protracted fight against the charges. In February 1983, he won one skirmish when the presiding judge insisted that Strike Force prosecutors Jeff Anderson and Marvin Rudnick be replaced by other prosecutors since they were likely to be called as witnesses. Still, the judge found there was sufficient reason to continue the proceedings, and the trial was scheduled for April.

Sarno kept making the rounds of Las Vegas casinos, gambling as if he had no tomorrow. He half-thought that he didn't.

Finally, on the eve of his trial, Sarno pled guilty to criminal contempt, paying a $250 fine and avoiding jail. The money was nothing, but the threat of jail, as well as the new legal complications a conviction would bring, aged him. He already had no money to build his casino. His option on Peccole's land on Industrial Road had lapsed; he now had nowhere to build it. And here was a fresh black mark on his record that the Gaming Commission would note if he ever applied for a casino license.

By year's end Sarno was completely out of the casino business. Bennett and Pennington's Circus Circus Enterprises was prospering during a recession that saw other casinos declaring bankruptcy; their focus on the low-budget gambler fit the times. After opening the Reno Circus Circus, the company bought Slots-A-Fun, a small grind joint next to its Las Vegas flagship, as well as the nearby Silver City, another minor Strip property. Together with the Edgewater casino in Laughlin, Nevada, Circus Circus's portfolio of five casinos made it the biggest operator, by square footage, in the state.

Circus Circus was making both men incredibly wealthy. The last thing Bennett and Pennington wanted was for Jay Sarno to upset the apple cart by re-assuming control over the Las Vegas casino. The company was looking to get into Atlantic City, whose regulators would never license Circus Circus as long as Sarno was its landlord. When their option to purchase came up in 1983, they exercised it. With the proceeds of $72 million in a new first mortgage, Circus Circus Enterprises bought the casino from Ringmaster, Ltd., Sarno's holding company.

Sarno didn't pocket all those millions himself. He first paid off the $26.2 million in loans still outstanding to the Teamster Central States Pension Fund, as well as $15.5 million he had borrowed from the Nevada Public Employee Retirement System. Then there was Stan Mallin, who finally received his share of the casino: he never worried about money again, becoming active in Las Vegas philanthropy and enjoying life in a house on the Las Vegas Country Club. That still left Sarno a multimillionaire. But even as he signed the paperwork, those millions didn't mean anything to him. He wasn't a hotel man anymore.

Bill Bennett's first act of business as undisputed owner of Circus Circus was to evict Jay Sarno from his gilded penthouse. Seeing the last of his landlord plodding around the casino in his bathrobe and slippers was almost worth $72 million. Then, with the help of Michael Milken at Drexel Burnham Lambert, he organized an IPO for Circus Circus Enterprises. With Bennett's golden balance sheet and Milken's savvy, the shares disappeared in a matter of hours; Bennett and Pennington made millions selling some of their own shares while still retaining sizable positions.

As Jay watched his clothes and golf clubs being boxed up and carted out of the penthouse he had built, he felt the knife twisting. No matter how long you keep throwing the dice, sometimes your number just doesn't come up.

SEVENTEEN

Just Like That, Kid

Las Vegas had changed around Jay Sarno. He couldn't change with it. The Circus Circus cash-out money brought out lackeys catering to Mr. S's every whim, but it couldn't help him build a future. Sarno had never dreamed of a comfortable retirement, of reading the Sunday paper while relaxing in an overstuffed chair with grandchildren frolicking underfoot. He had always wanted to be where the action was. As a managing director of Caesars Palace, he was in the middle of the top joint in the top gambling town in the world. At Circus Circus, even as an absentee landlord, he had prestige. The papers called him "hotel man Jay Sarno," and in Las Vegas in those days, there was hardly a higher honor. But Sarno was now just a "former hotelier." As the months dragged on and investor after investor said no, Grandissimo slipped further and further from his reach. It became a dark joke.

"I'm going to make the Grandissimo eight thousand rooms," he told his son Jay. "After all, it costs just as much not to build eight thousand rooms as it does six."

His diabetes worsened, and he continued to ignore his doctors' advice. He couldn't walk more than a few feet without stopping and his eyesight was worse than ever. His gout flared up most days. Sarno was in physical pain nearly every day.

With his body falling apart and his dream of reclaiming the title of hotel man gone, he settled into a deep depression only slightly mitigated by non-stop gambling and serial sexual conquests. But even that got tired after a while. He reached the point where nothing made him happy. Still, he went through the motions—eating, golfing, gambling, chasing women—mechanically. It was the only thing he knew how to do.

By January 1984, he realized that he wasn't ever going to be a hotel man again.

As his fortunes declined, Sarno wasn't alone. His old friend Evel Knievel, who still walked with a limp thanks to injuries sustained in his Caesars Palace crash, had also fallen on hard times. After beating his erstwhile promoter Sheldon Saltman (breaking the tell-all author's left arm), Knievel pled guilty and served a five-month jail sentence; a civil court later awarded Saltman $13 million in compensation. The IRS and then the state of Montana began hounding him for millions of dollars in back taxes.

But he still stood by Jay. Despite his flashy clothes and Hollywood lifestyle, Knievel never had enough money to invest in Sarno's hotels, though he made a few small investments in his smaller enterprises, like the bumper cars. He always made his money back, something that few of those who invested with Jay could say. Knievel even bought Israel bonds on Sarno's advice, and he sincerely regretted not being able to help Sarno launch Grandissimo.

To cope with his problems, Knievel spent more time in Las Vegas, parking his huge RV at the Las Vegas Hilton, between the Las Vegas Country Club and the casino. He and Sarno golfed together, gambled together, and talked long into the night. Despite the millions he had earned as a daredevil and product endorser, Knievel often had to borrow money from Sarno to gamble. Sometimes he returned the favor.

One night, after playing golf, Sarno pulled up to Knievel's motor home in his Rolls Royce.

"Kid, I need $10,000," was all he could say.

"Okay. I'll go over to the Hilton and sign a marker," Knievel replied.

They went over to the casino. As promised, Knievel got the marker and handed Sarno $10,000 in cash.

"I'll meet you back here in a half an hour," Sarno told Knievel, "at the crap tables."

Forty-five minutes later Knievel couldn't find Sarno. He wasn't at the crap tables, he wasn't anywhere. Then Knievel saw Sarno sitting in the coffee shop, alone.

"Jay, what the hell are you doing here?" he asked. "Did you win or lose?" Sarno said nothing. "I guess you must've lost if you're in here."

Sarno looked up. "Bing, bing," he said, smacking his hands together. "Gone, just like that, kid." He flashed his empty palms to the sky, like a dealer clapping out, his eyes watery. The aging stuntman offered his usual condolences.

"Oh, I'll get them tomorrow," Sarno said, brushing off his bad luck. "Hey, do you need some money?"

"Yeah, I could use it."

"Well, go over to Circus. Let me make a phone call. It'll be in the cage for you." And it was. Sarno always repaid his debts to Knievel.

The pair spent most of their time together on the golf course. Sarno still loved to play, despite being cheated.

With his usual partner, Sarno couldn't do much about it. But with Evel at his side, things were different.

"Robert, watch my ball," Sarno would say.

"Boys, you all know what I've got in the bag," Knievel had already warned the other golfers. "It'll talk six times and go bang, bang, bang. I don't want to catch you cheating this man—or me."

Incredibly, given Knievel's reputation, some of the rounders still tried to take advantage of them. Once, Knievel pulled a gun on a couple of cheaters; they called the police. Clark County sheriff Ralph Lamb himself showed up to adjudicate.

"Look, we know what happened," Lamb told him after hearing it from both sides. "We know who these guys are. But, Evel, it's the only game in town. You're not going to get action like that anywhere else."

"They're cheating us," Knievel told Sarno. "You're an honorable good guy. Why do you expect all these filthy, no good, chickenshit thieves to have the same kind of class?"

The clique of Country Club hangers on were merciless when it came to cheating Sarno at golf and gin, stripping him of millions over the years. Sarno had gotten awards for his community work, but his real charity was on the greens of the Las Vegas Country Club.

But since they couldn't get any honest players to bet $30,000 a game with them, Sarno and Knievel kept playing with the Country Club irregulars.

In his more honest moments, Sarno was aware that he was, as he put it, "a maniac" when it came to golf and gambling. But he couldn't stop himself. Nor could Knievel, who lost more than a million dollars at the Hilton alone in one stretch, prompting casino executives to beg him not to play anymore.

"Jesus Christ, don't gamble your money away out on those tables," casino manager Jimmy Newman begged Knievel. "You're not going to win." But neither he nor Sarno were ever barred from the casino or refused credit.

Sarno knew he couldn't change his nature. At one point he wrote to each casino imploring to be cut off. "Do not let me sign a marker," he candidly told them. "I will not pay you." It was the only way he could think of to control his gambling.

But he soon lost his resolve and convinced the casinos to tear up the letters. When it became clear that he still had enough money to pay off even the biggest marker, he was treated like a king. Usually.

One night, Knievel needed $20,000 to repay Sarno for cash he had been fronted and lost; Sarno wanted to gamble and this was the only money he could get. Knievel went to the Hilton's credit desk to sign a marker. But there was a problem. Casino manager Johnny Oaks stood in front of the clerk and swirled his finger around his ear, as if he was playing with an earring.

"What the hell's this?" Knievel asked.

"Let me have the earring," Oaks responded, gesturing at Knievel's eight-carat diamond showpiece.

"How do I know you're not going to switch the diamond?"

"Well, if you don't want to do it, to hell with you. You want the marker, you leave the diamond."

Knievel gave him the earring and took the money. "I'll be back to get it in a little while," he warned Oaks. Sarno was standing outside the cage, waiting. Knievel gave him the money.

An hour later, Knievel strode into the credit office. "Here's your money," he said to Oaks, slapping down a wad of bills on the desk. "Give me my earring, you cheap little asshole." Jay had won at the craps table and given Knievel back all of the money he had borrowed.

But Knievel wasn't around in Sarno's final months to share the burden of winning and losing. With his dream fading, Sarno began his last race, a final contest to see which would run out first: his money or his life.

Things couldn't have played out any differently. All his life, Sarno had lived for action. He wouldn't change when the time for settling accounts came near. He would double down on living how he had always wanted: like a Caesar.

Others pleaded with him to slow down.

"I heard you've lost $20 million," Stan Mallin said to him. "You've got to stop."

"I don't care."

"You don't care about your kids? Don't you want to leave them some security?"

"I want to gamble. I don't care what happens after that."

In late June, while she was at her Prudential Securities office in Beverly Hills, September got a call from Carol Freeman.

"September, your dad lost $250,000 last night."

"Oh shit," was all September could manage before hanging up.

Despite watching her father escalate his losing for nearly a year, she had never faced the possibility that it might all be gone. She had known abstractly that the Circus Circus windfall would eventually run out, but now she realized it might not take him very long to gamble away tens of millions of dollars.

September had never confronted her father. Even when she worried about his spending, she kept her conversations with him upbeat, convinced that before the bottom fell out he would luck into an investor for the Grandissimo. But she called him with no pretenses this time.

"Dad, I'm really upset," she blurted when he picked up. "Carol called me. I know what you lost last night."

"You know there's ups and downs. I'll get them tomorrow," her father answered by rote.

"We're scared, Dad," September responded, feeling the panic begin to rise inside her. "Heidi and Freddie and I are scared about our future." But her father remained calm.

"What's the matter? Do you need something you don't have?"

"No."

"Do you have everything you need?"

"Yes."

"Has your daddy always provided for you?"

"Yes."

"Then you've got to trust me. I'm still going to take care of you, no matter what."

"But dad, I know how much money you had a year ago and I know what you have now. I'm worried."

"Honey, you have to remember one thing," Jay said, as calmly as ever. "It's my money and I can do anything with it that I want."

Then they hung up. Shaken by the confrontation, September didn't talk to her father for three weeks. Before long, she started to feel guilty about questioning him.

She decided to offer him an olive branch. A friend of hers, hearing stories of how generous Jay was with his dates, had been pestering her for months to introduce them. September finally gave in to Mimi Morton and told her that fine, she would set her up with her father.

As long as he's giving his money away to every woman in Vegas, she thought, why not give it to a girl who says she's my friend?

"Remember that gorgeous girl I told you about?" she asked her father. "The one who had the affair with that government dignitary?"

"Oh, yeah."

"Well, she wants to have a date with you. She's coming into town on Friday. Her boyfriend from Texas isn't getting in until noon Saturday, and she'll be at the Desert Inn."

"Great, great, give me her number." Jay thanked his daughter and hung up. It was the last time they ever spoke.

Finally, it was Friday. Sarno bided his time until his date with Mimi. He made a few phone calls and didn't get any closer to building the Grandissimo than he had been the day before. He played 27 holes of golf. He played cards and won some money. It was a perfect day.

Finally, the moment arrived. Sarno pulled up to the Desert Inn's porte cochere in his limousine. He angled his head to get a look at Mimi from inside the car, but couldn't see more than a blur. Then his driver opened the door, and she sat down next him.

"Jay Sarno?" she cooed. "I'm Mimi Morton. It's just so wonderful to finally meet you."

She was, without a doubt, the most beautiful woman Jay had ever seen. He was actually speechless for a moment. But as the limo pulled away from the Desert Inn and prepared to make a U-turn and head south to Caesars, he felt back in control. It didn't hurt that Mimi was hanging on his every word, nodding along as he talked about his last triumph at the Caesars craps tables.

His driver opened his door with a flourish after helping Mimi out of the limo, and the infamous hotel man and the statuesque blonde turned heads as they walked into the hotel, the recently-remodeled stepped lights of the porte cochere softly illuminating them both. Here, Jay was still an emperor. There wasn't a door that wasn't held for them. Before settling in at his usual dice table, Sarno paused and looked around at the oval space that used to be his casino. With the lanky stickman waiting for the come-out roll, Sarno had to admit that the Perlmans had kept the place looking great.

Trying to impress Mimi with his prowess at craps, Sarno lost $50,000 before he had even finished explaining the game to her.

"Don't worry, honey, I'll be back for it," he said to her as they headed off to the Bacchanal. Truth to be told, she didn't look that concerned that he had just blown enough to buy a four-bedroom house.

As usual, the staff at the Bacchanal couldn't fuss over Sarno enough. Whether it was the way they treated him, or the wine, or just his improbable magnetism, Mimi Morton found herself attracted to him. She could see herself dating him seriously. He was such an important man, but he didn't have anyone to take care of him, she thought. He needs someone to put him right, she mused, as he looked at her with shining eyes, and that someone might as well be me.

"You've got to go to Pritikin," she declared after Jay had talked about his struggles with his weight. One of my…friend's wives spent six weeks there and lost 30 pounds."

"No way, kid. I couldn't handle that place. I'd be bored in twenty minutes," Jay responded.

"What if I go with you?" she asked.

"Why? You don't need to lose weight."

"No, baby, I'll go *with* you. Try it for a week, at least. I'll be there with you the whole time. I'll stand on the treadmill next to you and keep you going. You can do this."

"Maybe you're on to something," Jay said after thinking about it. "Why not? I'll do it. With you."

This girl, he thought, as he couldn't stop looking at her, is the greatest girl in the history of the world. I'm in love.

His throat felt a little dry, even after the wine they'd drunk. His chest was tight. But he felt hope for the first time in a while.

I can do it, he resolved. I can really do it with her. I'm going to get focused. I'm going to get healthy. I'm going to build the biggest hotel in the world. It's all going to happen.

"I've had a wonderful time with you tonight," Mimi said to fill a pause.

"You're not the only one, kid. Let's do it again next week. You'll come up here and stay in my Fantasy Suite with me. It's got a Jacuzzi. You ever sit in a Jacuzzi?"

"Oh, I have. That room sounds like heaven. I wish I didn't have to be back at the Desert Inn tomorrow to see my friend."

"Don't worry about it. I think I'm going to play a little golf and relax a little anyway. Why don't I get up early and pick you up at 10:30 tomorrow morning? I'll take you to get two mink coats— one for you and one for September. I owe her for giving me your number."

"That sounds great, but what am I going to do until 10:30?"

"Why don't we head back to the dice table?" Sarno was already anticipating a big win. "I didn't get to finish teaching you to play craps. And I'm sure you'll be bringing me good luck tonight."

"I've got a better idea. Why don't you show me that suite? I want to know what I'm getting myself in for." She smiled at him, and he would have taken her to Australia if she would have asked. Jay left a tip even more generous than usual and they headed toward the elevators.

"Wait," Jay said before they got there. "Let me run into the gift shop and buy this Herbal Essence stuff. It's the best bubble bath around. We can sit in the Jacuzzi and relax."

Sarno bought the bubble bath and they headed up to the room. He was as giddy as a little kid even though his neck and shoulders felt tight, heavy.

But Mimi made him feel better. She had almost fallen over when she had seen the view from the room. They enjoyed the Herbal Essence and the Jacuzzi, then made love without shame. Then they returned to the Jacuzzi, though Jay was far more tired than he should have been at midnight.

"Honey, you don't look so good," Mimi said, starting to get concerned. "Maybe I should call a doctor."

"No, don't bother," Jay protested. "It's just indigestion." But suddenly he couldn't get enough air into his lungs. "Maybe you should call the front desk…have them send someone…"

The rich food at the Bacchanal, the wine, the exertion all caught up to his diabetes-weakened heart. Suddenly, he wasn't thinking about a second go-around with Mimi. He was scared and alone as he heard her calling the front desk, then moving around the suite, getting dressed and straightening things up.

Jay was still alert but not talking much when the doctor showed up a few minutes later. He called for an ambulance and asked Jay what he was feeling, how long he had felt sick. Between sharp intakes of breath, Sarno answered as best he could.

He was having a heart attack.

He was still conscious when paramedics loaded him onto a gurney and wheeled him towards the ambulance idling in the porte cochere. He could see the casino lights only dimly, but the sounds of the casino—coins smacking metal, gamblers whooping and cursing, waitresses flirting—were as loud as ever. People gambling in his casino. It was the sweetest music he had ever heard.

Just before they hit the doors, someone sevened out.

His eyes were closed as the paramedics grunted and lifted him into the ambulance, though he heard the siren as it pulled out of the taxi lane. He didn't see his fountains, the glorious fountains that he had dreamed of in his cousin Marian's living room, the fountains that had almost killed his friend Evel, the fountains that were still there, against all odds.

The ambulance pulled onto Flamingo Road, heading for Sunrise Hospital. But Jay Sarno never made it to the emergency room. Somewhere along the way, his heart quit on him and his struggles ended, just like that.

EIGHTEEN

The Greatest Hotel Man

In Encinitas, California, Jay C. Sarno and his wife, Bonnie, were still up when the phone rang a little after midnight.

"Oh hell, I bet my dad died," was Jay's gut reaction. His father had looked awful when Jay had last seen him a month before.

"It's your dad," his father's chauffeur told him. "You've got to come home. He's not doing well."

"What's wrong with him?"

"I don't know. He's taken ill. You should really get here quickly."

As he was figuring out how he' would get up to Las Vegas in the middle of the night, his uncle Louis called.

"Jay, I'm sorry, I've got really bad news. Your dad had a heart attack and I'm afraid he died."

It wasn't unexpected. Jay didn't cry. He had long ago gotten over his adolescent squabbles with his dad and had begun to accept him for who he was. In his own way, Sarno was proud of his son, even though he didn't become a hotel man. On a trip to La Costa, he had come over to see a building his son had built for a company he was president of.

"That's nice. Getting a good return?"

"Yeah, we're going well. But the guys keep teasing me about something."

"What?"

"They keep asking me if I'm going to put a fountain out front."

Sarno had smiled. This was his son.

But now that was all far away. Jay knew that he had to get back to Las Vegas. As he was starting to consider the drive, September called, hysterical.

She had been out that night. It had been a rough week for her, and she had vented to her date about her father's mounting losses. She had barely gotten back home when she got a phone call from Caesars.

"You need to come home now," the voice on the other end said. "Your father is sick. They're sending an airplane for you." This was Caesars' charter jet, used to ferry high rollers to and from the casino. Sarno had ridden it many times to the casino's villa near La Costa.

September told her brother about the jet, but not much more. He and Bonnie packed and waited by the phone for further instructions. Meanwhile, Jay reached Freddie, then a junior at the University of San Diego spending the summer near school, and broke the news.

Jay eventually got a call and was told to go to a private terminal at the San Diego airport. Jay met Freddie there, and they waited, and waited. Finally, a harbor patrolman told them that their plane was landing at Palomar airport, in Carlsbad, miles away. Jay and Freddie started driving north.

Around four in the morning, Jay, Bonnie, and Freddie piled into the Caesars Palace Learjet at Palomar; September was already inside. They touched down in Las Vegas at 5 a.m., just as the sun was coming up.

A cheerful young woman came out to greet them. Thinking they were a group of high rollers getting a late start on the weekend, she laid on the charm.

"Hi, welcome to Las Vegas," she started, as they shuffled off the plane. "I bet y'all are here for an exciting weekend of gambling!"

"No, our father just died," Jay mustered, almost feeling sorry for her. Couldn't someone have told her?

The four of them went to the Rancho Bel Air house. A crowd of domestic help, girlfriends, and other retainers was milling around.

The children knew that their first priority was to get Heidi home. She had just graduated from the Bishop's School in La Jolla and was on a class trip in Eastern Europe. It took over a day for Jay, working through the school, to get in touch with her. It took her another day to get on a plane bound for Las Vegas.

Meanwhile, Jay had assumed the brunt of the funeral planning responsibilities. September was beside herself with grief and was only able to catch a few hours sleep after she helped herself to one of her father's sleeping pills. Freddie was still a college kid, and Heidi wasn't there.

So Jay fielded calls from the press and a motley group of strangers he had never met, each asserting a claim on his father's friendship. His mother flew up from Louisiana to support her children, but Carol circling around the house only added to the tension. Though Joyce had remarried, she still couldn't forgive her husband's mistress.

His father's sister Sara Corash called.

"Jay, it's so terrible," she said. "We're all so upset. We're all flying out there. Will you please send the car to meet us and get us rooms at Caesars?"

"Sara," Jay told her, "the guy who could do that for you just died."

"Well, won't they give you rooms out of respect?"

"I doubt it," Jay responded, "I don't have time to be a travel agent right now. Could you take care of it on your own?"

Jay, Freddie, and September went to Palm Mortuary to make the funeral arrangements. When they looked at caskets, he saw a silver and black model.

He turned to September. "It looks like his Rolls. Let's get him that one."

She agreed.

Returning to the house, Jay found friends of his father looting it, as if it were the palace of an assassinated Caesar.

"We're just trying to help," they told him. "We're getting this stuff out of here for tax reasons."

"Just leave it alone," was Jay's response. Meanwhile, the staff, worried about getting paid, was discussing how to break into Sarno's safe to get the cash inside. Several girlfriends, acquaintances, and flings were showing up, hoping that Sarno would be as generous in death as he was in life. Surely he had left something for them. Jay did his best to shoo them away.

He asked his brother, who knew his father's friends far better than he did, to pick the pallbearers. Jay then asked Carol to pick out a suit for his father to be buried in. Grateful, she charged off to the closets with a sudden sense of purpose.

The calls kept on coming: queries from the media and condolences from casino executives. Then the chauffeur pulled Jay aside.

"A couple of people asked if there's going to be a private viewing separate from when everybody else is going to be there. There are certain people who'd like to pay their last respects, but they can't be around when…"

"If you think I'm going to set up a second viewing for the hookers in this town," Jay cut him off, "you're fucking nuts. Forget it."

The family scheduled the funeral for Tuesday afternoon. With well-wishers, opportunists, and thieves swooping through the house and their concerns over Heidi, none of the siblings got much sleep over the next three days.

Finally, at 11 AM on July 24, Jay Sarno's children, with Jay's wife, Bonnie, got into a limo that took them to the Palm Mortuary. It was time to say goodbye to their father.

The funeral chapel was already crowded when the children arrived, and they immediately went to work greeting the mourners while camera crews started setting up in the back.

Carol Freeman said as she approached Jay. "I don't know where it's appropriate for me to sit."

Jay replied, "If you're asking me where the mistress is supposed to sit at a funeral, I don't know. And I don't care. You can sit anywhere you want."

Needless to say, Jay Sarno didn't have a typical funeral. It certainly wasn't a traditional Jewish funeral. The preparations flouted most of the usual customs. Religious Jews bury their dead in simple white shrouds which represent how completely death erases the distinctions of wealth and privilege, and with burial usually taking place the day after death.

This later became a source of family strife. At the time, Jay insisted that the service be non-religious because of his father's hostility towards religion. He thought it would be hypocritical to give a man who "thought religious people were idiots" a pious sendoff.

Later, he realized that funerals are more for the benefit of the living than the dead. "I would have made it more Jewish," he admitted, "to pacify the people who were still alive." Mostly, that meant his father's three sisters, Phyllis Dunetz, Hannah Saal, and Sara Corash. Brother Louis was there, but as usual he wasn't bothering anyone.

The sisters bristled at the news crews and their cameras, saying that it wasn't proper to turn their brother's funeral into a circus. To them, he was still a darling little brother who was smart as a whip and so ambitious. They still couldn't fully understand the world he had built for himself as an emperor of Las Vegas.

The service started. As Sarno's friends took turns telling stories about the wild times they'd shared with him, the nights out, the big golf games, the sisters turned ashen. Each peccadillo was another knife to the heart.

Sara got a chance to restore some dignity, speaking about what a wonderful provider he had been, what a public-minded man, the pride of his family.

Then Jay offered a few words. He looked at the crowd of casino guys, golf hustlers, hard women. These were his father's people, no doubt about it.

"What my dad really wanted was to be famous. Go outside and look around at the Strip. He got his wish." He talked for a few minutes about the casinos, about the schemes, before putting down his notes and looking directly at his aunts.

"If any of you have been shocked by anything said here today, please keep in mind who we're burying today. It's all perfect."

That said, the funeral party left the chapel and lowered Jay Sarno's body into plot 270G in the Garden of Honor, the section of Palm Mortuary dedicated to military veterans. The headstone was eventually paid for by the Veterans Administration.

The kids went back to the house and watched coverage of the funeral on the news, while everyone sat around and talked, snacking on food the hotels had sent over.

Jay Sarno was really gone: there would be no roller coaster casino, no six thousand-room hotel.

The papers gave him his due respect. The *Las Vegas Sun* obituary noted that he "made his first dollars as an enterprising student at the University of Missouri." After detailing his ownership of Caesars Palace and Circus Circus, the paper said that his latest "dream," the

Grandissimo, "remains uncompleted with his death." It was a telling choice of words. Most entrepreneurs have projects; only guys like Jay Sarno have dreams.

After brushing aside "legal conflicts involving the Internal Revenue Service, the Teamsters Union, and federal courts," the obituary went on to speak of his good works: "[he] was a supporter of nearly every charitable and philanthropic cause in Nevada."

"We are extremely proud of him—he created 20,000 jobs," September was quoted as saying. "He was a genius not without faults, but a genius in the true sense of the word."

The *Los Angeles Times*, whose brief notice focused on Sarno's success with Caesars Palace, credited him with "the initial vision of the Roman-style resort with its colonnaded structures and statuary," briefly mentioned Circus Circus and the Grandissimo, but didn't touch on his legal troubles.

In death, Jay Sarno had become almost respectable.

With time, Sarno's death became another "Jay story" that got bigger with each telling, making the Vegas rounds with a chuckle and a shrug. The simple facts themselves, that he had succumbed to a heart attack after a tryst with a woman decades younger in a Fantasy Suite weren't quite fantastic enough for Jay Sarno. So they were embellished.

Some said he dropped dead at the craps table after winning a million dollars. Others insisted that it was after he had *lost* a million dollars. Most of those who told the story correctly placed him in a Fantasy Suite, and, as was said about John Garfield's passing, neither alone nor unappreciated. But once someone switched Mimi's role from "date" to prostitute, the tale became grander. He passed away after servicing two working girls, one version went. Or it was three, four, or, according to one oldtimer, no less than five girls who shared Sarno's final hour.

Even in death, Jay was larger than life.

Soon, the whole story was crystallized into an anecdote—it was too serious to call it a joke, too profane to be a parable—that circulated throughout the bars and dealer's lounges of Las Vegas.

"Jay Sarno died the way every man wishes he could. He departed this life in the most fantastic suite inside the most gorgeous hotel in the world with a beautiful girl, owing the IRS a million bucks."

It's now been more than twenty-five years since Jay Sarno died. The world is a much different place now than it was when Sarno began to change Las Vegas. The week that Caesars Palace opened, outraged citizens burned Beatles albums en masse after John Lennon asserted that Christianity was doomed to perish, that at that very moment his band was more popular than Jesus Christ. Ministers organized record-burnings, and the band received numerous death threats.

But Las Vegas was in a bubble: the emperor Nero had his own Nook at Caesars Palace. Here, the notorious persecutor of Christians presided over lounge entertainment, in spirit if not in body. Yet there were no demonstrations against a commercial establishment that celebrated a man some early Christians considered the Anti-Christ.

Forty years later, the Beatles returned to Las Vegas. In early 2006, the Cirque du Soleil entertainment troupe partnered with Apple Corps, the Beatles' licensing corporation, to present Love, a "re-imagination" of the Fab Four's music, at the Mirage casino resort. It's a true Vegas spectacle. An ethereal woman floats through the air during "Something." Acrobats bounce on trampolines for "Revolution." Audience members, many of whom weren't born when the Beatles broke up, pay up to $310 for seats in the $100 million custom-built theater. Commerce and counter-culture have reached a rapprochement.

Not even in his most grandiloquent moments would Sarno have claimed that he was responsible for bridging that gap. But his properties paved the way for the massive success of Las Vegas in the 1990s, and they anticipated the major shifts in personal morality and entertainment that American culture would take.

Sarno's influence eventually extended over all of Las Vegas, though few would realize it. Steve Wynn integrated Sarno's vision with his own, but with one crucial addition: he was able to convince bankers and fund managers to fund his dreams. Five years after Sarno's death, his former apprentice turned the world on its head with The Mirage, a 3000-room mega-resort with waterfalls, a volcano, and its own rainforest. It was a Sarno casino on steroids, built with Wall Street money that Jay never could have gotten. Within ten years, there were a score of Mirage imitators, and Wynn would be celebrated as the inventor of modern Las Vegas.

Wynn wasn't the only one Sarno inspired. Circus Circus Enterprises, building on the success of Sarno's slots-first philosophy, opened a 4,000-room medieval mega-resort, Excalibur, followed by the pyramidal Luxor. In 1999, with the completion of Mandalay Bay, a South Seas-themed resort, the company ditched the big top and officially changed its name to Mandalay Resort Group. Six years later, it was acquired by MGM Mirage, the company created when Kirk Kerkorian's MGM Grand, Inc. bought up Steve Wynn's casino empire. The casinos built by Sarno's one-time landlord, his former lessees, and his star pupil now had a single owner. Though there's a world of difference between the Bellagio and Circus Circus, all the casinos in the MGM Resorts' portfolio had one thing in common: there's a little bit of Sarno in each of them.

Caesars Palace had a more complicated legacy. Clifford Perlman prospered at the helm of Caesars World, as the casino became the most famous in the world. But then things started to go wrong. Perlman and his brother were forced to step down from the company after New Jersey regulators balked at their dealings with Alvin Malnik, a Miami Beach lawyer and partner of Samuel Cohen, who'd been ensnared in Meyer Lansky's skimming operation at the Flamingo. Without the Perlmans, Caesars World was permitted to keep its Atlantic City casino, though it soon became a takeover target. In 1995, ITT bought Caesars World, including Caesars Palace and casinos in Lake Tahoe and Atlantic City, for $1.7 billion, adding to a portfolio that included Sheraton hotels, the Desert Inn casino, Madison Square Garden, the New York Knicks, and the New York Rangers.

But Caesars Palace didn't bring ITT much luck. Three years later, hospitality giant Starwood Lodging Trust swallowed up ITT. Less than 18 months later, Starwood decided it didn't want to play emperor; tired of the volatility and high costs of the VIP casino business, it sold its Caesars World casinos, which now included outposts in Indiana, Mississippi, Delaware, and management contracts on three continents, to Park Place Entertainment.

Park Place had been formed from the spinoff of Hilton Hotels' casinos, including the flagship Las Vegas Hilton, originally built by Kirk Kerkorian. Park Place also caught the Caesars bug: in early 2004, it renamed itself Caesars Entertainment, acknowledging the supremacy of the Caesars brand. But the company didn't remain supreme for long; the following year, Harrah's Entertainment bought it. In 2010, Harrah's changed its name to Caesars Entertainment, tempting fate, or perhaps thinking that it wouldn't be as snake-bitten as its predecessors.

So today, Jay Sarno's stamp is all over Las Vegas. Caesars Entertainment owns ten casinos; MGM Resorts owns another ten; Steve Wynn owns two; and Sheldon Adelson's Venetian and Palazzo have applied Sarno's theme idea to another Italian locale.

While Sarno's name wasn't on any marquees, those in the know acknowledged his contribution.

"It was Jay who brought Las Vegas the first concept that the place itself is the show, from top to bottom, stem to stern, the costumes, the architecture," Steve Wynn said in a 1998 Associated Press story celebrating his own role in re-inventing Las Vegas. "He thought that the design should be an imagination excursion. And Caesars Palace did that.

"Somebody, if not me, would have picked up on what Jay was trying to do in Las Vegas. We just got there first."

Wynn was speaking as he was on the cusp of building what he called "the most romantic hotel in the world," the Bellagio, across Flamingo Road from Caesars Palace. Wynn was in the process of designing its ample water feature—an artificial lake with fountains that shot water two hundred feet into the air. Sarno, lover of water and romance, would have loved it.

Sarno's colleagues came to acknowledge his vision. In 1989, Wynn gave a speech at Sarno's induction into the Gaming Hall of Fame; it was a vindication of Sarno's importance to the business he changed so profoundly. At the time, the industry gathered annually at the World Gaming Congress and Exposition in Las Vegas to buy the latest technology, network, and trade gossip. In 1989, the show's organizers decided to pay tribute to some of the casino business's luminaries by creating a Hall of Fame. Its inaugural class included E. Parry Thomas, the banker who helped build most of the hotels of the Strip, northern Nevada casino legend Bill Harrah, and Jay Sarno.

At the induction ceremony, fittingly held at Caesars Palace, September, Heidi, and Freddie were on hand, as was Steve Wynn. Presented with their father's honor, the daughters let Freddie say a few words on behalf of the family.

"We'd like to thank the World Gaming Congress for remembering our dad," he said. "As I speak to you from the most famous hotel in the world, there's a special, warm feeling in our hearts. We are so proud of him.

"Our father was a unique and creative man—it was apparent in his work. He would strive to build anything but ordinary. Caesars Palace will always be the standard that everything else is compared to.

"But he wasn't just creative. He had a passion for gambling. He loved this town. And all of his ideas, in a broad scope, enriched this industry and this town.

"We are delighted, touched, and appreciative of the recognition given to our father tonight. Thank you very much."

The industry still acknowledges its debt to Sarno. Each year at the Global Gaming Expo, the highest honor bestowed upon an architect or visionary is the Sarno Award for Lifetime Achievement.

In the 1990s, Heidi began working to address some of the wrongs she felt had been perpetrated on her father's legacy. She was most concerned about her father's final resting place. The spartan headstone didn't seem a fitting tribute to her father:

JAY J. SARNO
JULY 2, 1921 – JULY 21, 1984

So she added a Jewish star above the name and, below the date:

THE GREATEST HOTEL MAN

Almost as an afterthought, the lowest line reads:

BELOVED FATHER AND GRANDFATHER

Heidi wasn't content with embroidering her father's resting place. She wanted to create a more public monument to him.

In some cities, having a street named for you is the ultimate honor. In Las Vegas, it's usually less about civic accomplishment than star power or old-fashioned juice. The first street most Vegas visitors see is Wayne Newton Boulevard, a feeder road for McCarran International Airport and a fitting monument to

"Mr. Las Vegas." A small road running behind the University of Nevada Las Vegas's Thomas and Mack Center is named for Jerry Tarkanian, the beloved—and beleaguered—basketball coach who guided the Running Rebels and the town to unprecedented glory in the early 1990s. There's even a road named for Mel Tormé, probably not so much on the merits of his velvety voice as for the fact that his sister, Myrna Tormé Williams, was a longtime Clark County commissioner.

So Heidi set about having a street named for her father, eventually settling on an access road inside the Caesars Palace acreage. Running from Caesars Palace Drive, the Strip-front entrance to the property, past the Colosseum, under the Forum Shops mall, and back to Frank Sinatra Drive, employees, guests, and delivery trucks use Jay Sarno Way every day.

Officially renamed in 2005, just as the Harrah's purchase became final, the street is the only memorial in Las Vegas that bears Jay Sarno's name. Yet there are other places that he is remembered. His daughter September hasn't visited his grave in years. He's not there, she insists. When she wants to feel close to her dad, she'll go to the Caesars Palace baccarat room and place a few high-stakes wagers. That's where she finds his spirit is strongest.

If you walked into Caesars Palace today, you'd hardly believe it was the same place that Jay built. The Circus Maximus theater is gone; the Bacchannal gourmet room is gone, its name given to a buffet; room 1066 hasn't been the finest suite for years; that honor now falls to the 10,000 square-foot Constantine villa overlooking the pool. But one thing hasn't changed: the fountains that welcome visitors. They are an oasis of calm amidst the boulevard's frenzy, and they look exactly the way Jay Sarno designed them, down to the Winged Victory that Sarno planted at their crest—a fitting symbol of the hope that never dies. And it's fitting, because although Las Vegas has reinvented itself several times since Sarno's 1984 death, it's still a city built in his image. Whether as a high roller haven, themed retreat, or family-friendly vacation spot, Las Vegas has only gone where Jay Sarno pointed the way.

Sometimes, the city loses sight of Jay's vision, but at times of crisis, it comes back to him. Scrambling to redefine itself in the post-9/11 gloom, an ad writer with R&R Partners created a slogan, "What Happens Here, Stays Here," that defined the Las Vegas Convention and Visitor Authority's promotional efforts for the next decade. The new Las Vegas, with nightclubs, celebrity chefs, world-class shopping, and five-diamond suites, wasn't about the mundane; it was a release from a threatening world, an oasis of 24/7 freedom. People wanted to hear this message, and they flocked back to Vegas.

Those were the boom years, when anything seemed possible. Otherwise-sober gaming executives caught the fever, betting big that the future would bring only better news—a gambler's outlook if every there was one. The same lenders who would have scoffed at Sarno for wanting to build 6,000 rooms in 1979 thought nothing of wagering that the Strip could absorb tens of thousands of new luxury rooms.

Even through the subsequent slowdown, the worst in the city's history, the image of Vegas as a fantasy world remained strong. Most of its homeowners might have been underwater on their mortgages; unemployment may have been high; people might have stopped moving to the desert to chase the American dream. But for those who visited Las Vegas, it remained a place where they can be the people they only dream about being back home.

In other words, exactly how Jay Sarno knew Las Vegas had to be.

And that—more than Caesars Palace, more than Circus Circus, even more than the Grandissimo concept that foresaw a generation of super-resorts—is Jay Sarno's final gift to the city that let him, for a time, reign as emperor.

Notes

2 THE WINDSOR KNOT

13   Jay's feelings about his father: Oral History Interview with Jan Corash, July 13, 2007, 1; Oral History Interview with Lillian Sarno, February 8, 2007. New York City. 9.

13-4 Life in Szczuczyn: Martin Gilbert. *The Routledge Altas of Jewish History*. Sixth Edition. London: Routledge, 2003. 72-3, D; Dombrovska, Abraham Wein and Aharon Vai . "Szczuczyn"in *Encyclopedia of Jewish Communities. Poland*. Volume 4. Jerusalem: Yad Vashem, 1976-99. 445-8. accessed at *In Memory of Szczuzyn* website, URL: http://www.szczuczyn.com/index.htm.

14   Alexander's early years in the United States: Lillian Sarno, 15.

15   Alex and Nellie's early years in St. Joseph: Jan Corash, 1. Lillian Sarno, 9.

15   Stench around Indiana Street house: Lillian Sarno, 15-6.

15   Young Jay being bullied: Einbender, 1.

15   Nellie taking control of the family: Lillian Sarno, 13.

16   The Sarnos' employment in the 1920s: Jan Corash, 3.

17   The Sarnos' commitment to Jewish observance: Lillian Sarno, 17-8.

17   Jay's lack of religiosity: Oral History Interview with Paul Sarno. July 13, 2007. Las Vegas, Nevada. Cited hereafter as P. Sarno. Recorded over telephone.

17   Herman's asserting control over the family: Jan Corash, 4.

18   Herman's successes in business: Larry Corash, 4.

18   Herman's losses at cards: Jan Corash, 5.

18   Sam and Herman's disagreements over money: Rosenbloom, 7.

19   "We were a poor family…" "$15 Million Las Vegas Spot," *St. Joseph News-Press*, October 13, 1968. 10A.

20   Sarno' second thoughts about the marriage: Paul Sarno. 5.

20   Jay walking out of Windsor: Rosenbloom, 6; Larry Corash, 6; Paul Sarno, 5.

21   Jay's reconsidering: September Sarno, 4; Paul Sarno, 5.

22   Joyce blocking Jay's view of golf courses: Rosenbloom, 6.

3 JIMMY LENDS A HAND

23-4 Stan Mallin's background: Oral History Interview with Stan Mallin. January 29, 2008. Las Vegas, Nevada. Cited hereafter as Mallin. 1.

24   Contrast between Mallin and Sarno: Oral History Interview with Allen Greenberg. February 7, 2008. New York, New York, 11; Mallin, 1.

24   Mallin's desire to join with Sarno: Mallin, 2.

24-5 Lake of the Woods craps game: Einbender. 6.

25   Sarno's gambling in Atlanta: Mallin, 18.

25   Descriptions of Sarno's latest project: Fred Hartley. "Atlanta Cabana Plush, Pampering," *Atlanta Journal*, December 5, 1958.

26   Morris Abram biography: William Honan. "Morris Abram Is Dead at 81; Rights Advocate Led Brandeis." *New York Times* Mar 17, 2000. C19.

26   How Sarno and Mallin met Abram: Mallin, 5.

27   Hoffa's habits Arthur A. Sloan. *Hoffa*. Cambridge: The MIT Press, 1991. 54, 61.

27   Melvin Grossman's Miami career: Eric P. Nash and Randall C. Robinson Jr. MiMo: Miami Modern Revealed. San Francisco: Chronicle Books, 2004. 73, 74, 91, 101.

28   Jo Harris's biography: John G. Edwards. "Visions of an Empire." *Las Vegas Review-Journal*, December 20, 1997. 1D.

28   Jo Harris's initial meeting with Sarno: K.J. Evans. "Dream Weaver," in A.D. Hopkins and K. J. Evans, editors. *The First 100: Portraits of the Men and Women Who Shaped Las Vegas*. Las Vegas: Huntington Press, 2000.

28-9 The Atlanta Cabana's design: Fred Hartley. "Atlanta Cabana Plush, Pampering," *Atlanta Journal*, December 5, 1958; "Swank Motel Here Holding Open House, "*Atlanta Constitution*, December 6, 1958.

29   The Cabana' s pool: Atlanta Cabana brochure; Hugh Park. "Operator of a New Motel Has His Early Problems." *Atlanta Journal,* December 10, 1958; Fred Hartley. "Atlanta Cabana Plush, Pampering," *Atlanta Journal*, December 5, 1958.

29   The Cabana's opening: Fred Hartley. "Atlanta Cabana Plush, Pampering," *Atlanta Journal*, December 5, 1958.

30   Cabana's Teamster disrepute: Oral History Interview with Evelyn Spinks Cappadonna. August 1, 2008. Las Vegas, Nevada. 1.

30   Sarno's office: Cappadonna, 2.

30   Alex Sarno's lack of creativity: Paul Sarno, 1, Jan Corash, 11.

30   Sarno's design aesthetic: Einbender, 7.

31   News accounts of the Cabana: Fred Hartley. "Atlanta Cabana Plush, Pampering," *Atlanta Journal*, December 5, 1958.

31   Standard Town and Country Club: Lillian Sarno, 32.

31   Sarno's pants-splitting: Ed Miles. "Jay Steams Forward Despite Rip in Stern," Newspaper article, date unknown.

32   Sarno's performance in the 1958 City Amateur Championship: Mickey Logue. "Sarno Duels 'Dolly' Today," Newspaper article, date unknown.

33   Sarno's windowless room concept: Jan Corash, 9.

33   Sarno's praise of Jimmy Hoffa: J.C. Sarno 2, 11.

34   September 1959 Teamsters CSPF meeting: Ralph James and Estelle James. *Hoffa and the Teamsters: A Study of Union Power*. Van Nostrand, New York, Van Nostrand, 1965. 252-5.

34   Jack Ruby and the Dallas Cabana: *Report of the Warren Commission on the Assassination of President Kennedy*. New York: Bantam, 1964. 312.

34   Sarno and Raquel Welch: Mallin, 8.

35   Palo Alto Cabana: Marc Igler. "Our Town: The Cabana's Return." *Palo Alto Weekly,* December 30, 1998; Email communication with Matthew Bowling, September 5, 2008.

35   Wedding photographs: Oral History Interview with Arlene Bates. September 12, 2008. Las Vegas, Nevada. 2.

35   Nero's Nook and the Goddesses: Bates, 1-3.

36   Caesar's Seizure: Bates, 18.
36   Doris Day, Marty Melcher, and the Cabanas: Mallin, 8.
36   Palo Alto Cabana's renown: Email communication with Matthew Bowling,
        September 5, 2008.
36-7   Westover Drive home: Jay C. Sarno 1, 1.
37-8   Evelyn Spinks's introduction to Sarno: Cappadonna 2, 7.
38   Sarno and Carol Freeman: Bates, 4, 17; Cappadonna, 11, 17.
39   Joyce teaching Carol to golf: Personal communication with September Sarno.

4 Las Vegas Comes to Jay Sarno

40   Jay's claimed introduction to Las Vegas: George Stamos. "Caesars Palace."
        Las Vegas Sun Magazine, October 14, 1979. 6.
40   Sarno and Mallin's Flamingo junket: Mallin, 6.
40   Morris Lansburgh: "Flamingo Hotel Sold." *New York Times*. May 30, 1960.
        22.
40   Flamingo tour packages: "News and Notes from the World of Travel. *New
        York Times*. April 23, 1961. 533.
41   Lansburgh's management of the Flamingo: Dick Odessky. *Fly on the Wall:
        Recollections of Las Vegas' Good Old, Bad Old Days*. Las Vegas: Huntington
        Press, 1999. 131.
41-2   Strip architecture in 1963: Alan Hess. *Viva Las Vegas: After-Hours
        Architecture*. San Francisco: Chronicle Books, 1993. 53.
42   Sarno settling in to gamble immediately: Mallin, 6.
43   Flamingo's entertainment policy: Forrest Duke. "Show Biz 'Breakthroughs'
        scored in Vegas in '62," *Las Vegas Review Journal*, January 1, 1963. 1.
43   Robert Goulet at the Flamingo: "Flamingo Prepares for Goulet Stint,"
        Las Vegas Review-Journal, February 8, 1963; Forrest Duke. "The Visiting
        Fireman," *Las Vegas Review-Journal*, February 10, 1963
43   Sarno's reaction to the Flamingo: Mallin, 6.
44   Sarno's boredom with Las Vegas 1963: Cappadonna, 9.
44   Perceptions of early 1960s Las Vegas: Peter Wyden. "How Wicked is
        Vegas?" *The Saturday Evening Post*. November 11,1961. 17-8; Bill Becker.
        "A Desert Babylon." *New York Times*. July 16, 1962. 43.
44   Sarno's trip around town: Mallin, 7.
45   Grant Sawyer's diversification drive: Gene Shearman. "Nevada Seeks
        Industry to Reduce Its Long Dependence on Gambling." *Los Angeles
        Times*, May 12, 1961. 2.
45   Esquire profile of Las Vegas 1961: Arthur Steuer. "Playground for Adults
        Only." *Esquire*. August 1961. 41-2.
45-6   Nick Dandalos: Steuer, 46; Peter Wyden. "How Wicked is Vegas?" *The
        Saturday Evening Post*. November 11,1961. 18.
46   Teamster involvement in Las Vegas: James and James, 381-4.
46   "Get Hoffa" squad: Arthur A. Sloane. *Hoffa*. Cambridge: The MIT Press,
        1991. 176.
46   Federal perceptions of Hoffa in Las Vegas: "Vegas Gaming-Crime Probe

Reports Said Exaggerated." *Nevada State Journal.* November 7, 1961. 1.

47   Sarno investigated because of Hoffa ties: Gene Blake and Jack Tobin. "Doris Day and Toots Shor Figure in Teamster Loans." *Los Angeles Times*, October 22, 1962. A1.

47   Nevada gaming's black book: David G. Schwartz. *Suburban Xanadu: The Casino Resort on the Las Vegas Strip and Beyond.* New York: Routledge, 2003. 137-41.

5 From St. Peter's Square to Flamingo Road

53   Sarno's plans to build in Las Vegas: Mallin, 7.

54   Kirk Kerkorian's biography: Dial Torgerson. *Kerkorian: An American Success Story.* New York: Dial Press, 1974. 95, 154.

54   Kerkorian buying land from the Backers: Clark County Assessor's records: 140-140-001.

55   Kerkorian's impressions of Sarno: Personal communication with Kirk Kerkorian, October 19, 2007.

55   Morris Seidelbaum is a pseudonym.

55   Introduction to Nathan Jacobson: Mallin, 7.

56   Nate Jacobson biography: John L. Scott." Palace Really Fit for Caesar." *Los Angeles Times*, July 4, 1966. D16.

56   Sarno and Mallin's agreement with Jacobson: Mallin, 7.

56   Jacobson's gambling problem: Mallin, 7.

57   Clifford Jones biography: George McCabe. "A Life of Adventure—Nevada Style," *Las Vegas Review-Journal*, March 4, 1993. P. 1C.

58   James Ford is a pseudonym; the SA in question's name was nowhere in the FBI's official version of events.

58-60 Sarno's conversation with Ford: FBI Airtel dated 2/11/1962, LV 92-1256..

60   Hoffa's conviction: Gerald Kurland. James Riddle Hoffa. Charlotteville, New York: Samhar Press, 1972. 28-9.

61   Reaction to Sarno interview: FBI Teletype dated February 13,1964, 67-5; FBI General Investigative Division memo, February 13, 1964, 67-5

62   Kerkorian's lease to Sarno: Clark County Assessor's records: 140-140-001; FBI Memo dated October 19, 1973, LV 156-21.

62   Rosenstein's loan: Cappadonna, 10.

64   Sarno's stay with Sara Corash: Larry Corash, 7-8.

65   Sarno's stay with Marion Portman: Telephone interview with Marian Portman. February 21, 2007.

65   Marshall Logan is a pseudonym.

65   Burton Cohen biography: Oral History Interview with Burton Cohen. Interviewer, Claytee White. Las Vegas, Nevada. January 9, 2009. 1.

66   Sarno's meeting with Cohen: Oral History Interview with Burton Cohen. Interviewer, David G. Schwartz. Las Vegas, Nevada. January 26, 2010. 2, 6-7.

67   Sarno's introduction to Jerry Zarowitz: Mallin, 9.

67   Jerry Zarowitz biography: Dan E. Moldea. Interference: *How Organized*

Crime Influences Professional Football. New York: William Morrow and Company, 1989.59, 243.

67-8   Zarowitz's presence in the casino: Mallin, 9; Oral History Interview with JoeyTrujillo, Interviewer, David G. Schwartz. Las Vegas, Nevada October 8, 2008. 13-4.

68   Harry Lewis as a shareholder: Gaming Commission transcript, 05/20.1966 meeting, p. 36

68   Zarowitz's actual role at Caesars Palace: Mallin, 9; Wynn, 15.

6 BUILDING A PALACE FOR CAESARS

69   Taylor Construction as Caesars Palace builder: Oral History Interview with Stuart and Flora Mason. Las Vegas, Nevada. February 27, 2010. Conducted by David G. Schwartz. 5-6. Hereinafter cited as "Masons."

69   Early days of Caesars construction job: Masons 1, 10.

70   Harry Wald gets hired: Bates, 1.

70   Harry Wald biography: "Harry Wald, former head of Caesars, Dies," *Las Vegas Sun,* May 8, 1996; "Wald Remembered as Vital to LV Economy," *Las Vegas Sun,* May 9, 1996.

70   Everyone at the Palace a Caesar: Jay Barrows. "Jay Sarno: The Man Who Dreamed Las Vegas and Blazed the Trail for Others to Follow." *Las Vegas Style.* May 1994.

71   Jo Harris's influence on the Caesars theme: A.D. Hopkins. "Jay Sarno: He Came to Play." In Jack Sheehan, ed. *The Players: The Men Who Made Las Vegas.* Reno: University of Nevada Press, 1997. 95.

71   Screen block in Miami Modern architecture: Eric P. Nash and Randall C. Robinson. *MiMo: Miami Modern Revealed.* San Francisco: Chronicle Books, 2004. 39.

71-2   Sarno's design of Sarno Block: J.C. Sarno 1, 27.

72   Evelyn Spinks's move to Las Vegas: Cappadonna, 3.

73   Jay and Joyce's marital problems: September Sarno, 8.

74-5   The Sarnos' move to Las Vegas: Jay C. Sarno 1, 4-5.

75-6   Sarnos and Masons socializing: Masons 1, 3-4, 9.

77   Carol Freeman's house and car: http://redrock.co.clark.nv.us/assrrealprop/pcldetail.aspx?hdninstance=pcl7&hdnparcel=162-03-610-009; Cappadonna, 18.

77   Joyce's unhappiness in Las Vegas: September Sarno, 8.

77-8   Evelyn's unhappiness in Las Vegas, and Sarno's solution: Cappadonna, 5.

78-9   Entertainment listings of Caesars Palace and Aladdin: John L. Scott. "New Hotel Lists Big Names." *Los Angeles Times,* March11, 1966. C12.

79   Nate Jacobson discusses Caesars: John L. Scott." Palace Really Fit for Caesar." *Los Angeles Times,* July 4, 1966. D16.

79-80   Steve Wynn discusses Caesars:Wynn, 5.

80-1   Caesars Palace licensing hearing: Nevada Gaming Commission meeting minutes, May 18, 1966. 6-7, 34-8, 64-5, 76-7..

81-2   Announcement of Caesars opening party: Display Ad 24. *Los Angeles*

Times, July 27, 1966. A2.

82-84 Caesars construction details: Masons, 10-11, 15-16, 8.

7 THE TRIUMPHS OF CAESAR

86 Caesars opening plans: John L. Scott. "Caesars Palace Creates Setting Fit for the Gods," *Los Angeles Times,* August 8, 1966. C1.

87 Caesars Palace opening invitation. Jay Sarno Collection, UNLV Special Collections.

89 Caesars/Versailles fountains comparison: Jerry Hulse. "Plush Vegas Hotel Forgot Fig Leaves." *Los Angeles Times,* August 21, 1966. E 13.

90 Interior design of Caesars: Stamos, 6.

91-2 Furniture installation triage: Masons, 9.

92 Stuart Mason's feet: Masons, 9.

92-3 "Merlin" appears: Masons, 10.

94 Perceptions of the Caesars opening: Wynn, 5.

94 Opening mishaps: Peter Bart. "Vexation Time in Vegas," *New York Times,* August 14, 1966. 101.

95 Circus Maximus design: John L. Scott. "Caesars Palace Creates Setting Fit for the Gods."

96 Celebrities at Caesars opening: Mike Weatherford. "An Era Ends," *Las Vegas Review-Journal.* September 1, 2000. 3J.; Peter Bart. "48-Hour Party Opens Newest Las Vegas Hotel," *New York Times.* August 8, 1966. 22.

96 Opening remarks at Caesars: John L. Scott. "Caesars Palace Creates Setting Fit for the Gods;" Peter Bart. "Vexation Time in Vegas," *New York Times,* August 14, 1966. 101.

96 Andy Williams's performance: Mike Weatherford. "An Era Ends."

97-8 The fireman: "Oral History Interview with Bob Stupak." Las Vegas, Nevada, January 9, 2009. 23.

98 Costs of Caesars opening: Stamos, 7.

99 Steve Wynn in room 1066: Wynn, 6-8.

100 Reaction to Caesars' opening: "The Talk of the Town." *New Yorker,* August 20, 1966.

8 A PALACE COUP

101 Zarowitz's carpet speech: Claytee D. White. "An Interview with Milton I. Schwartz." Oral History Research Center at UNLV. 2007. 5.

101-2 Argument over the trees: Jane Wilson. "A Double Roman Holiday," *Los Angeles Times,* June 18, 1967. A39

102 Celebrity weddings: http://www.reviewjournal.com/weddings/celebrity/50s-60s.html

103 First Caesars wedding: "Cugat Weds Charo in Las Vegas," *New York Times,* August 8, 1966. 21.

103 Sarno's seduction techniques: Trujillo, 5; Mallin, 8.

104 Bacchanal: Jane Wilson. "A Double Roman Holiday."

105 American Express junket: Paul J.C. Friedlander. "500 Europeans Inspect

U.S. on $500,000 Guided Tour," New York Times. November 13, 1966.

105   *A Funny Thing* chariot race: Margaret Malamud. "Brooklyn-on-the-Tiber," in Sandra R. Joshel, Margaret Malamud, and Donald T. McGuire, Jr., eds. *Imperial Projections: Ancient Rome in Modern Popular Culture*. Baltimore: The Johns Hopkins University Press, 2001. 206.

106   "Good night Sands:" Wynn, 8.

106-7 Howard Hughes' arrival in Las Vegas: Robert Maheu and Richard Hack. *Next to Hughes: Behind the Power and Tragic Downfall of Howard Hughes by His Closest Advisor*. New York: HarperCollins, 1992. 166-7.

107-8 Howard Hughes memos: Michael Drosnin. *Citizen Hughes*. New York: Holt, Rinehart, and Winston, 1985. 107.

108   Sarno and Jacobson borrowing from the Caesars cage: Wynn, 11.

108-9 Problems with Zarowitz: Mallin, 9-10.

110   Rumors of mob control of Caesars: FBI memorandum, LV 156-21.

110   Federal allegations of mob influence at Caesars: "Gang Ownership in Casino Charged," *Los Angeles Times*. August 4, 1966. 3.

110-1 Federal wiretaps of Nevada casinos: David G. Schwartz. *Cutting the Wire: Gambling Prohibition and the Internet*. Reno: University of Nevada Press, 2005.

111   Jacobson's threat to sue the *Sun-Times*: "Gang Ownership in Casino Charged," *Los Angeles Times*.

111   Jacobson's denials: "Casino Denies Hoodlum Link,' *New York Times*, August 18, 1966. 13.

111   Milton Keefer's response to Caesars inquiry: "Gambling Inquiry Widens in Nevada," *New York Times*, August 21, 1966. 68.

111   Chicago bookmaking raid: Robert Wiedrich. "Raiders Here Find Cash, Link to Vegas," *Chicago Tribune*. September 29, 1966. 5.

112   "Little Apalachin:" Gene Blake and Bob Jackson. "Grand Jurors Here Probing Gathering of Big Gamblers," *Los Angeles Times*. December 18, 1966. C1.

112   Big Apalachin: Schwartz 2005. 76-7.

112   Federal grand jury investigating meeting: "Crime: A Showgirl and Law of Omerta." *Los Angeles Times*. December 25, 1966. B5; Gene Blake and Bob Jackson. "Grand Jurors Here Probing Gathering of Big Gamblers."

112-3 Outcome of grand jury investigation: "Lazarus Sentenced on Perjury Counts in 'Apalachin' Case," *Los Angeles Times*, May 28, 1968. A1.

113   "Good Housekeeping stamp of approval:" Geoff Schumacher. *Howard Hughes: Power, Paranoia, and Palace Intrigue*. Las Vegas: Stephens Press, 2008. 54

113   Hughes' impact on Nevada: Omar V. Garrison. *Howard Hughes in Las Vegas*. New York: Lyle Stuart, 1970. 67.

114-5 Frank Sinatra's argument with Carl Cohen: Wynn, 9.

114   Carl Cohen's reputation: Oral History Interview with Jack Binion. Las Vegas, Nevada. October 17, 2008.

115   Sinatra's promise to Cohen. Schumacher, 54.

9 You Want It All or You Don't Want Nothing

117 Allen Dorfman's reputation: "The Silencers," *Time*, January 31, 1983.

117 Allen Dorfman among his friends: September Sarno, 7.

120 Evel Knievel's Long Beach jump: "Daredevil is at Long Beach Honda," *Los Angeles Times*, December 3, 1967, P3; Gilbert Rogin. "He's Not a Bird, He's Not a Plane." *Sports Illustrated*. February 5, 1968. 66.

120 Knievel's presence in Las Vegas: Ace Collins. *Evel Knievel: An American Hero.* New York: St. Martin's Press, 1999. 103.

120-1 Knievel's biography: Rogin, 62, 69.

120 Knievel's ethos: Collins, 19, 99, 60.

121 Knievel's first sight of Sarno: "An Interview with Evel Knievel," May 15, 2007. By David G. Schwartz. 1.

122 Knievel's campaign to jump at Caesars: Collins, 105-7.

122 Knievel's contract: Pete Peters. "Cyclist Seriously Injured in Leap Over Fountains." *Las Vegas Review-Journal*. January 2, 1968. 2.

122 Weather on January 1, 1968: http://www.almanac.com/weatherhistory/oneday.

123 John Derek filing Knievel's jump: Collins, 109.

123 Knievel comes clean with Sarno: Collins, 107.

123 Knievel on the day of the jump: Collins, 111.

123-4 Knievel's preparations for the jump: Pete Peters. "Cyclist Seriously Injured in Leap Over Fountains."

124 "Nothing ever gets done if you wait till you feel right," Collins, 112.

125 Details of the jump: "Evel Knievel at Caesars Palace" video accessed on YouTube.com, January 6, 2008: http://www.youtube.com/watch?v=kYGGCVE2lKY.

125 Knievel taken to Southern Nevada Memorial Hospital: Pete Peters. "Cyclist Seriously Injured in Leap Over Fountains." SNMH is today the University Medical Center.

125 Knievel's official prognosis: "Cyclist in Fair Condition Mon." *Las Vegas Review-Journal,* January 3, 1968. 1; Pete Peters. "Cyclist Seriously Injured in Leap Over Fountains."

125 "Oh yeah, he's fine." Conversation with Jay C. Sarno, March 10, 2008.

125 Knievel leaves the hospital: "Hollywood Trick Cyclist Leaves Hospital." *Los Angeles Times*, February 13, 1968. 22.

126 Sarno conversation with Knievel: Knievel, 2.

10 Raising the Big Top

134 Sarno's initial ideas for Circus Circus: United States v. Jay Sarno & Stanley Mallin: LV-CR-74-35. Sarno testimony. 6; Cohen 2, 2.

136 Homer Rissman biography: Greg Blake Miller. "The Architect's Architect," *Architecture Las Vegas*, Fall/Winter 2001. 12-4.

136-7 Circus Circus plans: Rissman and Rissman Associates. Circus Circus Preliminary Plans, November 17, 1967.

137 Circus approval: "LV Circus Casino Approved; No Topless Shoeshine

Girls." *Reno Gazette-Journal?* February 23, 1968.

137   Circus's ownership: "McIntosh and Mallin again on 'Sarno Team.'" *Las Vegas Review-Journal*, October 18, 1968.

138   "My decision…" "McIntosh and Mallin again on 'Sarno Team.'" *Las Vegas Review-Journal*, October 18, 1968.

138-9 Cohen's work with Sarno on Caesars, Cohen 2, 7.

140-1 Cohen's arguments with Sarno: Cohen, 2, 7, 10.

141   Circus Circus fountains: "Gigantic Circus Circus Opens Friday," *Las Vegas Review-Journal,* October 18, 1968. 32.

141   The Great Montyne: "Fierce," *Las Vegas Review-Journal*, October 17, 1968.

141   "World's most unusual sign:" Display ad, *Las Vegas Review-Journal*, October 17, 1968.

142   Monorail of beauty: "Gigantic Circus Circus Opens Friday," *Las Vegas Review-Journal*, October 18, 1968. 32.

142   Ed Sullivan at Caesars Palace: Display Ad. *Las Vegas Review-Journal*. Undated.

144-5 Sarno's feelings on Circus's opening: "Gigantic Circus Circus Opens Friday," *Las Vegas Review-Journal*, October 18, 1968. 32; Display ad, *Las Vegas Sun*, October 15, 1968. 14.

145   Don Drysdale: "Drysdale Opens Circus Circus," Las Vegas Review-Journal, October 15, 1968.

145   "Ain't kids stuff:" Display ad, *Fabulous Las Vegas*. October 12, 1968.

146   Cohen's winning the restroom argument: Cohen 2, 6.

11 RINGMASTER

147-8 Opening of Circus Circus: Frank Winston. "Circus Sets Record at LV Opening." *Las Vegas Sun*, October 19, 1968. 1; Harold Byman. "$15 Million Circus Circus Opens Tonight," *Las Vegas Sun*, October 18, 1968. 1.

148   "Circus Circus Premiere Week:" "Laxalt Lauds Circus Circus," Las Vegas Review-Journal, October 18, 1968.

148   Sarno's thoughts on Circus Circus: Frank Winston. "Circus Sets Record at LV Opening."

149   "Only for you:" Cohen 1, 14.

149   Sarno falling asleep: Cohen 1, 14.

150   Dining selections at Circus Circus: "Food, Beverage Spots Galore." *Las Vegas Review-Journal*, October 18, 1968. 33.

150   "Piece-Full Palace" review: Bill Willard. "Circus Circus," *Fabulous Las Vegas*. October 26, 1968. 22-4.

150-1 Tourist reactions to Circus Circus: "Midway on the Strip." *Time*. November 29, 1968. 80.

151   Cohen's meeting with the creditors: Cohen 2, 2-3.

153-4 "His partners are wondering…" Display ad 79, Los Angeles *Times*, November 26, 1968. G16.

155   Cohen leaves Circus Circus: Cohen 2, 1.

155   Denny's to buy Caesars: "Agreement Reach on Denny's Plan to Buy

Caesars Palace," *Los Angeles Times*, December 25, 1968. H8.

156   Denny's later attempts to buy casinos: John Abele. "Parvin-Dohrmann Gets Suitor, *New York Times*, June 6, 1969. 59; Myrna Oliver. "Harold Butler, Founder of Denny's Chain," *Los Angeles Times*, July 11, 1998. B-8.

156   Lum's buying Caesars Palace: "Lum's Closes Deal to Buy Las Vegas Spa," *Chicago Tribune*. October 1, 1969. C11.

156   Caesars faces pressure for hosting "unsavory" characters: "Caesars Palace Faces Possible $100,000 Fine," *Los Angeles Times*, June 13, 1969. 12.

157   Sarno and Mallin's difficulty in collecting money from Lum's: Mallin, 10.

157   Federal raid at Caesars Palace: Gene Blake. "U.S. Siezed $1.5 Million in Las Vegas Raid," *Los Angeles Times*, December 15, 1970. 3.

157-8 SEC action against Lum's: "SEC Sues Lum's, Others in Purchase of Caesars Palace," *Los Angeles Times*, December 7, 1971. D7.

158   Caesars buys the Thunderbird: "Crafty Caesars," *Chicago Tribune*, December 20, 1972, C7.

158   Burton Cohen works for Caesars: Cohen 1, 15.

158   Disposition of SEC suit: Robert Rosenblatt. "SEC Forces Caesars to Tighten Procedures," *Los Angeles Times*, April 11, 1974. D13.

159   Jerry Rosenthal: A. E. Hotchner. *Doris Day: Her Own Story*. New York: William Morrow and Company, 1976. 171; Roger M. Grace. "Uncle Jerry Wants to Kiss and Make Up," *Metropolitan News-Enterprise*, October 22, 2007. 7.

159   Sarno's opinion of Jerry Rosenthal: Oral History Interview with Lillian and Jonathan Sarno. February 8, 2007. New York, New York. 31.

159   Rosenthal's control over Cabana Management: Hotchner, 185; Grace, 7.

160   Rosenthal's collapse: Hotchner, 230, 279-82.

160   Disposition of Dallas Cabana http://www.dallas-sheriff.com/Detentions.html

160   History of Palo Alto Cabana: Marc Igler. "Our Town: The Cabana's Return." *Palo Alto Weekly*, December 30, 1998.

160   Demise of Atlanta Cabana: "Architectural Obituary: Once a symbol of modern glamor, the Atlanta Cabana is no more." *Creative Loafing Atlanta*: http://clatl.com/atlanta/architectural-obituary/Content?oid=1236528

161   Cab driver's revolt: Stupak, 25-6.

162   Circus Circus regulatory difficulties culminating in Sarno's resignation: "It's still showtime under the big top," *Las Vegas Sun*. April 30, 1969.

12 What'll It Take to Make You Happy?

163   Sarno returns to Circus Circus: "DA slates meet over Sarno's bid," *Las Vegas Sun*, January 26, 1970.

163-4 Life for the Sarno children: September Sarno, 13-4; Jay C. Sarno I, 11.

164-5 Sarno's largess to his extended family; "Why don't you guys:" Rosenbloom, 9-10.

165   "Look, I've got a reputation here:" Portman.

166   Jonathan Sarno's investment and Lillian's response: Lillian Sarno, 34.

166   Brown Circle home: Jay C. Sarno 2, 4.

167   Joyce's work: Jay C. Sarno 2, 3.

167   Hughes on Circus Circus: Drosnin, 118.

168-9 Sarno's film debut: *Diamonds are Forever*. Directed by Guy Hamilton. EON Productions. 1971.

169   Meeting with Nick Civella: Mallin, 20.

170   Circus Circus expansion plans: FBI memorandum, LV 156-21, 11.

172   The Sarno suite: Jay C. Sarno 2, 9.

173   "I'm having some problems…" Greenberg, 13.

174   Sarno's marriage falls apart: September Sarno, 8-9.

13 Friends, Hustlers, and G-Men

176   Knievel and Dorfman in Sarno's suite: Knievel, 5.

177   Jack O' Lantern lodge: Jay C. Sarno I, 7.

177   Dorfman Winter Olympics: September Sarno, 7-8.

177-8 Evelyn's sentiments on the winter trip: Cappadonna, 15-6.

179   "What are you doing there?" Sarno 2, 10-11.

179   Sarno's breakfast meetings: Stupak, 2-3.

179   Sarno's gambling increases: Stupak, 30.

180   "I'm not a golfer," Wiretap transcript, January 29, 1974. 26.

180   Gin rummy: Einbender, 10.

180   Cheating at golf: Oral History Interview with Freddie Sarno, February 9, 2010. 8-9.

181   Giving away clubs: Wiretap transcript, December 27, 1973, 7.

181   "I've given away…" United States v. Jay Sarno & Stanley Mallin: LV-CR-74-35. Sarno testimony. 46.

181   Sarno's friends tampering with his clubs: Freddie Sarno, 11.

181   Sarno's golf bag: Freddie Sarno, 11.

181-2 The Special Performance Takeoff: Jay C. Sarno 2, 12-4.

183   Bomb extortion plot: Lou Dolinar. "Sarno Helps Bust Casino Bomb Plot," *Las Vegas Sun*, June 27, 1973.

184   Harvey's Wagon Wheel explosion: Ed Vogel. "Casino Explosion Nearly Forgotten," *Las Vegas Review-Journal*, August 27, 2005.

183-4 Sarno's role in the FBI investigation of the Strip bomb plot: Dolinar.

184-5 Frank Fitzsimmon's animosity towards Sarno: FBI memo, "Jay Jackson Sarno—victim." 11/13/1973. LV 166-2216.

185-6 "Big Ben" Harrison's alleged contract to kill Sarno: Memo, Las Vegas to Director, Phoenix 10/19/1973 Jay Jackson Sarno—victim. LV 166-2216.

186   "Currently under investigation…" FBI report, "Jay Jackson Sarno." 01/11/1974. LV 92-1256.

187   "I don't know quite when I became under audit…" United States v. Jay Sarno & Stanley Mallin: LV-CR-74-35. Sarno testimony. 8. Trial heretofore cited as "U.S. v. Sarno & Mallin."

187   Extent of IRS audit: U.S. v. Sarno & Mallin. Main trial transcript. 485.

187   Larry Corash learns his uncle is under investigation: Larry Corash, 8-9.

188   "Actually, I know quite a lot about that…" Larry Corash, 9.

188   Mr. Arnold's demand: U.S. v. Sarno & Mallin. Sarno testimony. 27, 31.

188   Arnold overruled: U.S. v. Sarno & Mallin Sarno testimony.28, 70.

188   Arrival of criminal tax investigators: U.S. v. Sarno & Mallin Main trial transcript. 279.

189   Sarno claims gambling losses: FBI report, "Jay Jackson Sarno." 01/11/1974. LV 92-1256; U.S. v. Sarno & Mallin Main transcript.179.

189   Sarno's refund request: U.S. v. Sarno & Mallin Main trial transcript. 377.

189   Sarno and Mallin's plans for their refunds: United States v. Jay Sarno, Stanley Mallin, & Leo Crutchfield, Grand Jury Indictment. 11.

189   Circus Circus's hard times: U.S. v. Sarno & Mallin Main trial transcript. 415; U.S. v. Sarno & Mallin Mallin testimony. 23-4.

190-1 Bill Bennett and Bill Bennett biography: A. D. Hopkins. "Del E. Webb: Man of the Years." Hopkins and Evans; A. D. Hopkins. "William G. Bennett: Savior of Ailing Resorts." Hopkins and Evans; Peter Earley. *Super Casino: Inside the "New" Las Vegas*. New York: Bantam Books, 2000. 77-9.

14 A Brutal Thing

192   Mallin's introduction to Crutchfield: U.S. v. Sarno & Mallin Mallin testimony. 6.

193   Crutchfield gets Circus Circus rental car office: U.S. v. Sarno & Mallin Crutchfield testimony. 8.

193-4 Crutchfield under invesgiation: U.S. v. Sarno & Mallin Crutchfield testimony. 10-11, 18; U.S. v. Sarno & Mallin Turner testimony. 8. At the trial, Turner denied that he'd ever mentioned wanting to meet a girl.

194   Turner agrees to accept a bribe: United States v. Jay Sarno, Stanley Mallin, & Leo Crutchfield, Grand Jury Indictment. 2-3. U.S. v. Sarno & Mallin Turner testimony. 12-16.

195   Turner speaks about Agent Smith: U.S. v. Sarno & Mallin Main trial transcript. 103.

195   Crutchfield agrees to get Smith introduced: U.S. v. Sarno & Mallin Main trial transcript. 119.

195   Casino owners' sloppy tax records: U.S. v. Sarno & Mallin Main trial transcript. 157-8.

195   Robert Ray Smith's real identity: U.S. v. Sarno & Mallin Main trial transcript. 163.

195-6 Sarno and Mallin speak about Crutchfield: U.S. v. Sarno & Mallin Sarno testimony.12.

196   Smith complains to Crutchfield: U.S. v. Sarno & Mallin Main trial transcript. 293.

196   "Get lost…" U.S. v. Sarno & Mallin Sarno testimony.13.

196   Bingham tells Sarno he's not getting his refund: U.S. v. Sarno & Mallin Sarno testimony.13.

196-7 Crutchfield's call to Sarno: U.S. v. Sarno & Mallin Sarno testimony.18.

197   Crutchfield arranges the steam room meeting: U.S. v. Sarno & Mallin

Crutchfield testimony. 102, 108.

197   Crutchfield's ambitions: Mallin, 15.

197   "I'm not saying anything…" U.S. v. Sarno & Mallin Crutchfield testimony. 193.

197   "It was like a Mexican standoff…" U.S. v. Sarno & Mallin Sarno testimony. 18.

198-9 Smith's proposition to Sarno and Mallin: U.S. v. Sarno & Mallin Mallin testimony. 22.

200-1 Sarno and Mallin agree to the bribe: U.S. v. Sarno & Mallin Mallin testimony. 22

201   Sarno gets his refund check (and pays Smith): United States v. Jay Sarno, Stanley Mallin, & Leo Crutchfield, Grand Jury Indictment. 4.

201-2 Sarno and Mallin arrested, largest bribe in IRS history: "Sarno Faces Bribery Charge," *Las Vegas Review-Journal*. March 8, 1974. 1.

202   Mallin posts bail: Mallin, 16.

15 The United States v. Jay Sarno

204   Oscar Goodman biography: John L. Smith. *Of Rats and Men: Oscar Goodman's Life, From Mob Mouthpiece to Mayor of Las Vegas*. Las Vegas: Huntington Press, 2003.

205   Goodman as attorney in Lansky, Zarowitz cases: Smith, 49, 51.

205   Sarno wrests Goodman from Mallin: Mallin, 14.

205   Harry Claiborne biography: Smith, 161-2.

205   Pretrial motions: Ann Henderson. "Sarno Bribery Trial Begins." *Las Vegas Sun*. February 19, 1975.

205   Jurors excused: "Links to Tokes Excuse Jurors," *Las Vegas Sun*. February 19, 1975.

206   Foley's pretrial instructions to the jury: U.S. v. Sarno & Mallin Main trial transcript. 3-5.

206   Prosecution case: U.S. v. Sarno & Mallin Main trial transcript. 786-7.

206   Claiborne challenges IRS agents' narrative: U.S. v. Sarno & Mallin Main trial transcript. 109-12.

206   Turner's testimony: U.S. v. Sarno & Mallin Turner testimony. 161.

206-7 Smith's testimony: U.S. v. Sarno & Mallin Main transcript. 185, 194-8, 206.

207   Smith claims to send money to a Swiss bank: U.S. v. Sarno & Mallin Main transcript. 252.

207   "I'll level with Smith…" U.S. v. Sarno & Mallin Main transcript. 255.

208   "Bob, let me tell you…" U.S. v. Sarno & Mallin Main transcript. 258-9.

208   Smith tells Sarno about Swiss banks: U.S. v. Sarno & Mallin Main transcript. 263, 274/

208   Claiborne's cross-examination of Smith: U.S. v. Sarno & Mallin Main trial transcript. 291-92, 204, 368, 394-5.

209   Turner takes the stand again: U.S. v. Sarno & Mallin Main trial transcript. 336-9.

209   Claiborne's opening statement: Ann Henderson. "IRS Agent Berated,' *Las Vegas Sun*, February 28, 1975. 1.

209 Testimony of Ash Resnick: U.S. v. Sarno & Mallin Main trial transcript. 457-9.

210 Testimony of James Faso: U.S. v. Sarno & Mallin Main trial transcript. 480, 487, 491, 497.

210 Leo Crutchfield testifies: U.S. v. Sarno & Mallin Crutchfield testimony. 128.

211 "I was working…" U.S. v. Sarno & Mallin Crutchfield testimony. 196.

211 "There are no bad ideas…" U.S. v. Sarno & Mallin Sarno testimony. 6.

211 Sarno's recollections of Smith: U.S. v. Sarno & Mallin Sarno testimony. 8, 13.

211 "We wanted to…" U.S. v. Sarno & Mallin Sarno testimony. 26-7.

212 "If I killed every guy…" U.S. v. Sarno & Mallin Sarno testimony. 45.

212 "I put him on…" U.S. v. Sarno & Mallin Sarno testimony. 46.

212 Sarno's "dead man" explanation: U.S. v. Sarno & Mallin Sarno testimony. 59.

212 "I'm not saying I'm the holiest man alive…" U.S. v. Sarno & Mallin Sarno testimony. 51.

212 "The trick…" U.S. v. Sarno & Mallin Sarno testimony. 53.

213-4 Sarno's reasons why he shouldn't be sent to prison: U.S. v. Sarno & Mallin Sarno testimony. 63-4.-5

214 "I didn't say it was sensible…" U.S. v. Sarno & Mallin Sarno testimony. 99.

214 "You know how many guys…" U.S. v. Sarno & Mallin Sarno testimony. 96

214 "Mallin, you don't need…" U.S. v. Sarno & Mallin Sarno testimony. 102.

214 "If you choose that interpretation…" U.S. v. Sarno & Mallin Sarno testimony. 92-3.

215 "I'm excited…" U.S. v. Sarno & Mallin Sarno testimony. 128

215-6 Sarno "fires" Goodman: Goodman, 2-3.

216-7 Mallin's testimony: U.S. v. Sarno & Mallin Mallin testimony. 24, 45, 57, 63.

217 Mention of Spilotro at trial: U.S. v. Sarno & Mallin Mallin testimony. 97.

217 "He's the type of individual…" U.S. v. Sarno & Mallin Mallin testimony. 153.

218 "I can't get any character witnesses…" U.S. v. Sarno & Mallin Main trial transcript. 503.

218 "He's going to win…" Goodman, 3.

218 Mallin's character witnesses: U.S. v. Sarno & Mallin Main trial transcript. 504-6.

218 "Just ask him about me…" Goodman, 3.

218 John R. Young's testimony: U.S. v. Sarno & Mallin Main trial transcript. 507-8.

219 Sarno gets a character witness: U.S. v. Sarno & Mallin Main trial transcript. 507-13.

220 Request for dismissal: U.S. v. Sarno & Mallin Main trial transcript. 598.

220 Threat charges tossed: U.S. v. Sarno & Mallin Main trial transcript. 743.

220 Goodman's closing argument: Ann Henderson. "Sarno Defense Rips Feds in Closing Blast." *Las Vegas Sun*, March 11, 1975. 4.

220 Duff's closing argument: Crimson Lewis. "Sarno-Mallin Tax Trial Ends in Roar," *Las Vegas Review-Journal*, March 12, 1975. 1; Ann Henderson. "Sarno Defense Rips Feds in Closing Blast."

221 Foley's instructions to the jury: U.S. v. Sarno & Mallin Main trial transcript. 811.

221 Jury leaves at 5:00: U.S. v. Sarno & Mallin Main trial transcript. 839.

221 "You'll just have to rely…" U.S. v. Sarno & Mallin Main trial transcript. 872.

221　"There comes a time…" U.S. v. Sarno & Mallin Main trial transcript. 873.

221　"You must take your time…" U.S. v. Sarno & Mallin Main trial transcript. 879.

222　Sarno and Goodman bet: Personal communication, Oscar Goodman, August 20, 2013.

222　Jury admits it is deadlocked: U.S. v. Sarno & Mallin Main trial transcript. 893.

222　Foley declares a mistrial: U.S. v. Sarno & Mallin Main trial transcript. 894-6.

222　"There necessarily being a reasonable doubt…" U.S. v. Sarno & Mallin Main trial transcript. 896-7.

222　"SARNO BEATS IRS TRAP…" Ann Henderson. "Sarno Beats IRS Trap," *Las Vegas Sun*. March 16, 1975. 1.

223　"Didn't see any threat…" U.S. v. Sarno & Mallin Main trial transcript. 389.

223　Sarno as victim of government plot: "Time: Fitzsimmons Was IRS Informer," *Boston Globe*, August 24, 1981. 1.

224　Sarno's legal woes continue: Ken Langbell. "Jay Sarno Indicted Again." *Las Vegas Sun*, October 31, 1975. 1.

224　Charges against Sarno and Mallin finally dismissed: Criminal docket, No. 75-1972.

16 GRANDISSIMO DREAMING

232　Retains right to room 1410: Oral History Interview with Mel Larson. March 8, 2007. Las Vegas, Nevada. 2.

232　Sarno's relationship with Bill Bennett: Larson, 2.

233　Bennett's success with Circus Circus: A. D. Hopkins. "William G. Bennett: Savior of Ailing Resorts." Hopkins and Evans; Earley, 86-8.

234　Mel Larson biography: http://www.lvms.com/documents/mel_larson.pdf

234-5 Sarno's driving lesson: Larson. 2-3.

235　Centurion hotel: Note to Bill Willard, in Sarno Collection, UNLV Special Collections.

235-6 Sarno's announcement of Grandissimo: Daryl Gibson. "Sarno to build 3,000-room hotel." *Las Vegas Review-Journal*, December 22, 1976.

236　Grandissimo plans: Grandissimo, Inc Registration Statement, filed December 14, 1979. 15-6.

237　"Miniature Disneyland…" "Sarno reveals Grandissimo plans." Las Vegas Review-Journal, November 3, 1979. 1.

238　Sarno gets option on land: Grandissimo, Inc Registration Statement, filed December 14, 1979. 24.

238　Planned Grandissimo IPO: Grandissimo, Inc Registration Statement, filed December 14, 1979. 37.

237　Grandissimo's board of directors: Grandissimo, Inc Registration Statement, filed December 14, 1979. 30.

238　Potential windfall of Grandissimo IPO: Grandissimo, Inc Registration Statement, filed December 14, 1979. II-2.

238-9 *Wall Street Journal* article: "In Gaudy Las Vegas, Grandissimo is to Be Gaudissimo." *Wall Street Journal*. July 23, 1980. 1.

239　Sarno's reaction to WSJ article: Jay C. Sarno 2, 1.

240-1 Sarno's typical weekend day: September Sarno, 10-1.

241 Sarno's open-heart surgery: "Jay Sarno recuperating," *Valley Times*, September 15, 1977.

241-2 Beverly Hills diet: http://articles.latimes.com/2007/oct/26/local/me-mazel26

242-3 Sarno's adopting the Beverly Hills diet: September Sarno, 12.

243 Sarno's subsequent diet regimen: Freddie Sarno, 3.

243 Allen Dorfman's legal troubles: Dorothy Robyn. *Braking the Special Interests: Trucking Deregulation and the Politics of Policy Reform*. Chicago: University of Chicago Press, 1987. 43-5.

243-4 "He's involved with…" Freddie Sarno, 13.

244 "We're a team…" U.S. v. Sarno & Mallin Sarno testimony. 113

244 "I very often turn a deaf ear…: U.S. v. Sarno & Mallin Mallin testimony. 89.

244-5 Sarno's growing relationship with Steve Wynn: Wynn, 14.

245 Sarno honored by Anti-Defamation League: Anti-Defamation League 1980 Luncheon pamphlet.

245 Aetna's loan to Caesars World: David G. Schwartz. "Mothballing the Mob." *Vegas Seven*, July 27, 2011. http://weeklyseven.com/blogs/felt/2011/07/27/legacies-lanni

246 Sarno's difficulties in getting financing: Greg Blake Miller. "A Man of Appetite." *Las Vegas Life*. August 2001.

246-7 Sarno's presentation to the Wall Streeters: Larson, 5-6.

247 Flying Larson's helicopter to Pahrump: Freddie Sarno, 10.

247 "That was Jay…" Larson, 5.

247 Sarno's frustrations with getting Grandissimo backers: Freddie Sarno, 17.-8.

247 Allen Dorfman's indictment: Dan McCaughna. "Dorfman follows Hoffa again," *Chicago Tribune,* January 21, 1983. 12.

248 Allen Dorfman's murder: Douglas Frantz. "Dorfman freed on firm's stock, $1 million bond," *Chicago Tribune*, December 18, 1982. W1; Dan McCaughna. "Dorfman follows Hoffa again."

248 Sarno's contempt charge from no-show at Linton trial: Jane Ann Morrison. "Sarno may face contempt charges for trial no-show." *Las Vegas Review-Journal*, November 13, 1982. 1C

249 Sarno's contempt trial rescheduled: "Sarno wins round." Las Vegas Review-Journal, February 1, 1983.

249 Sarno's contempt plea: "Sarno pleads guilty to criminal contempt," *Las Vegas Review-Journal*, April 1, 1983.

249 Sarno bought out of Circus Circus; company's subsequent expansion: Circus Circus Annual Report, Year Ended January 31, 1984. 6-7, 17.

249 Sarno's proceeds from Circus Circus sale: "Circus Circus is Raising $72 Million to Buy Hotel It Leases in Las Vegas," *Wall Street Journal*, June 27, 1983.

250 Circus Circus IPO: Earley, 100-101.

17 JUST LIKE THAT, KID

251 Sarno's prestige in Las Vegas: Knievel 5.

251 Sarno's "plans" to enlarge Grandssimo: Jay C. Sarno 2. July 25, 2008.

252   Sarno's cycle of hedonism: September Sarno, 19.

252   Evel Knievel's difficulties: Ace Collins. *Evel Knievel: An American Hero*. New York: St. Martin's Press, 1999. 203-5, 209.

252   Knievel and Sarno remain close: Knievel, 1.

252   Sarno borrows gambling money from Knievel: Knievel, 7-8.

253   Knievel's reaction to Sarno being cheated at golf: Knievel, 5-6.

254   Sarno continues playing with cheats: Knievel, 8.

254   Sarno asks casinos to exclude him: Knievel, 2.

254-5 Knievel leaves his earring as a deposit: Knievel, 3-4.

255   "I heard you lost $20 million…" Mallin, 12.

255-6 September challenges Sarno's gambling: September Sarno, 20.

256   Elaine Morton is a pseudonym.

256   Sarno's final conversation with September: September Sarno, 21.

257-9 Jay's final day: September Sarno interview, 21.

18 The Greatest Hotel Man

261   Jay C. Sarno learns his father has died: Jay C. Sarno 2, 26.

261   "That's nice…" Jay C. Sarno 1, 13.

262   "You need to come home now…" September Sarno, 22.

262   Jay and Freddie's catching the Caesars plane: Jay C. Sarno 2, 26.

262   The siblings locate Hedi: Jay C. Sarno 2, 27.

263   September Sarno, 22.

264-5 Jay Sarno's funeral: Jay C. Sarno 2, 31-2.

265-6 Newspaper accounts of Sarno's death and life: "Hotelman Jay J. Sarno dies." *Las Vegas Sun*. July 22, 1984. 4C; "Jay Sarno, 63;One of Caesars Palace Founders." *Los Angeles Times*, August 4, 1984. B13.

266   "Jay Sarno died the way…" Jay C. Sarno 2, 33.

268   Caesars later history: "ITT offers 1.7 billion for Caesars World." *Los Angeles Times*, December 20, 1994; "ITT will expand two Caesars World casinos." *New York Times*, June 26, 1996; Gary Thompson. "Starwood chief sees further growth." *Las Vegas Sun*, December 11, 1997.

269   "Someone, if not me…" "Big bad wolf won't blow down Steve Wynn's hotels," *Reading Eagle*, March 12, 1995. B3.

270   "We'd like to thank…" Freddie Sarno. Notes for Gaming Hall of Fame induction speech.

Index

Pages with photos are indicated with italic font.

About the Author

Photo: Scott Roeben

David G. Schwartz, the Director of the Center for Gaming Research at the University of Nevada, Las Vegas, has written or edited seven books about gambling and Las Vegas. An Atlantic City native with hands-on experience in the casino industry, Schwartz has been at UNLV since 2001.

In addition to being an active consultant and speaker, Schwartz is Gaming and Hospitality editor for *Vegas Seven* magazine, where he writes the biweekly "Green Felt Journal" column and regular feature and long-form pieces about gambling, history, and hospitality in Las Vegas and elsewhere.

Schwartz earned his bachelor's degree (a double major in anthropology and history) as well as his master's degree (American History) from the University of Pennsylvania before receiving his doctorate in US History from UCLA. He lives in Las Vegas with his wife and two children.

You can learn more about Schwartz's work on his website, www.dgschwartz.com.

Also by David G. Schwartz

Roll the Bones
The History of Gambling

Cutting the Wire
Gambling Prohibition and the Internet

Suburban Xanadu
The Casino Resort on the Las Vegas Strip and Beyond

As editor

Frontiers in Chance
Gaming Research Across the Disciplines

(with Pauliina Raento)
Gambling, Space and Time
Shifting Boundaries and Cultures

For more information, see
http://dgschwartz.com

Printed in the United States
151451LV00003B/1/P